Human Traffic and Transnational Crime

Human Traffic and Transnational Crime

Eurasian and American Perspectives

EDITED BY SALLY STOECKER
AND LOUISE SHELLEY

ROWMAN & LITTLEFIELD PUBLISHERS, INC.
Lanham • Boulder • New York • Toronto • Oxford

ROWMAN & LITTLEFIELD PUBLISHERS, INC.

Published in the United States of America
by Rowman & Littlefield Publishers, Inc.
A wholly owned subsidary of The Rowman & Littlefield Publishing Group, Inc.
4501 Forbes Boulevard, Suite 200, Lanham, MD 20706
www.rowmanlittlefield.com

P.O. Box 317, Oxford OX2 9RU, UK

British Library Cataloguing in Publication Information Available

Library of Congress Cataloging-in-Publication Data

Human traffic and transnational crime : Eurasian and American perspectives / edited by
    Sally Stoecker and Louise Shelley.
        p.   cm.
    Translated and updated edition of Torgovlëiìa lëiìud'mi.
    Includes bibliographical references and index.
    ISBN 0-7425-3029-9 (cloth : alk. paper) — ISBN 0-7425-3030-2 (pbk. : alk. paper)
    1. Human smuggling—Russia (Federation) 2. Human smuggling—Ukraine.
3. Prostitution—Russia (Federation) 4. Prostitution—Ukraine. 5. Women—Crimes
against. 6. Transnational crime. I. Stoecker, Sally W. II. Shelley, Louise I. III.
Torgovlëiìa lëiìud'mi.
    HQ281.H86   2005
    306.3'6—dc22

                                                            2004015912

Printed in the United States of America

♾™ The paper used in this publication meets the minimum requirements of American
National Standard for Information Sciences—Permanence of Paper for Printed Library
Materials, ANSI/NISO Z39.48-1992.

≈ଶ≈ଶ≈ଶ

Contents

※ ※ ※

Acknowledgments

W e would like to thank several individuals for their time and commitment to our research on human trafficking and for helping to develop it into a book. Susan McEachern, vice president and executive editor for area studies and geography of Rowman & Littlefield acquired our manuscript and enthusiastically supported our work. Matt Hammon, also of Rowman & Littlefield, helped to produce the book. The Department of State enabled us, through several grants, to conduct research on human trafficking in Russia and the former Soviet states of Ukraine, Moldova, and Georgia. We thank the Department in general, as well as several colleagues there: Susie Baker, Carla Menares-Bury, Sally Neumann, Amy O'Neill Richards, and James Puleo. Thomas Firestone, formerly the Department of Justice resident legal adviser in Moscow, provided excellent commentary on some of the chapters and helped us in our analysis of federal human trafficking cases in the United States. We also thank our blind peer reviewers for helpful suggestions.

Several researchers in Russia worked tirelessly to provide assistance to us and to our authors: Maria Buriak in Vladivostok, Tatiana Sudakova, Vika Shakina, and Vitaly Shakin in Irkutsk and Moscow. Joyce Horn, formerly managing editor of the journal *Demokratizatsiya*, edited and formatted the book, which was no easy task. As always, her professionalism and skill contributed to the clarity and accessibility of this volume. Our two translators, Saltanat Sulaimanova and Irina Morozova, deserve special mention for their knowledge of the subject matter, which helped fine-tune their impeccable translations.

Finally, Keeli Nelson, Irina Morozova, and Karen Saunders of TraCCC are recognized for their untiring assistance in proofreading the text, obtaining permis sions to reprint, and gathering and translating other key documents that support the research in this book.

≪ी≪ी≪ी

Introduction

Sally Stoecker and Louise Shelley

Human trafficking is a despicable and growing transnational criminal phenomenon. Although it is not a new phenomenon, it has spread to new regions of the world and become a larger part of the illicit global economy.[1] Russian and Eastern European women were trafficked into prostitution in the pre-revolutionary period in Argentina and China.[2] The phenomenon ended when the USSR was established and the country's borders were sealed in the 1920s. During the Soviet period, internal migration and foreign travel were strictly limited, eliminating the possibility of both domestic and international trafficking.

Until the late 1980s, the trafficking of women was primarily an Asian phenomenon.[3] But with the collapse of the USSR, thousands of Russian and Ukrainian women were trafficked into sexual exploitation across the globe—to Asia, Latin America, and the Middle East, as well as to Central and Western Europe and the United States.[4]

The ill-conceived post-Soviet transition from a centralized economy to one based on market principles proved to be particularly traumatic for women. The elimination of job security, the decline of the economy, and the collapse of the social welfare system placed women in an extremely precarious position. Women had limited opportunities to function in the legitimate economy and to earn adequate wages. The speedy privatization process deprived women of jobs because enterprises downsized their workforces and, in most cases, eliminated female workers.

The rise of organized crime groups in the perestroika period and their phenomenal growth in the first years after the collapse of the Soviet Union also in

1

creased the vulnerability of women.[5] Corrupt bureaucrats and members of organized crime groups acquired most of the countries' wealth. Because women in Russia and Ukraine had little access to the spoils of the corruption and organized criminal activity, they were left without capital or property. They sought offers of employment abroad in a desperate effort to support their families. Others, without financial alternatives, answered advertisements to work abroad in a variety of venues, from bars and dance clubs to restaurants, business firms, and private homes, without understanding the perils that faced them outside their country. Once under the control of the traffickers, they had almost no chance to escape or buy themselves out of enslavement.

The arrival of numerous Slavic women in the brothels of Western Europe aroused considerable concern. Women's groups were particularly vocal in Belgium and the Netherlands where Eastern European gangs used violence to keep women enslaved in brothels.[6] As a result of citizen activism—especially their publicizing of the enslavement and abuse of women in these brothels—parliamentary hearings were held, government reports were produced, and the European Union began to focus seriously on the issue of human trafficking. The unprecedented growth of the trafficking problem in Europe, the United States, and Asia led to the creation of a United Nations Protocol against the trafficking in women and children that was adopted along with the United Nations' Convention on Transnational Crime. The Protocol was adopted by the General Assembly in November 2000 and presented for signature at a high-level meeting in Palermo, Italy, in December of that year.[7] Russia, an early signatory to the Convention and the Anti-trafficking Protocol, committed itself to fighting this phenomenon as well as other serious forms of organized crime.[8]

Despite considerable activism and legislative activity in response to the trafficking problem, surprisingly little is known about the actual dimensions of the problem internationally and within individual countries. There is a paucity of rigorous research into the origins of the crime groups, their size, level of organization, or the most effective strategies to deal with the trafficking problem. Considerable research and analysis exists on trafficking in Asia, particularly Southeast Asia.[9] This is understandable considering the longevity of the phenomenon and the tens of thousands of children and women who are trafficked to this region of the world. The post-Soviet states lack a similar volume of analytical material. Much of the information on trafficking in the former USSR is anecdotal or has been prepared by governmental or nongovernmental organizations not trained in research techniques or lacking access to the data needed to prepare sophisticated analytical studies.

This publication is the first English-language compilation on human trafficking from Russia and Ukraine to the United States. The collection, first published in Russia in 2002 as *Torgovlia Liud'mi*, is unique in both the authors' level of access to materials and the variety of research methodologies used to address the topic.[10] The English language book differs from the Russian original as new material has been added and the original chapters have been updated. Truly interdisciplinary, it combines the strengths of law, political science, sociology, demography, and criminology in analyzing human trafficking. Produced with the cooperation of the Transnational Crime and Corruption Center's (TraCCC's) network of research centers within Russia, this book capitalizes on the centers' affiliations with law schools, law enforcement academies, and the criminal justice community and the unique data supplied by those institutions and their scholars.

Although the law enforcement community is often cast as corrupt in Russia, it is misleading to view the whole organization as such. Many of the investigators with whom our scholars worked were forthcoming in providing data and proactive in their approaches to human trafficking crimes in their regions. Many investigators are deeply troubled by the rise of human trafficking, its impact on Russian women and children, and its contribution to the growth of organized crime within Russia. Consequently, they were ready to help us in Siberia and the Russian Far East, areas from which many Russian women are trafficked. First-hand interviews with law enforcement personnel who deal with trafficking and some of their official files were utilized in the research and analysis included in this collection. Hence, the studies present a fuller view of the picture of organized crime and trafficking than previously available.

The sensitivity of the information is reflected in the fate of a journalist who popularized the research of Ludmila Erokhina on the connection between the travel industry and human trafficking in the Russian Far East. In spring 2002, the journalist was severely beaten and required medical treatment. (One might surmise that Erokhina was spared a similar fate because she was doing research in TraCCC's Washington offices during this time period.) This suggests that those who are at the front lines of this struggle to expose trafficking and document its penetration into the Russian economy face enormous personal risks.

Despite the growth of human trafficking into the United States, law enforcement in this country did not respond aggressively to the problem. Finally, in 1999, a coalition of Republicans and Democrats in the U.S. Congress formed and crafted antitrafficking legislation. Their efforts culminated in the passage in 2000 of a strong U.S. law against trafficking entitled "The Victims of Trafficking and Violence Protection Act." The law requires increased prevention, protection, and prosecution of human trafficking crimes in the United States, as well as an annual report on the state of human trafficking internationally.[11] American law enforcement agencies are now expected to do more to target trafficking rings, secure convictions, and protect victims so that they may stand trial in trafficking cases. As a consequence of this new law, more than eighty trafficking cases were initiated in 2001 and 2002 alone—double the number that had been started prior to the passage of the law.[12] Although few cases have yet resulted in convictions, the growth in the number of cases nevertheless represents a dramatic change in U.S. response to human trafficking.

Although only a few criminal cases involve women from the former Soviet Union, we chose to highlight them by including a chapter by Beatrix Siman Zakhari on the trafficking of women from the former USSR to the United States since the passage of this law.

Scholar Selection

The rest of the collection represents contributions by the original participants in the research. These Russian and Ukrainian scholars were selected for this research based to an open grant competition conducted by TraCCC and sponsored by the Bureau of Educational and Cultural Affairs (ECA) of the U.S. Department of State. When the ECA grant was awarded in 2000, there were few Russian experts on human trafficking. The challenge was to find good specialists in different regions of the country who, with the provision of research materials and guidance from TraCCC's analysts, could develop expertise in trafficking research. Dozens of applications were received in response to our advertisement, which was circulated through the Internet to research centers in law enforcement, gender studies, and social sciences, and through the listservs of activists concerned with combating trafficking. After reviewing the applications and writing samples received, Stoecker, Shelley, and Repetskaia selected the best candidates. The researchers chosen have excellent scholarly credentials and their expertise was easily adaptable to this topic, although at the time few had actually done research on trafficking. For example, Elena Tiuriukanova, an accomplished demographer and the editor of the Russian-language edition of this book, had done extensive research on women's migration and labor issues that could be used to understand the problem of trafficking within the larger context of women's migration.

Human trafficking exists in every region of the Russian Federation, although the groups involved and the destinations of the women may differ. Because the trafficking problem is not confined to one region of Russia and its manifestation differs from region to region, it was important to attract researchers from diverse areas. Our researchers represent Vladivostok in the Russian Far East, Irkutsk in Eastern Siberia, Omsk in the Urals, and Moscow in European Russia. As suspected, their findings differed according to their geographical location. Analysis by Liudmila Erokhina originating in the Russian Far East focuses more on the trafficking of women to Asian countries, whereas the analysis of Elena Tiuriukanova from Moscow examines the problem of trafficking and migration headed primarily to Western Europe. Similarly, we found that the decline of the military-industrial complex left many women in the Urals and Siberia displaced and impoverished. Therefore, unemployed women in this vast region became a key source for the perpetrators of trafficking schemes and deserved significant representation in the study.

A Ukrainian researcher from Kharkiv was also selected to provide a comparative perspective on the antitrafficking legislation. Ukraine's economy suffered tremendously with the collapse of the Soviet Union and quickly became a major "source" country from which women were trafficked abroad. In response, Ukraine was the first post-Soviet state to adopt an antitrafficking law. Although hundreds of cases were initiated—some of which actually resulted in convictions—the efficacy of the law is controversial and is discussed in chapter 7, "An Evaluation of Ukrainian Legislation to Counter and Criminalize Human Trafficking." Nonetheless, Ukraine's commitment to the issue at the highest political levels is admirable. Comparable figures have not yet been achieved in Russia.

Conceptualizing the Problem

Together with our Russian and Ukrainian contributors to this collection, we formulated a common conception of the problem of human trafficking and a shared analytical framework. Our Russian authors conceptualized the problem broadly: they sought to provide a comprehensive view of the ways people could be traded, rather than focus solely on the sexual exploitation of women and children. They view Russia's human trafficking problem as a composite of an organized crime problem, a labor problem, and a consequence of regional conflict within the country's borders. This differs from the traditional perspective of many American scholars, who focus on the sexual dimensions of human trafficking, and Western European scholars, who are especially concerned with massive illegal immigration.

Russia's regional conflicts in the Caucasus, which have deep historical roots in Russian and Soviet history and its history of forced labor, were subthemes that the Russian authors felt needed to be integrated into the collection through analyses of the vulnerability of men to exploitation in civilian and military situations.[13]

Labor exploitation also has a long history in Russia. In Anna Repetskaia's chapter she provides an analysis of not only the forms of coercion applied to people, but also the various sectors in which people can be exploited, including physical and physiological exploitation. She makes the point that in the labor exploitation sector, individuals can be exploited not only for sexual labor, but also as military combatants.

Although the scholars worked with a common conceptual framework of trafficking, all faced enormous challenges in collecting reliable and uniform data. The complexity of the trafficking phenomenon makes it very difficult to gather data on a crime that is rarely reported because of the closed nature of the organized crime groups involved. These crimes are usually detected only after extensive undercover work and lengthy investigations. What constitutes being a victim of trafficking is varied: immigrants are smuggled and trafficked into Russia from other countries by diverse crime groups, as Kleimenov and Shamkov point out. Many women leave Russia on what appear to be legitimate tourist visas, only to become trafficking victims in the country of their destination. The book's contributors suggest a variety of forms of coercion applied against the women and men who are trafficking victims. The type of sexual exploitation also varies: some women are forced to work long hours in strip joints, while others are pushed into prostitution.

The chapters by Erokhina, Repetskaia, and Kleimenov and Shamkov focus on the crime groups within Russia that engage in human trafficking and almost all of them fall under the Russian definition of organized crime, as they are comprised of a group of individuals with sustained activity. However, the composition of such groups is diverse as well; many are very small groups of individuals that are moving only a small number of women, whereas other groups are much more coordinated and involve many more actors.

The criminal groups are flexible organizations that often have educated members, including former members of the state security apparatus. Many crime groups have entered into the trafficking business in Russia and Ukraine because the financial capital needed to engage in this business is insufficient and the chance of detection is limited. One can conduct business in Russia and Ukraine with few obstacles. Given the widespread corruption in law enforcement, it is possible to obtain the documents necessary to move people abroad illegally; further, traffickers can bribe border guards and custom officials if they are suspected of trafficking. In the rare case in which a member of the organization is apprehended, the whole operation is not brought down because it has a flexible network structure that is difficult for either domestic or international law enforcement to penetrate.

Chapters in the Collection

The collection in this book addresses the full range of complex issues surrounding the trafficking problem. These include the reasons for the rise of the problem, the forms it takes, the intersection of migration and trafficking, and law enforcement responses to the problem.

Sally Stoecker presents an overview of the human trafficking phenomenon as it emerged after the collapse of communism and the demise of the Soviet Union. The loss of a seventy-year ideology coupled with the breakup of the USSR into fifteen states caused enormous upheaval. The resulting chaos flowed nicely into the hands of criminal entrepreneurs, who took advantage of the situation and deceived and lured many desperate women into criminal trafficking schemes. The profits were enormous and the risks were low. Since the early 1990s, many activists have pressured the Russian state to address human trafficking at both the federal and local level. American activists began later to press for action by law enforcement personnel and legislators. Therefore, the United States is only now beginning to address the problem and much remains to be done.[14] Many markets for human labor (sexual and otherwise) exist in the United States, and Stoecker calls for rigorous research in this area.

Mikhail Kleimenov and Stanislav Shamkov provide a fascinating and comprehensive look at the phenomenon of criminal transportation of persons. They also discuss the movement of persons for political purposes, such as deportation, for which Russia has a long and rich history. Kidnapping persons for ransom is also a form of criminal trafficking in persons prevalent in Chechnya today. Kleimenov and Shamkov report that approximately 150 criminal groups operate in Chechnya and more than one hundred criminal cases involving kidnapping have been opened. Some estimates suggest that between 1997 and 1999, as much as $600 million in ransom was paid to Chechen militants. They report that among the causes of the increase in criminal trafficking in persons are low moral standards, military conflict, and the lack of legal mechanisms to fight these crimes.

Anna Repetskaia was the first of our authors to develop typologies of the human trafficking phenomenon in a systematic fashion. Her contributions to our collective conceptualization of the problem have proven to be invaluable and have informed and promoted more research into the chief elements of human trafficking: recruitment, movement, and exploitation. As she reveals, victims of human trafficking are not only exploited in a sexual or labor manner, but physiologically. Women become surrogate mothers and give birth to children for large fees; children smuggle heroin in their stomachs from Central Asia to Moscow; vital organs such as kidneys are removed and sold on the black market through corrupt individuals for exorbitant sums of money. It should also be noted that Repetskaia's research has been disseminated widely in Eastern Siberia, and law enforcement agencies have begun to open departments to deal with human trafficking crimes.

Louise Shelley's chapter contrasts human trafficking in Russia and China. Although both of those formerly closed socialist societies have become active traffickers of women for sexual exploitation, the trafficking in those countries assumes different forms. She suggests that the trafficking in the two countries reflects prerevolutionary business traditions. Whereas the Chinese have traditionally been traders, the Russians have been sellers of natural resources. These long-term differences prevail in the area of trafficking—Russians trade women as they have their natural resources with no concern for the future. Chinese trafficking is a business that contributes to the country's economic development.

Liudmila Erokhina offers interesting insight into the specifics of human trafficking crimes in the Russian Far East. Having interviewed law enforcement officials and studied documents in several regions of the Far East, she illustrates the varied law enforcement responses to such crimes. For example, she finds that law enforcement agencies in Khabarovsk take human trafficking crimes much more seriously than those in other regions. They have taken concrete measures to conduct proactive investigations, rescue victims, and arrest perpetrators. In Primorskii krai, in contrast, the attitude is more complacent and law enforcement officials tend to view trafficked women as deserving of their fate. They purport that they have more serious crimes to investigate. This difference in law enforcement attitudes may be explained in part by the different levels of corruption and criminalization of the top leadership in the two locales.

Elena Tiuriukanova has been studying and writing about migration for several years. In her chapter, she delves into the problem of the "feminization" of migration. The free migration law adopted by the Russian Duma in 1993 posed numerous advantages and disadvantages for Russian citizens—among them the evolution of Russia into a "gender migration" regime, whereby women migrants become "cheap labor" abroad, taking jobs that are well below their educational level. In many cases, they have become victims of human trafficking schemes. Beginning in 2001, the Russian Ministry of Foreign Affairs started to address the discriminatory policies of destination countries, such as the United States, toward Russian migrants. However, much remains to be done to redress the imbalance and protect Russian women from exploitation in foreign countries.

In addition to the articles published in the Russian collection, we have made two changes. First, we added a chapter by Olga Pyshchulina, who is actively working on human trafficking at a leading Ukrainian research institute in Kyiv. Pyshchulina examines the Ukrainian legislation against trafficking and its implementation through 2002. She finds enormous growth in the number of cases, from two in the first year to 107 in the fifth year. She reveals that there is a lack of incentive for prosecutors to take on these complex cases, and the absence of witness protection also makes it difficult to bring convictions in the cases. Despite the enactment of legislation, there is little political will in Ukraine to address the problem of trafficking from her country.

This collection also contains a chapter by Beatrix Siman Zakhari, not published in the Russian-language edition, analyzing three of the completed antitrafficking cases concerning women from the former Soviet Union. American law enforcement personnel were reticent in sharing case materials for analysis, but certain antitrafficking experts within the Department of Justice, including Tom Firestone, the Department of Justice representative in Moscow, helped us to secure case materials for analysis and helped to critique the case analysis presented here.[15] These cases from Texas, Alaska, and Illinois show that the trafficking problem is not confined to only the major cities of the United States but has a broader reach. Deception and coercion are part of the trafficking into the United States, and the Internet has helped to facilitate the international communications necessary to conduct them. Unfortunately, as this research indicates, securing convictions with meaningful sanctions against the traffickers has not been easy. Clearly, law enforcement personnel have still to learn how to apply the antitrafficking law effectively.

Recent Russian Response to the Problem

When this collaborative research was initiated, there had been legislative response to trafficking in Ukraine, but little to none in Russia. Much has changed in the legislative arena since Russia's signing of the Convention on Transnational Crime and the companion Protocol against Trafficking and Smuggling of People in 2001. The scholars in this collection have assumed an active role as advisers to the Russian parliament in drafting an antitrafficking law.

The broader conception of the problem of trade in humans presented here has appealed to a wide range of communities within Russia. Members of the military, advisers to the security committee of the Russian Duma, and members of the law enforcement community identify with the trafficking issue because trade in human beings—especially kidnapping—is part of the ongoing war in

Chechnya, where Russian soldiers and law enforcement personnel have been captured and sometimes traded. This broader conception of trade in people has been important in winning support for the legislative initiative.

From October 2002 until April 2003, at the initiative of the State Duma Committee for the Legislation and Judicial Reform and with the support of the Office of the Plenipotentiary Representative of the President of Russia in the Central Federal District, a draft Federal Law to Combat Trafficking in Persons in Russia was developed. An interagency working group was created to elaborate this law; Elena Mizulina, State Duma deputy from the liberal pro-reform party Union of Right Forces (SPS), chaired the group. The working group brought together representatives of relevant ministries, the State Duma, local countertrafficking NGOs, and international organizations, including the Organization for Security and Cooperation in Europe's Office for Democratic Institutions and Human Rights. Elena Tiuriukanova and Liudmila Erokhina, two contributors to the collection, worked actively behind the scenes and in public meetings on this process. Three seminars and several public discussions, including the public Parliamentary Readings in February 2003, were held with the financial support of the U.S. State Department and the U.S. embassy in Moscow.

The purpose of the draft law is to prevent, identify, and suppress trafficking in persons as well as to protect the individual, public, and state against trafficking in human beings through the eradication of its causes, and to provide legal framework for the support and social rehabilitation of those who have become victims of trafficking. The draft law fully met the requirements of the international standards set forth in the UN Protocol, including the definition of human trafficking, the concept of exploitation, and the important provision that the consent of a victim of trafficking to the intended exploitation shall be irrelevant.

The draft law has not yet been adopted, although it passed the second reading in the State Duma. However, in October 2003 President Putin introduced the amendments to the Criminal Code of the Russian Federation criminalizing human trafficking and providing punishment of up to fifteen years of deprivation of liberty. In introducing the new Criminal Code provisions to the State Duma, the president defined human trafficking as a modern form of slavery, a form of organized crime, and a source of funding for terrorism. He stated that the human trafficking market in Russia can flourish because of existing loopholes in national legislation. Those amendments were adopted in December 2003.

Although an entire antitrafficking law has not been passed and Deputy Mizulina was not elected to the newly constituted parliament, others legislators appear willing to continue pressing for more legislative change in Russia.

Scholars and Activists

In the year and a half since this book's publication in Russia, the authors have become well-known not only within Russia's legal, gender, and policy communities, but also to a larger international community. Many of them are now busy lecturing throughout Russia, mentoring younger specialists, speaking at domestic and international conferences, and reaching a broad audience.

These researchers now constitute an important network of scholars who, following their first steps that culminated in the vital contributions included in this collection, have continued to produce important research in the field. Erokhina and her junior associate, Maria Buriak, from Vladivostok have produced an important volume, *Torgovliia zhenshchinami i det'mi v tselakh seksual'noi ekspluatatsii v sotsial'noi i kriminologichieskoi perspective* (Moscow: Profobrazovanie, 2003). This book is currently being used by Russian law enforcement personnel all over the country to help them to understand the phenomenon of human trafficking and to develop the capacity to address it.

The TraCCC regional research center on organized crime and corruption in Irkutsk, headed by Anna Repetskaia, has engaged in training and outreach throughout the Siberian region. They have collaborated with NGOs and with local and regional governments to raise awareness of human trafficking at all levels. At the Baikal Women's Forum in July 2002, attended by hundreds of women activists, there was great interest in the original Russian-language version of this book. A special session was held at the forum where antitrafficking activists from all over Siberia met with the books' contributors from Moscow, Omsk, Irkutsk, and Washington to discuss the practical applications of this study. A follow-up meeting on the topic occurred in mid-2003. Recently, the Russian Ministry of Interior's crime branch for Siberia, based in Novosibirsk, approached the Irkutsk Center for assistance in analyzing and fighting organized crime in the Siberian region. Additionally, Anna Repetskaia and her fellow scholars have been using their analysis to support a police antitrafficking unit recently formed in the Irkutsk region to address the problem. Such anti-trafficking units are being established in other parts of Russia.

Elena Tiuriukanova, based in Moscow, has been called on to advise a Ministry of Interior working group on human trafficking. She is frequently asked to advise various committees of the Duma interested in trafficking.

Olga Pyshchulina has moved from the provincial city of Kharkiv to Kyiv. She now works in a strategic studies institute under the national government where part of her work concerns antitrafficking policy. Her research analysis is now applied to government policy in this area.

Future Directions

Although a brave and vital beginning, this volume is by no means the "definitive" work on human trafficking from the former Soviet Union. Much more research needs to be done on the geographical variations of human trafficking in Russia, the state and nonstate actors involved, the linkages to other forms of organized crime, and the utilization of the proceeds of the crime. Rigorous research is needed in the key countries of "destination" to which Russian and Ukrainian victims are trafficked, such as the United States and Western Europe. Although we have intelligence figures on the scale of trafficking to the United States—18,000 to 20,000 victims per year—little is known about the traffickers, clients, methods, and links to transnational criminal groups, or the percentage of traffickers originating from the countries of the former Soviet Union and Central Europe.

We hope that this book will provide new impulses for further research on human trafficking both within and from the former Soviet Union and other regions of the world. Serious study is needed to address this contemporary form of human slavery. Without careful analyses, effective strategies cannot be developed to address the problem.

Notes

1. Karen Colligan-Taylor, introduction to *Sandakan Brothel No. 8* (Armonk, N.Y.: M. E. Sharpe, 1999), xx–xxvii.

2. For a discussion of the story of Rachel Liberman, a Russian émigré woman trafficked into prostitution in Argentina, see www.news.cornell.edu/Chronicle/00/4.20.00 /Teatrotaller.html (3 February 2004); Eileen Scully, "Pre-Cold War Traffic in Sexual Labor and Its Foes: Some Contemporary Lessons," in *Global Human Smuggling: Comparative Perspectives,* ed. David Kyle and Rey Koslowski (Baltimore: Johns Hopkins University Press, 2001), 74–106.

3. See for example, International Organization of Migration, *Combating Trafficking in South-East Asia: A Review of Policy and Programme Responses* (Geneva: IOM, 2000); Asian Development Bank, *Combating Trafficking of Women and Children in South Asia,* Asia Development Bank, ADB headquarters, 27–29 May 2002, report released July 2002.

4. See for example, James O. Finkenauer, "Russian Transnational Organized Crime and Human Trafficking," in *Global Human Smuggling: Comparative Perspectives,* ed. David Kyle and Rey Koslowski (Baltimore: Johns Hopkins University Press, 2001), 166–86; Bertil Lintner, *Blood Brothers: The Criminal Underworld of Asia* (New York: Palgrave Macmillan, 2003); Victor Malarek, *The Natashas: The New Global Sex Trade* (Toronto: Viking Canada, 2003).

5. See Sally Stoecker, "The Rise in Human Trafficking and the Role of Organized Crime," *Demokratizatsiya* 8, no. 1 (2000): 129–44; Louise Shelley, "The Trade in People in and from the Former Soviet Union," *Crime, Law and Social Change* 40 (2003): 231–49.

6. See for example, Foundation against Trafficking in Women www .bayswan.org/FoundTraf.html (4 February 2004); Monika Smit, "Trafficking in Women: Dutch Country Report," Amsterdam, 25–26 April 2003, www.newr.bham.ac.uk/ pdfs/Trafficking/Netherlands1.pdf (4 February 2004).

7. "Summary of the United Nations Convention against Transnational Organized Crime and Protocols Thereto," The United Nations, Office of Drug Control and Crime Prevention, Vienna, December 2000, published in *Trends in Organized Crime* 5, no. 4 (Summer 2000): 11–21.

8. Victims of Trafficking and Violence Protection Act 2000, *Trafficking in Persons Report* (Washington, D.C.: U.S. Department of State, 2001), 95.

9. See for example, Pasuk Phongpaichit, Sungsidh Piriyarangsan, and Nualnoi Treerat, *Guns Girls Gambling Ganja Thailand's Illegal Economy and Public Policy* (Chiang Mai: Silkworm Books, 1988).

10. Elena V. Tiuriukanova and Liudmila D. Erokhina, *Torgovlia Liud'mi: Sotsiokriminolgickii analiz* (Moscow: Academia, 2002).

11. See the first report, *Trafficking in Persons Report* (Washington, D.C.: U.S. Department of State, 2001).

12. *Trafficking in Persons Report*, 2003 www.state.gov/g/tip/rls/tiprpt/2003/21262.htm#usgefforts (5 February 2004).

13. Mikhail Kleimenov and Stanislav Shamkov, "Kriminal'noe peremeshchenie liudei: Vozmozhnosti protivodeistviia," in *Torgovlia Liud'mi* (Moscow: Academia, 2002), 90–134.

14. See for example, Peter Landesman, "The Girls Next Door," *New York Times*, magazine section, 25 January 2004, 30–39.

15. For his analysis of the problem see Tom Firestone, "The Russian Connection: Sex Trafficking into the US and What the US and Russia Are Doing about It," *International Organized Crime* 51, no. 5 (2003): 39–41.

Chapter 1

Human Trafficking: A New Challenge
for Russia and the United States

Sally Stoecker

The trafficking of women and children from their home countries abroad for purposes of sexual exploitation and forced labor has become a global industry and a serious transnational criminal phenomenon.[1] Recent intelligence estimates put the total number of women and children deceived, recruited, transported from their homes, and sold into slavery throughout the world at 800,000 to 900,000 per year.[2] Several factors are facilitating the growth of this phenomenon, including the globalization of the economy, the increased demand for personal services in the developed world, the shortage of employment opportunities for women in developing countries and countries undergoing political and economic transition, and the rapid and unregulated enticement and movement of human capital via the Internet. It is a sad commentary on the state of the global economy at the beginning of the twenty-first century that women and children are being traded as quickly as commodities, stocks, and bonds without adequate legal and humanitarian protection. This phenomenon can be called the "commodification of persons."[3]

Since the collapse of the Soviet Union, which ended seventy years of centralized political and economic controls and at least fifty years of a comfortable social contract that guaranteed employment and social security for all, unemployment in Russia has hit the entire population extremely hard. President Putin has made considerable progress in addressing the problem of wage arrears in Russia. Yet only a few years ago studies indicated that nearly half of Russian adults are out of work and only a quarter of those employed are getting paid on a regular basis.[4] The population that is hardest hit by unemployment and poverty is women and the children they support. These bleak labor trends have flowed nicely into the hands and coffers of criminal organizations seeking to exploit the fluid and chaotic situation by luring desperate, jobless women and their children in many cases unknowingly—into forced prostitution, sweatshop labor, and domestic servitude.

In the early to mid-1990s, in the wake of globalization and the weakening of the Russian state, criminal organizations assumed the roles that the state previously played, asserting their own form of authoritarianism. These criminal organizations exploited the chaos and high unemployment trends in Russia and intimidated the populace in a manner not unlike the coercive KGB informants and operatives of the Soviet era.[5] Criminal organizations penetrated the financial structures and political circles and impeded efforts to foster the growth of civil society in Russia. Although the Russian economy has improved in the past few years, Russian society continues to be penetrated by corrupt officials, despite concerted efforts to oust them or reduce their influence. This corrupt environment combined with an undeveloped respect for law or "legal consciousness" (*pravosoznanie*) has hindered efforts to create economic and political institutions capable of serving the Russian citizenry.

By most accounts, human trafficking is a highly attractive business for criminal groups because it is low in risk and high in payoffs. The U.S. Federal Bureau of Investigation estimates that perhaps three thousand Russian mobsters control gangs in American cities that involve the forced prostitution of more than eight thousand women, many of whom are of Slavic origin.[6] According to one UN estimate, criminal organizations generate up to $3.5 billion per year in profits from illegal migrant trafficking alone.[7] The head of operations for a UN crime prevention center remarked bluntly, with respect to trafficking in women from the former Soviet Union, "The earnings are incredible. The overhead is low—you don't have to buy cars and guns. Drugs you sell once and they are gone. Women can earn money for a long time."[8]

Market Demand and Employment Opportunity

Currently, the market for Slavic women and children in the "developed" countries of North America, Europe, and North Asia is among the hottest and largest and is drawing on a vast supply of impoverished and vulnerable citizens of the former Soviet Union. The International Organization for Migration (IOM) calls this rise in demand for Slavic women the "fourth wave" of victims of trafficking involving women and children from Central and Eastern Europe, including Russia and Ukraine, that began in the early 1990s and continues to the present time.[9] Prior waves included the Thai and Filipino women (the first), Dominicans and Colombians (the second), and Ghanaians and Nigerians (the third). The number of victims from Central and Eastern Europe more than doubled in Belgium and tripled in the Netherlands between 1992 and 1995. German crime statistics show that there were more female victims of trafficking into Germany from the countries of the former Soviet Union than from anywhere else, Poland coming in second and Thailand dropping to seventh place. German investigators of human trafficking crimes describe it as a major branch of organized crime.[10] In the German region of Nordrhein-Westfalen, human trafficking as a branch of severe sexual crimes ranked second in the hierarchy of violent crimes committed in 2001.[11]

Research conducted by IOM and other nongovernmental organizations identified the sources and flows of women trafficked from European Russia into Western Europe. One report documented the extent to which Slavic women trafficked to Belgium, the Netherlands, Poland, and Switzerland, had overtaken the traditional caste of African, South American, and Asian women. For example, in 1994, 17 percent of the artist visas granted to "dancers" in Switzerland were granted to Russians.[12] The underworld has enticed numerous Slavic and Baltic women from Russia, Ukraine, Latvia, Lithuania, and Estonia, as well as women from the former East Bloc countries of Hungary, Poland, Romania, and Czechoslovakia. These women are seen as exotic and desirable in the "developed" industrial countries of Europe, North America, Asia, and the Middle East.[13] According to some reports, there are more than 5,000 Russian prostitutes in Thailand recruited in the Russian Far East for job opportunities there. Slavic women are in great demand by Asian businessmen from Japan and China who work in Thailand, and by wealthy Thai men.[14] Throughout Southeast Asia, Russian women are considered to be "a symbol of social prestige."

The Russian Federation is losing an invaluable source of human capital as women are trafficked abroad and exploited. Many of the Russian women exported and enslaved tend to be well educated. They answered advertisements for positions in the service sectors for which they are frequently overqualified. This appears somewhat counterintuitive, because most of the international development literature has shown education as a means of liberating women from enslavement and abuse. If anything, education should enhance their status in society.[15] The common profile of a woman trafficked from the less-developed countries of South Asia or Africa, for example, is a woman who lives in poverty, is uneducated, and is discriminated against for reasons of gender or ethnicity. For impoverished peoples such as the Tamang in Nepal, becoming a prostitute is deemed socially acceptable and a means of providing for one's family.[16] Indeed, the family often promotes this line of work for its daughters.

In the Soviet era, women represented the backbone of the Russian labor force and Russia had a very small gender gap. The Soviet social contract and planned economy offered women generous child support systems that enabled and encouraged them to work outside the home. With the transition from a command to a market-style economy, women have lost out to men in many aspects of the labor market. A UNICEF report suggests that women in the Russian Federation lost seven million jobs between 1990 and 1995, while men lost two million jobs.[17] Most of women's work opportunities are in the public sector, as

opposed to the private sector, partially because of their perceived family responsibilities and associated nonwage costs. Moreover, gender stereotypes about
"women's work" and "men's work" are well entrenched and show no signs of
abating. Small private businesses have blossomed in Russia and it was hoped
that they would absorb a large percentage of state workers and create a new
middle class. However, *Goskomstat* figures reveal that very few women are
hired to work in private businesses and those who are hired are for part-time
positions.[18] According to a sociological survey, in the early 1990s the average
working wage for women was nearly 70 percent that of men, but at the end of
the decade it had dropped to 56 percent.[19]

Historical Context and Current Trends in Human Trafficking

The similarities in the human and social costs of political and economic transition between the postcollapse Russia in the early 1990s and postrevolutionary
Russia are striking. In the 1920s and 1930s, the upheaval associated with the
communist revolution, civil war, the Volga famine, and the New Economic Policy (NEP) had a deleterious effect on the cohesiveness of families in Russian
society. Those disruptions resulted in the proliferation of abandoned children
and unemployed and widowed or single mothers. As American historian Wendy
Goldman stated,

> Large numbers of women were forced to leave the workforce after the civil war
> and entire branches of industry closed in the shift to cost accounting under
> NEP. Sharp cutbacks in spending hurt social welfare agencies and state indus-
> tries, sectors where female workers predominated. Thousands of medical per-
> sonnel, state employees, daycare staffers, and nutrition and communications
> employees lost their jobs. [20]

Similarly, the Petrograd Bureau of Labor in 1922 reported that 67 percent of
the 27,000 registered unemployed persons in the city were women.[21] The same
statistics could be used to describe the situation in the Russian Federation today
where it is estimated that a substantial proportion of the urban female population
is currently unemployed, particularly those under thirty years of age or over fifty
years of age.[22] It is also important to remember that women predominated in
industries such as textile factories and other light industries that were especially
hard-hit by the economic decentralization and privatization processes.[23]

In postrevolutionary Russia, as the competition for jobs increased, women
lost out to men. The plight of divorced, nonworking women was especially
acute. Such women were labeled *netrudnyi* (nonlaborers), who out of despera-
tion turned to the street. In addition to the dislocations and suffering associated
with famine and war, a contributing factor was the change in family codes of
1918 and 1926 that made divorce much easier.[24] Increased divorce left many

single parents (especially mothers) with children they could not support. In turn, desperate women turned to the streets and were known to solicit sexual services everywhere from public toilets and baths to passenger cars on trains to earn money.[25]

Homelessness (*besprizornost'*) left countless children susceptible to various forms of labor and sexual exploitation and to becoming criminals themselves. Homelessness was called the "mother of juvenile crime." Starving young girls were driven to perform sexual acts in exchange for a piece of bread.[26] Begging, theft, and prostitution were then, as today, the most common methods homeless children used to find food or obtain train fares. Children who hovered over cafeteria tables in search of leftovers were known as *tarelochniki* (those who sought plates).[27] Children also begged for food and money at markets, bazaars, and churches; they made up stories, feigned illness, and sang songs on the street for alms. In fact, the head of the Soviet Secret Police (*Cheka*), Felix Dzerzhinsky, was so moved by the plight of these children that he took on the battle against *besprizornost'* almost single-handedly.[28] In 1921, he created a commission for the improvement of children's lives that was attached to the All-Union Central Executive Committee. This commission, comprised of representatives from other child welfare agencies, the People's Commissariat for Education (*Narkompros*), and other commissariats of health and food, survived for two decades. The chief responsibility for the rehabilitation of street children lay with the Division of Social and Legal Protection of Minors (SPON).[29] SPON was responsible for combating juvenile homelessness and delinquency and establishing guardianships. Despite the creation of those and many other commissions to deal with homelessness and rehabilitation, the number of homeless children grew unabated and the agencies grew perplexed as to how to care for the children, who were increasingly turning to crime as a means of survival.

Soviet analysts estimate that there were between five million and seven million homeless children roaming the streets of Russia after the revolution, about 5–7 percent of the population.[30] Adjusting for population differences (approximately 145,000,000 in 2002 versus 100,000,000 in 1926), 2 percent of the current Russian population consists of homeless and unsupervised children.[31] Moreover, the capacity to care for them and offer medical, nutritional, and psychological services appears to be just as bleak as it was decades ago.[32] The following statistical information from one of Russia's leading criminologists illustrates the severity and complexity of these problems.

> Every year some 500,000 children and teenagers lose a parent. Nearly 40 percent of all juvenile crimes are committed in these families. More than 160,000 children are raised in state institutions (including orphans of living parents who have lost custody). Annually, in attempts to save themselves from cruel physical and psychological abuses, about 2 thousand children and teenagers commit suicide, 30 thousand leave their families, and about 6 thousand leave children's orphanages. More than 24 thousand children and teenagers have disappeared and are being searched for by the police. Another 27 thousand are becoming victims of crime.[33]

Homelessness and juvenile crime are phenomena that plague many parts of Russia, such as the Far East.[34] There are simply not enough orphanages to accommodate the growing population. Whereas war, famine, industrialization, and collectivization created enormous social and familial dislocations in the Soviet Union of the 1920s and 1930s, today's unsupervised children (*beznadzornye*) and, to a lesser extent, *besprizornye,* are largely products of the problems associated with the abrupt loss of social guarantees and protections.[35] The new "army" of street kids is highly vulnerable to enticement by criminals all over the world into a variety of unsavory and often criminal activities, from narcotics trafficking to prostitution and pornography rings. Children are increasingly being used as "mules" to transport heroin from Central Asia to Moscow in their stomachs.[36] Many poverty-stricken single mothers lack state support in the form of maternity leave, child care, and other child-rearing subsidies so prevalent in the Soviet era. In their efforts to put food on the table, they must work two or three jobs in addition to trying to supervise their children. Their inability to give their children adequate attention has exacerbated the problem of juvenile delinquency.

A federal law focused on combating the problem of increased homelessness and neglect of children was adopted by the Russian Federal Assembly in July 1999.[37] Based on the UN Convention on the Rights of the Child, the new law seeks to protect the human rights of minors for the first time in Russian legal history. For example, in an effort to protect the rights of minors, a court order is needed to bring a homeless child into a center for temporary shelter. Yet a court order cannot be obtained without proof that a child either broke the law or does not have a permanent place of residence in the region. In most cases, the child rarely breaks the law and in most cases has a place of residence. Therefore, he/she is refused a hearing in court, is refused admittance to the shelter, and returns to the street.[38] Analyses of the homelessness problem in Vladivostok reveal that options previously available for caring for street children are curtailed by the new law—only one institution opens its doors to the homeless, and that regional social-rehabilitation center for minors is already overcrowded. As a result, children are returned to their homes and to alcohol- or drug-addicted parents. Some practitioners suggest that the new law *should* be violated until more accommodations can be created for the growing homeless population because "violating this unsatisfactory law is less of a crime than what is currently happening to children in the city of Vladivostok."[39]

During interviews, representatives of agencies involved in implementing the new law in Irkutsk, Siberia, indicated their belief that this law has a lot to offer and with time should improve the plight of homeless children.[40] At the present time, implementation of the new law has led to increased homelessness in Russia because of the restricted role of the Ministry of Internal Affairs (MVD) and failure thus far of social welfare agencies to take a proactive role in removing children from the streets. In the past, the MVD's juvenile affairs units conducted periodic sweeps of their jurisdictions and took all homeless children (offenders and nonoffenders) to shelters overnight. In some cases, the juvenile case workers continue that practice out of necessity, in defiance of the new law, even though the law restricts their ability to deal with children who are not juvenile offenders.[41] The new law provides for social welfare agencies and Russian courts to assume the main responsibility for locating and placing homeless children in shelters. However, most of the practitioners in those agencies lack the training and resources—and in some cases the knowledge that the new law exists—to take on the new responsibilities. Indeed, many of the agencies maintain a "pro-Soviet" character based on punitive, not individual, approaches to the children, because of shortages in funding and inertia.

As a result, the ever-growing pool of rootless and unsupervised children and teenagers has created auspicious conditions for ever-younger criminals. As researchers in the Vladivostok Center for the Study of Organized Crime have demonstrated, many children are drawn into criminal schemes through drug addiction.[42] They become dependent on their suppliers and then perform criminal acts to support their habits or become easy targets of labor and sexual exploitation. Russian criminologist Larisa Romanova believes that the average age of drug users in Russia is fifteen to seventeen years, and in some regions much younger than that. Most sociological research has estimated that 8 percent of Russian youth use drugs periodically; in the universities, the figure climbs to 30–40 percent.[43] The problem is especially acute in the port city of Vladivostok. The UNON (directorate for countering the illegal distribution of drugs within the Internal Affairs Administration of the Maritime Province) estimates that in the first half of 1999 more than 2,000 citizens of the province were charged with the possession and distribution of narcotics.[44]

Part of the explanation for the high incidence in drug addiction in this region of Russia is its geographic location. Bordering on the Sea of Japan and China, with easy access to Korea, Japan, and China, the Maritime Province is the perfect location for criminal activities because its vast borders and prolific shipping traffic cannot be adequately monitored. Specialists at Interpol believe that the Russian Far East will soon become the main transit corridor for narcotics being shipped to Asia and Europe.[45] Southern Manchurian hemp, from which drug manufacturers prepare marijuana and hashish, grows abundantly in the province. The province is also a main destination point for shipments of ephedrine (better known in Russia as *lyod* or "ice") from China and Korea and of opium from Central Asia, especially Tajikistan. Chinese couriers are said to carry contraband drugs across borders and thereby escape border control checkpoints. The couriers are accompanied and protected by Russian criminal organizations as they complete their deliveries. Perhaps most disturbing is the increasingly young age at which children and teens are using these drugs. Not only are the "elite youth" at institutions of higher education using them, but also seven to thirteen year olds. This trend, combined with the large population of homeless and unsupervised children in Vladivostok, has led to the growing problem of juvenile crime, with youth both committing crimes and suffering consequences. There are also many opportunities for the trafficking of children in the Maritime Province because vulnerable children can easily be illegally transported to shores of the Sea of Japan and shipped clandestinely to their final destinations in

Asia, North America, or other areas. Indeed, criminologists and law enforcement officials have recognized the severity of the human trafficking problem in the Far East and are actively investigating suspicious advertisements and tourist agencies.[46]

Although recruitment of children may be fairly straightforward and simple—offers of food, shelter, or toys—the illicit schemes for enticing young women into criminal activities are somewhat more sophisticated. Advertisements for positions as waitresses, baby-sitters, office clerks, and dancers in Europe, Asia, and the Middle East are the most commonly reported. The problem appears to be growing most rapidly in eastern Siberia, from the Urals to the Sea of Japan. Trafficking of women and girls from Irkutsk to China and Japan is becoming more common and is recognized as a growing crime problem by law enforcement officials serving the Irkutsk oblast. An example of methods used in Siberia is recounted in a recent newspaper report: A woman from Irkutsk named Lena left to visit her relatives in the Far East where she saw advertisements for a work-study program in China for restaurant chefs. She contacted the firm and received a contract that seemed to provide for everything—medical insurance, room, and board. She accepted the offer and traveled with a small group of women to a small Chinese town where they spent one month learning how to prepare native Chinese cuisine. Then, as many similar accounts reveal, the chef trainees' passports were confiscated and they were told that it would cost them $15,000 to get them back. Soon it became clear that there was no such restaurant and they had been deceived. One of the girls was sold to a group of traffickers from Macao and was sent there to work as a prostitute; others remained in the small Chinese town and were forced into prostitution, serving clients in bars and restaurants. They were abused by their "bosses" and were kept like slaves in locked quarters with little food. Finally, the girls escaped and traveled home to Irkutsk, often at the expense of serving more clients in exchange for travel money along the way.[47] Needless to say, this experience left deep emotional scars and necessitated extensive psychological counseling and rehabilitation.

Law enforcement officials have described the many and varied players or "links" involved in human trafficking chains. First, there are those who advertise the positions abroad and who tend to be of the same nationality as the women and children they seek to exploit. These criminal "entrepreneurs" work closely with brothel owners and organize and finance the transportation of women and children from their home countries to brothels in foreign countries. The second link consists of "middlemen," most of whom are from the homeland of the victims and work as couriers, smugglers, or passport and marriage document falsifiers. These middlemen are usually from the milieu of the drug addicts who see financial benefits and means of supporting their drug habits. In addition, there are those who issue invitations to Eastern European citizens, who exchange favors with officials in charge of local offices—such as the foreign office, real estate offices, or construction offices—whether monetary or sexual services in exchange for extension of residential or work permits of the victims.[48] This vast network of facilitators and others who accept bribes and relocate persons make the path difficult to trace.

Porous Borders Facilitate Human Trafficking

The pace and rate of movement of people today is so rapid and so vast that borders cannot be adequately monitored and literally invite the trafficking of persons. Migrant trafficking has become a large and lucrative business for crime groups that exploit the demand for illegal migration as a result of political entry restrictions imposed by industrialized states. The breakup of the Soviet Union, the creation of fifteen separate states (former republics), the loss of centralized controls, and visa-free entry policies with surrounding countries have exacerbated an already daunting border control problem. The Russian Federation represents an especially difficult situation, because it is now a federation comprised of eighty-nine subjects. Some of these subjects have crafted bilateral treaties and relationships with Moscow that give them considerable autonomy and have also created their own laws and regulations on migration, for example, that in some cases contradict federal laws. A new law on the temporary residence of foreign citizens and noncitizens in the Irkutsk region passed in 1998 has had virtually no effect. In fact, it has made the procedure for inviting foreign guests for professional purposes more complicated and costly while doing little to stem the tide of tourists, who make up the largest percentage of violators of the rules and whose visas are easily obtained or even come via visa-free schemes.[49] Although efforts to stem the tide of illegal migration through enhanced sanctions, fines, and other punishments may on the surface seem to be appropriate countermeasures, in fact they only serve to reinforce the attractiveness of this business to criminal groups who see in migrant trafficking extremely high payoffs and minimal risks.

Research conducted by IOM and other international organizations has identified some of the key transportation routes used by traffickers taking persons out of the Russian Federation. The *Baltic route* is said to be especially porous, with Lithuania among the most penetrable countries for illegal migrants traveling to Germany, Scandinavia, and the United States from Belarus and Ukraine. Criminal traffickers appear to believe that the Polish-Lithuanian border is especially easy to cross.[50] There were 9,787 illegal immigrants from Southeast Asia who were caught trying to cross from Ukraine into Poland in 1995.[51] The *Georgian transit route* has also expanded, due to an open-border policy with Turkey. Many women and children are being trafficked through Georgia to Turkey and Greece and on to the Mediterranean countries. Children, in particular, are at risk due to schemes involving the tampering of passports. These passports include the names of the children traveling with their alleged parents, who then proceed to "lose" the passport and with it the identity of their children; the children are then left without documentation and can be trafficked with impunity. The expansion of the *China and Siberia route* has been facilitated by an open-border policy created in 1992 to enhance tourism and goodwill. Chinese laborers are willing to take menial jobs that are unacceptable to Russians and the proliferation of Chinese citizens arriving on Russian soil with links to criminal groups appears to be a growing problem.[52] There is also considerable traffic from China via Moscow and Prague and on to Germany, according to Interpol sources that investigate alien smuggling flows.

Border control problems are by no means confined to the former Soviet Union. Indeed, the whole notion of "borders" is becoming obsolete in this era of global markets, increased tourism, and labor mobility. Administrative requirements and physical inspections of cargo are sorely outdated. Improvements are needed in transportation and navigational technologies capable of monitoring the movement of labor and capital. In addition, the private and public sectors need to collaborate in ways that will allow the speedy movement of labor and capital while providing adequate means of inspecting and controlling that movement.[53] Unfortunately, the present system is filled with opportunities for criminal intervention and the large amount of cargo stolen in transit on a regular basis is passed on to consumers in increased prices for goods.

What Has Been Done?

To combat human trafficking effectively, a comprehensive, transnational strategy needs to be developed. Such a strategy should involve methods for preventing women and children from being drawn into criminal schemes, investigating and prosecuting the crimes effectively, and protecting the victims of crimes who frequently end up in foreign countries as illegal aliens without rights. The United Nations Protocol to Prevent, Suppress, and Punish Trafficking in Persons, adopted in 2000, is a crucial first step in criminalizing human trafficking and protecting the victims at an international level. The legislatures of some countries have also passed antitrafficking legislation, such as the "Trafficking Victim Protection Act" in the United States. The architects of the UN protocol are hopeful that it may serve as a template for other countries around the globe to draft their own national laws, reflecting similar victim protection guarantees and punishments for the traffickers and their accomplices.

Victim Protection and Counseling

In Russia, victim protection and medical and psychological counseling is increasingly being provided by voluntary organizations and NGOs. Although these efforts were funded primarily by international organizations in the past, there is now evidence that city administrations within Russia are beginning to provide funds for victim protection and antitrafficking initiatives in local NGOs. An excellent example of a highly productive grass roots organization that is helping to prevent trafficking and protect victims thereof is the Angara Crisis

Center in Irkutsk, Siberia. In addition to publicizing the trafficking problem through educational workshops and the media, the crisis center collects information about firms and marriage agencies that advertise jobs abroad and disseminates practical information about the risks in taking jobs abroad. One Angara handout offers practical advice to those who accept jobs in other countries. Their recommendations to women and girls considering such employment include: keeping their passport and visa with them at all times; knowing the name and address of the employer, the salary, the living conditions, and the length of the contract; and leaving copies of passport documentation with parents or friends.

In the United States, the new "T" visa provides three years of temporary residence to trafficked victims. This not only provides a "safe haven" for them, but also enables them to receive psychological counseling and medical care, while preparing them to stand trial in trafficking cases. In many cases, victims of human trafficking are fearful of returning to their home countries. In some instances, the victims' involvement in sexual services—whether voluntary or not—is viewed as shameful to family and community members and may bring severe punishment against them. People in countries such as the Russian Federation frequently express concern for the victims' livelihood—as traffickers often make threats against them and their family members.

Training and Curriculum Development for Law Enforcement

Because human trafficking is a relatively new crime in Russia, law enforcement officials must be trained to recognize, investigate, arrest, and prosecute the perpetrators. In 2000, American University's Transnational Crime and Corruption Center received funding to work with researchers in Russia and other post-Soviet countries to study the problem of human trafficking in a multidisciplinary manner and create training materials and courses for use in police and procuratorial academies and institutes. Those training materials, translated into Russian, Georgian, and Romanian, focus on human trafficking as an organized criminal activity, as well as a violation of human, labor, and migration rights, and provide insight into investigative techniques and legal measures for police and investigators. The materials also offer strategies for protecting trafficked victims and providing them with temporary residence status in the countries to which they are trafficked. Methods of protecting the victims and witnesses of such crimes are covered at length in the training materials. In 2001, a week-long training seminar was held at the FBI Academy in Budapest, Hungary, attended by forty investigators and prosecutors from various regions of Russia, Georgia, and Moldova. A multinational and multidisciplinary faculty of scholars and investigators worked with the trainees to understand the elements of human trafficking schemes (deception, recruitment, movement, and exploitation), how they are designed and conducted by criminal organizations, and how to collaborate with authorities in different countries in the investigations of transnational human trafficking crimes. Many of the contacts made at this seminar have benefited the investigation of human trafficking cases in Russia, Moldova, and Georgia.

Public Outreach and Publicity Campaigns

Public outreach in Russia, Ukraine, and other NIS states is being performed by several nongovernmental organizations such as Miramed (Miracle Medicine), Winrock International, La Strada, and the International Organization of Migration. Those organizations reach out to vulnerable populations of young and unemployed women in the rural regions of Russia and Ukraine. Miramed has developed an antitrafficking coalition made up of numerous Russian NGOs connected by a very sophisticated and extensive Internet link. Through Internet links, conferences, and workshops, Miramed has educated graduates from orphanages—who are viewed as especially vulnerable to trafficking schemes—about the dangers of criminal deception and enticement into employment opportunities abroad.

Winrock International and the NIS-U.S. Women's Consortium based in Kyiv, Ukraine, have a trafficking prevention program that helps to promote economic opportunities for women and to prevent domestic violence through job skills and violence prevention training sessions at centers in Dnipropetrovsk, Donetsk, and Lviv. Those centers are managed by Ukrainian women's organizations that have links to health providers and legal resources in their respective regions. They expanded their activity to the Russian Far East in 2001 and now have offices in Khabarovsk.

What Is to Be Done?

Understanding and Addressing Demand for Trafficked Persons

The United States is a key destination country for some 18,000–20,000 trafficked persons per year. Therefore, the United States must address the demand for trafficked persons and attempt to reduce it. Unfortunately, little to no research has been done to identify the characteristics of demand, which would assist law enforcement investigators in dealing more effectively with human trafficking crimes. For example, what is the profile of a trafficker or of a client? Does trafficking occur mostly in cities? Are they and their clients usually male? In what types of services are trafficked victims engaged? Are they primarily sexual in nature, or is domestic servitude more widespread in the United States? How are children being exploited and by whom?

Preliminary findings, based on an examination of federal human trafficking cases in the United States, illustrate that in many instances, husband and wife teams have perpetrated the crimes. They have linked up with coconspirators in other countries and have designed and carried out crimes using the Internet and e-mail. The crimes are "entrepreneurial" in nature and do not appear to be linked to major organized crime groups. The geographic origins of criminal traffickers have been as diverse as large cities in Alaska and rural towns in Texas. Needless to say, rigorous research into the "demand" side of human trafficking should be a national priority.

Protecting Homeless Children from Exploitation

We need to pay more attention to the problem of child homelessness and neglect in countries such as the Russian Federation that are undergoing economic transition from command to market economies. As social protections disappear and change, children suffer the most and many end up on the street. Rootless children are extremely vulnerable to trafficking schemes and provide, as the Russians say, "human chattel" (*zhivoi tovar*) for criminal organizations seeking to exploit them for a variety of unsavory purposes. As mentioned above, children are increasingly being used as "mules" to transport narcotics—an extremely dangerous undertaking that could easily result in death. The psychological damage to children exploited sexually is enormous and can affect their ability to form relationships the rest of their lives. In many cases, neglected and sexually exploited children are becoming criminals—the juvenile crime rate continues to climb.

Programs to deal with child homelessness and neglect have been implemented in some regions of Russia, such as Kemerevo oblast, where local military authorities have placed street kids in educational settings at their own expense. Clearly, finding the funding for shelters and rehabilitation programs for street kids is difficult. However, successful business entrepreneurs are beginning to give charitable contributions to their home localities to provide shelters and staff. I visited one such shelter in Angarsk, Siberia.

There are many positive aspects of market economies and enhanced opportunities for mobility and opportunity in this global age. Unfortunately, the infiltration by organized crime into the global economy has made the social and human costs extremely high for the citizens of many underdeveloped countries and countries "in transition," such as Russia. These countries often are unable to compete effectively and are exploited and harmed by the global marketplace.

Notes

1. "Human trafficking" as used in this chapter refers to the criminal recruitment, deception, movement, and exploitation of persons. Anna Repetskaia elaborates on this definition in chapter 3, "Classifying the Elements of Human Trafficking Crimes."

2. Office of the Undersecretary for Global Affairs, U.S. Department of State, "Trafficking in Persons Annual Report, 2003," 7.

3. The idea of the "commodification of persons" was inspired by the phrase "commodification of women" studied by Daina Stukuls, "Body of the Nation: Mothering, Prostitution, and Women's Place in Post-communist Latvia," *Slavic Review* 58, no. 3 (Fall 1999): 537. Valerie Sperling also refers to the commercialization and objectification of women's bodies as processes that began in the mid-1980s with the onset of Gorbachev's glasnost reforms. See Sperling, *Organizing Women in Contemporary Russia: Engendering Transition* (Cambridge: Cambridge University Press, 1999), 77.

4. USIA Office of Research and Media Reaction, "Poverty in Russia: Just How Bad Is It?" *USIA Opinion Analysis* (Washington, D.C, 12 January 1999). According to this analysis, only half of Russia's 110 million adults work, one-third are on pensions, and one-tenth are employed. Russian citizens polled revealed that wage arrears was a more serious problem than unemployment, production stoppages, or low salaries. Putin has begun to address wage arrears and pensions and to restore trust in the public sector since he took office in 2000. See Linda Cook, "Social Cohesion in Russia: The State and the Public Sector," in *Social Capital and Social Cohesion in Post-Soviet Russia*, ed. Judyth Twigg and Kate Schecter (Armonk, N.Y.: M. E. Sharpe, 2003), 17–33.

5. Louise Shelley, "Post-Soviet Organized Crime: A New Form of Authoritarianism," in *Russian Organized Crime: The New Threat?* ed. Phil Williams (London: Frank Cass, 1997), 122.

6. Daniel Jeffreys, "Beauty and the Banker," *Moscow Times*, 18 September 1999.

7. International Organization of Migration, "Organized Crime Moves into Migrant Trafficking," *Trafficking in Migrants: Migration Information Program*, no. 11, June 1996, 1–2. "Migrant trafficking" has commonly referred to migrants who seek to emigrate from their home countries voluntarily and in this sense has differed from "human trafficking," whereby persons are deceived or coerced into slavelike conditions in other countries. The distinction between the two has become increasingly blurred and many international organizations are developing definitions that would respect the rights of persons exploited in other countries regardless of how they arrived in another country.

8. Interview with Michael Platzer, cited in Laura Barnitz, *Commercial Sexual Exploitation of Children: Youth Involved in Prostitution, Pornography, and Sex Trafficking* (Washington, D.C.: Youth Advocate Program International, 1998), 23.

9. *Trafficking and Prostitution: The Growing Exploitation of Migrant Women from Central and Eastern Europe* (Geneva: International Organization for Migration, 1995), 6–7.

10. Leo Keidel, "Menschenhandel als Phänomen Organisierter Kriminalität," *Kriminalistik* 5 (annual report, 1998), 322.

11. Dieter Schürmann, presentation on investigating human trafficking by the regional police in Nordrhein-Westfalen, 26 September 2003, Düsseldorf, Germany.

12. Keidel, "Menschenhandel als Phänomen Organisierter Kriminalität," 8.

13. N. Leskova, "100 Nalozhnits dlia Germanii," *Izvestia*, 27 September 1997.

14. E. Shteiner, "Russkie v Indokitae," *Nezavisimaia Gazeta*, 21 August 1997.

15. See, for example, Catherine Scott, *Gender and Development: Rethinking Modernization and Dependency Theory* (Boulder, Colo.: Lynne Reinner, 1994) and Joycelin Massiah, ed., *Women in Developing Economies: Making Visible the Invisible* (New York: Berg, 1992).

16. Renu Rajbhandari, *Girl Trafficking: The Hidden Grief in the Himalayas* (Kathmandu, Nepal: Women's Rehabilitation Center, 1997).

17. Gaspar Fajth and Jane Foy, eds., *Women in Transition: A Summary* (Florence, Italy: United Nations Children's Fund Regional Monitoring Report, no. 6, 1999), 4.

18. N. M. Rimashevskaia, ed., *Rossiia: 1999—Sotsial'no-demograficheskaia situatsiia* (Moscow: RAN Institute of Social Economic Problems of the Population, 2000), 209.

19. "Gendernye aspekty kadrovoi politiki na predpriiatii," in Rimashevskaia, *Rossiia 1999*, 214.

20. Wendy Goldman, "The Withering Away of the Family," in *Russia in the Era of NEP: Explorations in Soviet Society and Culture,* ed. Sheila Fitzpatrick (Bloomington: Indiana University Press, 1991), 131.

21. Goldman, "The Withering Away of the Family."

22. This is based on data provided by USIA, Office of Research, May 1999. The absolute number of unemployed women was comparatively higher in the 1920s, since the population for the Russian Federation (RSFSR) in 1926 was 100,858,000 compared with 144,978,573 in 2002. See *World Almanac and Book of Facts*, Robert H. Lyman, ed. (New York: Press Publishing Company, 1930), and Central Intelligence Agency, *World Fact Book 2002.*

23. Sperling, *Organizing Women*, 150.

24. Alan Ball, *And Now My Soul Is Hardened: Abandoned Children in Soviet Russia, 1918-1930* (Berkeley: University of California Press, 1994). This is perhaps the best single work to examine all aspects of child homelessness in the interwar period.

25. Ball, *And Now My Soul Is Hardened,* 132.

26. Ball, *And Now My Soul Is Hardened,* 56.

27. Ball, *And Now My Soul Is Hardened,* 45.

28. Ball, *And Now My Soul Is Hardened,* 91. See also Peter Juviler's discussion of the efforts by the People's Commissariat of Education to care for street children through communes and schools, "Contradictions of Revolution: Juvenile Crime and Rehabilitation," in *Bolshevik Culture: Experiment and Order in the Russian Revolution,* ed. Abbott Gleason et al. (Bloomington: Indiana University Press, 1985), 266–67.

29. SPONS was a subsection of *Glavsotvos*, a branch of the Commissariat of Enlightenment (*Narkompros*) responsible for combating child homelessness. See Ball, *And Now My Soul*, glossary.

30. Juviler, "Contradictions of Revolution," 264.

31. This is based on the figure of 2.5 million homeless and unsupervised children, reported by the chairman of the security committee of the Russian State Duma at an October 1997 international roundtable on combating the export and exploitation of women and children. This figure is similar to more current estimates by the Russian Ministry of Labor and the Russian Procuracy issued in 2002. It should be underscored that obtaining an accurate figure is extremely difficult and estimates of homelessness vary widely within organizations studying the problems of child welfare and juvenile crime. For example, UNICEF (United Nations Children's Fund) gives a figure of one million homeless children in the Russian Federation in its new report, Alexandre Zouev, ed. *Generation in Jeopardy: Children in Central and Eastern Europe and the Former Soviet Union* (New York: M. E. Sharpe, 1999), 69.

32. Stenographic Report of the Roundtable on International Cooperation in Combating the Illegal Export and Exploitation of Women and Children Abroad, State Duma of the Russian Federation, 9–10 October 1997.

33. A. I. Dolgova, *Prestupnost,' statistika, zakon* (Moscow: Kriminologicheskaia Assotsiatsiia, 1997), 10–11.

34. Viktoria Chernysheva, "The Attraction of Youth into Criminal Organizations in the Far East," *Organized Crime Watch*, TraCCC-American University, vol. 1, no. 1, 1998, 1–2.

35. *Besprizornye* is the Russian term applied to children without parents, orphans who wandered the streets and were not placed in orphanages or who escaped from them. *Beznadzornost'* is the phenomenon more prevalent today whereby children are poorly supervised by existing parents, albeit in many cases dysfunctional, or run away from home and take to the streets.

36. See, for example, "Narkotiki nachali privozit' v Moskvu v detskikh zheludkakh," *Moskovskii Komsomolets*, 3 August 2000, 2.

37. Federal'nyi zakon: "Ob osnovakh sistemy profilaktiki beznadzornosti i pravonarushenii nesovershennoletnykh" adopted by the Federation Council, 9 July 1999. See *Rossiiskaya gazeta*, no. 121, 30 June 1999.

38. Tatiana Oshchepkova, "Broshennye i zabytie," *Poslednie Izvestiia*, 19 October 1999, 3.

39. Galina Kushnareva, "Gde pomogut Mustafe?" *Vladivostok*, 20 October 1999, 8.

40. The author conducted these interviews in the summer of 2000 in Irkutsk, Russia. Those interviewed represented welfare, city administration, MVD, migration, and other city and oblast agencies dealing with homeless children.

41. Most railroad stations have "rooms for children" (*komnaty dlia detei*) where homeless youth can spend the night or wait until other arrangements are made by *Odel' po pravonarusheniiu nesovershennoletnykh* (Section on Juvenile Offenses duty officers).

42. Larisa Romanova, *Narkotiki, prestupleniia, otvetstvennost* (Vladivostok: Far Eastern University Press, 2000).

43. Larisa I. Romanova, *Nakomaniia i Narkotism* (St. Petersburg: Iuridicheskii Tsentr Press, 2003), 105.

44. M. Usova, "Geroinovye pobirushki," *Auf-Primore* 31 (1999).

45. Vitaly A. Nomokonov, ed., *Organizovannaia prestupnost': tendentsii, perspektivy bor'by* (Vladivostok: Far Eastern University Press, 1999), 106.

46. Ludmila D. Erokhina and Maria Iu. Buriak, *Torgovlia zhenshchinami i det'mi v tselyak seksualnoy ekspluatatsii v sotsia'lnoi kriminologicheskoi perspective* (Moscow: Profobrazovanie, 2003), 368–88.

47. Irina Ruzhnikova, "Russkaia Natasha, Masha, Liza . . . ," in *Chto Pochem* 33 (29 April 1999): 3.

48. Keidel, "Menschenhandel als Phänomen Organisierter Kriminalität," 324.

49. Sergei Skliarov, "Za zheleznyi zanaves—na zakonodatel'noi osnove?" *Inter-baikal*, no. 2 (2000): 29, 27.

50. IOM News Release, "Trafficking in Migrants: The Baltic Route," 24 January 1997.

51. *Reuters World News Service*, 11 June 1996.

52. The proliferation of *chelnoki* is also reminiscent of the interwar period when most private trade took the form of petty transactions in the streets. This trade was known as *meshochnichestvo* (bagging) and helped fill the gaps where the central government's distribution system fell short. The current system of *chelnoki* is similar in its ability to provide consumer goods to regions of short supply.

53. Stephen Flynn, "Globalization and the Future of Border Control," paper presented at Council on Foreign Relations Study Group Meeting, 26 October 1999.

Chapter 2

෯෯෯

Criminal Transportation of Persons:
Trends and Recommendations

Mikhail Kleimenov and Stanislav Shamkov

The term "human trafficking" is usually translated into Russian as "trade in people" (*torgovlia liud'mi*). However, we believe that is not an exact definition because "trafficking" includes transportation and relocation, not only trade. For example, the definition given by the international organization Global Alliance Against Traffic in Women is that trafficking is a complex phenomenon comprising all actions aimed at recruiting women and children in the countries of their residence and/or their transportation abroad for future exploitation through the use of violence or threats, abuse of power and corruption, debt bondage, fraud schemes, and other forms of coercion. The Irkutsk Center for Research on Organized Crime uses the following definition: trafficking in persons is transportation of any person from one location to another within the country of the person's residence or abroad by using force, threats, debt bondage, abuse of power, or breach of contracts, when a person is exploited and forced to work in conditions close to slavery.[1]

The key idea in these definitions is not so much the fact of trade in persons as transportation of people through the use of violence and fraud.

The following points should be taken into consideration in defining trafficking:

- Trafficking should be viewed as transportation and relocation;
- Trafficking is organized transportation that is supported and implemented though purposeful actions on the part of individuals and organizations;
- Trafficking does not always have profit earning or debt repayment as its objective. Persons can also be transported for political reasons;

29

- Human trafficking does not always involve criminal acts that result in human rights violations.

Summing up, we offer the following definition of human trafficking as criminal transportation of people. Criminal transportation of people is the involuntary transportation of a person or a group of people within the country or abroad through the use of violence or any other means that involves or can result in human rights violations.

Let us define the terms we have used in the above definition. *Criminal* does not always mean illegal. For example, if a state or a region has a law that legalizes human rights violations, an act committed within that jurisdiction will be considered legal according to the local laws, but will be criminal in the universal sense. Thus, when talking about *criminal* transportation one should rely on the universal international legal criteria. *Transportation* in this context should be organized. This definition presupposes criminal intent and purposefulness of criminal actions aimed at transportation of people. Moreover, criminal transportation is often performed by an *organization* that specializes in human trafficking. *Involuntary* transportation involves cases of physical and psychological coercion, as well as the situations when a person becomes an object of *manipulation* or *reflexive control*. *Human rights violations* are used as a criterion to determine the criminal nature of transportation and as proof of criminal intent for future criminal exploitation.

Criminal transportation of persons (CTP) is connected—intertwined—with such things as migration, exploitation, and so forth. That is why it is expedient to point out similarities and differences between them.

CTP and migration. In demographics, migration (in Latin, *migratio*— relocation) is defined as transportation of people (migrants) across the borders of territories and regions resulting in permanent or temporary change of residence. CTP is a type of migration that, first, is not voluntary; and second, is organized by a third party. The third party acts purposefully and studies demand and supply, conducts recruitment and advertising, uses a mechanism of psychological manipulation, spreads nets and sets traps in certain social groups, uses violence, frauds, and abuses trust.

CTP and criminal migration. Criminal migration is transportation that has criminal acts as its object as well as other movements that are part of criminal activity. Criminal migration involves movements of the criminals across territorial borders when they run from the law, vengeance, crimes committed by traveling criminals whose preferred type of crimes includes traveling, and so forth. CTP becomes criminal migration when illegal immigration becomes an organized business or when certain routes are created for transporting people who are involved in trafficking in drugs, weapons, and so forth.

CTP and labor migration. Labor migration can be used as cover-up for CTP. In such cases, several large-scale fraud operators act under the pretense of helping people to find jobs abroad.

CTP and trade in "human commodity." Trafficking in women and children is only part of CTP. There are many other parts that should be considered.

CTP and criminal exploitation. Criminal exploitation (work for low pay, performing manual jobs, criminal activities, sex slavery, and so forth) is the outcome of CTP. This is why it is important to study not only CTP but its outcomes as well. On the other hand, CTP is a mechanism used to create conditions for criminal exploitation (it is necessary to transport a victim to the site of future exploitation).

CTP and organized crime. Currently, CTP is an element of organized crime and is protected by it.

Types of Criminal Transportation of People

Criminal transportation of people in sociolegal terms has political and criminal motivation. There are two major types of CTP: political and criminal. The first type covers cases connected with the struggle for power and desire to stay in power, as well as performing the functions of the state, whereas the second involves forming criminal organizations, engaging people in criminal activities, criminal exploitation, and phenomena that are potentially dangerous to society. There is also a type of CTP where criminal transportation can be an element in the policy of certain states as well as a part of criminal business.

In addition, there is criminal transportation of people for political reasons: deportation, internment, exile, and repression. *Deportation* is an organized forced expulsion of people from the country of their residence or sending them to detention centers. One of the most common examples of internment is the arrest and forced relocation of foreign citizens by one of the conflicting or neutral sides in a war or military conflict. It is usually citizens of one of the states involved in a war, who live on the territory of another state, who are subject to internment. *Exile* is implementation of discriminative policies against certain groups aimed at motivating them to leave the administrative district. *Repression* is a type of criminal transportation of people caused by mass conviction for certain minor felonies and using the convicts as cheap labor force.

Criminal transportation of people for criminal purposes includes human trafficking, especially trafficking in women and children, trafficking in human organs for transplants, or organizing illegal labor migration, involving people in illegal trafficking in drugs, weapons, and so forth.

•   Trafficking in women includes organizing prostitution, creating a market offering sex services inside the country, and transporting women to other countries to work in the sex industry. Both "internal" and "external" aspects of prostitution should be considered, because the internal aspects create the condition for the external aspects and influences their quantitative and qualitative characteristics.

•   Trafficking in children is the sale or purchase of minors or any other transaction involving minors that results in giving them to other people.

•   Trafficking in human organs is transportation of donors for transplantation and involves illegal taking of organs that can be used as transplants and sold at transplant markets in the country of origin and abroad.

•   Recruiting people to become couriers for illegal goods (narcotic drugs, weapons, and so forth) is forcing people to transport illegal goods through debt bondage, violence, and threats.

The interim type of criminal transportation includes forcing victims to become slaves, mercenaries, and illegal immigrants. *Slavery* as a political phenomenon exists in states that implement criminal policies. From the criminal point of view, slavery involves kidnapping and turning victims into slaves. Victims are kept prisoners in places where they are forced to work or perform other services through threats of violence. *Kidnapping* involves capturing a person for future exploitation, for ransom, for sexual exploitation, or for satisfaction of the pathological needs of a criminal. *Turning victims into mercenaries* is forcing foreign citizens to participate in a military conflict or a combat operation for pay. Sometimes, people become mercenaries for ideological reasons, but usually it is for money. *Illegal immigration* is the illegal transportation of foreign citizens or persons without citizenship to a third country, or transportation of Russian citizens abroad to work or to become permanent residents that involves violating their human rights and laws of the destination country. This also includes illegal transit of foreign citizens through Russia—that is a relatively new direction in criminal business carried out by representatives of Russian and foreign organizations.

Therefore, criminal transportation of people can be studied as two separate concepts: CTP as an element of criminal state policy and CTP as a branch of criminal entrepreneurship. Sometimes, those two concepts become intertwined.

CTP as an Element of Criminal State Policy

For a long time, Chechnya has been the arena for the ancient criminal trade of kidnapping people for ransom. According to the Main Directorate for Fighting Organized Crime of Russia's Ministry of Internal Affairs, in 1999, twenty-seven organized armed criminal groups that specialized in kidnapping people for ransom were active in Chechnya. Their leaders for the most part were field commanders. Overall, according to the operations intelligence, as many as 150 organized criminal groups were involved in kidnapping. Their leaders and most active participants are the subjects of 159 criminal cases. Nasrudin Bazhiev, Chechnya's deputy minister of the interior, Movsar Baraiev, brigade general and former bodyguard of Zelimhan Iandarbaev, and Vaha Arsanov, former prime minister of the Chechen Republic of Ichkeria were charged in these cases. Operations intelligence shows that Arsanov was the mastermind and coordinator of many kidnappings within and outside of Chechnya. Also, Iandarbaev, former acting president of the Chechen Republic of Ichkeria, and of course, "field commanders" Basaev and Salman Raduev were involved in this criminal activity.[2] This shows that the current slave trade in Ichkeria emerged and developed under the protection of the Chechen authorities.

The slave trade has been immensely profitable for its organizers. The ransom paid for the Russian president's plenipotentiary in Chechnya was $3.5 million ($5 million according to other sources). Ransoms for journalists and foreign citizens were also very high. Experts estimate that more than $600 million in ransoms were paid to militants in 1997–1999. More than 1,000 people were freed from Chechen slavery.[3]

Although the war in the Caucasus stimulated slave trade in the region, slaves had been used in the Caucasus during Soviet times as well. In recent years, this business, along with trafficking in weapons and drugs, has become the basis of the criminal economy in Chechnya and Ingushetiya. Military actions have not only spurred an increase in the slave trade, but also have made it more diverse. Militants started kidnapping Russians, Chechens, and Ingush from neighboring villages. Slaves are being used not only for their labor or as commodities, but also as organ donors. Since the Khasavyurt Treaty was signed in 1996, the number of slaves and hostages kidnapped in the Daghestan, Ossetiia, Stavropol, and Krasnodar regions has increased. People have been kidnapped or tricked into coming to Chechnya or its neighboring regions where they were later sold to Chechens. Specialists in construction and oil processing were in the highest demand. Special agents have testified that criminal groups from Daghestan specialize in this type of business.

During the second Chechen campaign, every region taken by the Russian troops was thoroughly searched. According to witnesses, practically every household had a basement—called *zindan* by the locals—that was used for keeping slaves and prisoners of war.

Illegal immigration, which is relatively new in Russia, is a type of CTP that emerged after the new law on freedom of entry and exit was enacted. The Federal Agency for Migration estimates the number of illegal migrants at one million people. Specialists at the Ministry of the Interior say that there are between 700,000 and 2.5 million foreign citizens and people without citizenship in Russia.[4] Sociologists believe that this figure is 3–4 million people,[5] most of whom are citizens of the CIS countries who work in Russia illegally. However, more and more foreign citizens are coming to Russia as illegal immigrants.

Most illegal immigrants from foreign countries come from Afghanistan and Africa. There are also many illegal workers from China. Studies show that there may be as many as 500,000 Chinese working in Russia, including 300,000 in the border regions in East Siberia and Far East.

According to Alexander Shaikin, head of the Department of Border Control of Russia's Federal Border Service, from January 1999 until June 2000 more than a million Chinese citizens illegally entered and now reside in Russia. In that period, 1.5 million Chinese legally entered Russia. Only 237,000 of them registered; the rest disappeared somewhere in Russia. In Moscow city and region, only 12,000 Chinese of the 40,000–60,000 who reside there are officially registered. In official circles, that phenomenon is called the "quiet expansion" of China into Russia.[6]

At the same time, there is migration inside Russia, where people move from northern and eastern regions to the central and southwestern parts of the country. The population in the northern parts of the Far East has been decreasing dramatically. Since 1989, the population in the Chukotka and Magadan regions has decreased by half, in the Kamchatka region by 20 percent, in Sakhalin by 15 percent, and in the Far Eastern region as a whole by 10 percent.[7] If those tendencies continue and the government keeps ignoring problems in the Far East, the quiet expansion by the Chinese into that region rich in raw materials and natural resources is inevitable.

CTP as a Trend in Criminal Entrepreneurship

Survey Results

To determine the scale of the modern CTP, we surveyed various categories of people, including businessmen specializing in wholesale and retail. That category was chosen based on their personal experience in international travel (participating in so-called "shopping tours") and the environment in which they work, where they often discuss issues that are the focus of our survey. Therefore, those entrepreneurs know more, compared to other social groups, about criminal transportation of people. At the same time, their opinion should not be considered to be absolute and should be weighed against experts' opinion. For experts, we selected specialists from agencies combating violent crimes—deputy directors of violent crimes units in a number of cities in Siberia and the Far East, as well as officers in other law-enforcement agencies. We asked the same questions of criminal police officers in Omsk to determine the criminological situation in the field in question in that region. The results of the survey are shown in table 2.1.

Respondents' opinions on the scale of criminal transportation of people are shown in table 2.2. (Question: Mass media often report on cases when Russian citizens are transported abroad for future criminal exploitations. What is your opinion on the issue?) As the table shows, the majority commented that this is a rather widespread phenomenon. The numbers were even higher among the experts. Eighty-eight percent of law-enforcement officers who responded said that

Table 2.1 Methodology of Survey on the Criminal Transportation of Persons

Date of survey	Type of questionnaire (Number of questions)	Theme of questionnaire	Number of respondents
January 2000	Pilot questionnaire (5)	"Slavery in Russia"	198[a]
February–March 2000	Questionnaire (16)	"Criminal Exploitation of People"	559[b]
March–April 2000	Questionnaire (15)	"Criminal Transportation of People"	588[c]
March–December 2000	Experts' opinion (67)	"Criminal Transportation of People"	117[d]
September–December 2000	Opinion of officers in criminal police service (67)	"Criminal Transportation of People"	136

[a] Of those, 47.5% were students, 15.7% professionals, 7.6% representatives of the business sector, 4% workers, 3.5% representatives of law-enforcement agencies, 2.5% housewives, 1% pensioners, 0.5% unemployed; 17.7% declined to give their occupation.

[b] Respondents are entrepreneurs and persons working in sales at the wholesale fair "Torgovy Riad" in the city of Omsk. Of them, 43.8% were men (18–25 years old, 31.8%; 26–30 years old, 29.4%; 31–40 years old, 22.9%; 40 and over, 16.9%) and 56.2% women (18–25 years old, 33.1%; 26–30 years old, 18.5%; 31–40 years old, 31.5%; 40 and over, 16.9%).

[c] Of those, 52.9% were students, 22.8% professionals (state officers, economists, lawyers, medical personnel, teachers, academics), 6.6% unemployed, 5.8% entrepreneurs, 4.9% manual workers, 2.2% representatives of law-enforcement agencies.

[d] Average number of years in law enforcement—8.5.

Table 2.2 Opinion of Survey Respondents on the Extent of Criminal Transportation of People (percentages)

	Experts	Officers in criminal police service	Citizens
Never heard about it	1.4	1.0	7.1
Think it is a journalists' hoax	5.1	6.5	7.8
Know about cases like this	60.2	56.9	48.5
Believe it is a widespread phenomenon	33.3	35.6	36.6

Table 2.3 Purposes of Criminal Transportation of People As Seen by Respondents (percentages)

	Russia's criminal police service			Omsk City Police			
	Male	Female	Children	Male	Female	Children	Nonexperts
Exploited for their labor	69.2	38.5	17.9	79.5	38.6	13.6	39.6
Used as organ donors	30.8	30.8	56.4	22.7	13.6	47.7	33.2
Exploited in sex industry	10.3	84.6	51.3	2.2	75	16	43.4
Kidnapped for ransom	28.2	35.9	35.9	13.6	9	27.3	33.2
Taken hostage and robbed of possessions	15.4	12.8	5.1	13.5	11.4	2.3	14

the pretense most often used for criminal transportation of people is going abroad to work, 44 percent named tourism, 14.8 percent immigration, and 11 percent marriage. They also felt that 85.2 percent of women are criminally transported under the guise of looking for work, 44 percent for tourism, and 40.7 percent for commercial purposes. Women often use marriage to migrate. A majority, 59.3 percent, of the criminal police officers responding said that most cases of CTP are disguised as one of the activities mentioned above. Most of the time, adoption is used as cover for transporting children.

The majority (87.5 percent) of law-enforcement officers know of cases where persons were freed from criminal dependency. Of those, 41.7 percent said that victims were freed from various types of slavery when they asked a Russian consulate abroad for help, and 33 percent said that victims received help after they complained to their families who lived in Russia. In addition, 29.2 percent of the experts responding believe that victims had to buy their freedom; 25 percent said that asking for help from families abroad also helped victims; 20.8 percent said that local law enforcement helped; and 16.7 percent said that it was just luck.

Data used in table 2.3 help to form an idea about purposes of criminal transportation of people. It shows that in most cases criminal transportation of men leads to labor exploitation and that of women to exploitation in the sex industry, while children are used as organ donors.

Labor Exploitation

The majority of experts (80 percent) surveyed commented that most cases of CTP resulted in labor exploitation. CTP can be either intrastate or interstate. Most victims of internal CTP are homeless, unemployed people and other representatives of marginal groups, who have no family. These people are offered drinks, and when they are drunk are transported to the exploitation site. They are forced to work, and the only payment they receive is bad food, a place to sleep, and rarely, cheap liquor. CTP can take place either within a region (labor exploitation on construction sites) or abroad (mostly, labor exploitation on farms). CTP of other cheap labor takes people from Siberia to Central Asian states or to republics of the former Soviet Union (for example, from Omsk to Kazakhstan). The majority of the experts surveyed believe that the people who sell fruit in their respective cities did not make it a secret that most of the fruit was grown on farms in the former Soviet republics that used labor of Russian slaves.

The experts surveyed also mentioned cases where parents would sell their children. For example, some traditional families of little means in Central Asia sell their children to well-off neighbors. In return, they receive food and are allowed to use agricultural equipment. Thus, if they sell two or three of their children they can afford to feed the rest of the family. Sometimes, children are sold with all of their papers to wealthy individuals who use them not only for difficult work, but also for sexual services. The average price of a child in Tajikistan, for example, is \$200–\$300.

In Russia, labor exploitation has become almost legal. The recent construction boom in Moscow would never have been possible had it not been for slave labor of immigrants from other CIS countries. Many of them come to Russia, find jobs, and stay illegally. There are well-established recruitment agencies that have offices in neighboring countries and that specialize in supplying slave laborers to Russia. Local authorities choose not to notice this, as construction companies are major taxpayers to local budgets. Moreover, many officers in law-enforcement agencies as well as local government officials benefit from CTP into their regions. In Ukraine, Moldova, and Belarus, construction sites have become diaspora where the construction workers live. The laborers agree to work in conditions that are almost inhuman.

Criminal groups also use illegal migrants as potential slaves or recruit them to become criminals. "Construction slaves" have so few rights and so little protection that criminal elements have no difficulty finding potential criminals who are ready to do anything, including killing people for hire. That is why illegal immigration is a source of crime.

In recent years, the number of Russian citizens who go to the West looking for work has been growing. In most cases, these people become victims of illegal immigration. Very often immigrants from Russia fall prey to fraud schemes where a Russian guest worker (in German, *gastarbeiter*) is transported abroad where she or he is held financially dependent on the recruiter while working twelve- to fourteen-hour days on a private construction site. After a few months, the victim learns that he or she has earned almost nothing and all of the wages were kept by the recruiter.[8]

During a telephone interview, a native of Omsk, Evgenyi M., who had traveled to Portugal to work as a construction worker, stated

> I had worked as a retail salesperson at a market but, unfortunately, it was not enough to support my young family, which is why I decided to go work abroad. I had heard a number of stories about a friend of a friend who went to an economically developed country, found a job within a week, and a month later was sending as much money as he would make in a year in Russia back to his family. I made up my mind to go to a recruiting agency that specializes in finding work abroad and was pleasantly surprised to see a respectable looking office offering great customer service. It was explained that I would have a two-month visa, which should be enough for me to save up some money.
>
> I had to borrow money to pay for the trip, and I hoped that working in a rich country I would be able to pay it back very soon. Upon arrival to the country, we were greeted at the airport and taken to a hotel. Later we met with a representative of the recruitment agency. We had an option of either paying up front or later, when we had made some money, for his services. In the first few weeks, we made enough to pay the rent and pay off the debt to the agency, but there was nothing left to save. As soon as we paid off the debt and could afford saving we were fined by the local police as our papers had expired. We had no money to get home. On top of everything, our construction brigade was threat-

ened by a group of Russian racketeers. I guess we could have borrowed some money to buy tickets to go home, but at the very thought of going home after so much time, having earned nothing and with even more debt, we decided against it. So, we had to look for jobs illegally. And since then it has been a vicious circle. To get out of it, we [it was clear from the conversation that there was a considerable number of Russian illegal workers in the country] had to organize something like a credit union where all of us would pitch in to get enough money for one of us to go home, while the rest of us would have to look for more work.

At the end, Evgenyi said that his turn to take the money is coming up and he should be going home soon.

For the most part, recruitment of people for employment in foreign countries is illegal. According to Omsk regional law-enforcement agencies, in 2000 there were four legally registered agencies that recruited and transported Russian citizens to work abroad. The rest of them—sixty—worked illegally. Thus, the ratio between legal and illegal agencies was 1:15. In 2001, this ratio changed: there were two legal and ninety illegal agencies. Most of them were regional offices of Moscow and St. Petersburg agencies. When inspected by law-enforcement agencies, people at the offices could not show registration papers and the offices closed before they could be inspected again.

Potential immigrants and appropriate authorities should understand these issues better. In reality, no one is trying to solve the problem. Officials blame the fact that there are no immigration posts and say that the president's decree "On measures for introducing migration control" is not being implemented because funds are lacking.

The constitutional right for freedom of movement makes it almost impossible to track citizens' movement inside the country. Therefore, the problem should be solved by providing security for citizens who travel abroad (for example, as travel insurance). In this respect, preventive information programs that target potential victims of CTP are especially useful.

Trafficking in Women

Trafficking in women was the second most often mentioned and commented on type of CTP. A typical scheme of trafficking in women is: recruitment, transportation abroad, sale to the client/employer, and exploitation. The last stage is the end of the cycle. Only when a woman has been exploited can we talk about an act of criminal transportation, as we can clearly see its consequences.

This chain of actions shows that trafficking in women is organized crime.[9] It is evident that this is part of a larger industry—the entertainment industry. It is interesting to analyze the so-called "victim market." Potential victims of trafficking are women who are ready to take risks and are prepared to join a marginal group abroad provided that they will be well paid for their services. The results of our survey show that most of the recruited women are aware of or at least suspect what kind of work they are expected to do, even if the recruiters promise them that their services will not be of a sexual nature. Mass media have already formed a stereotypical image of the fate of a woman who goes to work abroad. This stereotype is confirmed by our respondents, 43 percent of whom said that in most cases women recruited tend to be sexually exploited abroad. Therefore, most people are aware of the potential dangers, and a woman who chooses to go abroad to work in show business realizes the potential danger of such a decision. She takes the risk because she hopes she will either have control of the situation or be lucky.

There is a large market of prostitutes in Russia and it is not difficult to recruit women who would like to work as prostitutes abroad. There is no need for recruiters to use complicated fraud schemes. In any Russian town there are a number of prostitutes who work on its main roads. In Omsk, such prostitutes charge 5–100 rubles and work without any protection. Hotels have their own groups of prostitutes, who charge 300–400 rubles. These groups work with pimps who keep all of the profits and later pay part of them to the prostitute. There are also call girls working with pimps who bring them to the client, take the money, and pick the prostitute up at a certain time. These prostitutes charge by the hour, and the prices are 150-350 rubles.

The prostitutes who work in hotels are professionals and are ready to serve any client or a group of them as long as they are paid for their services. Many prostitutes of this type are ready to travel abroad in the hope of earning more than they can earn in their home country. Therefore, they agree to work abroad even if it means taking more risks. Traffickers recruit most of their victims among these women. A much smaller portion of recruited women are those who hope to go abroad and work in a legal sphere.

A state that receives a large number of women exploited in the sex industry must assume a proactive role in investigations. For example, in summer 1999, about fifty young Russian women traveled to Cyprus to work as prostitutes. This incident provoked a wave of investigations on how the women entered Cyprus and what agency helped them. The authorities then tightened visa control, a step that was supported by the population. As a result, the number of prostitutes entering Cyprus decreased.

In some of the states, attempts on the part of the government to prevent the criminal transportation of migrants lead to discriminatory policies. For example, Australia's Immigration Service published a list of countries whose citizens, depending on their age and gender, are not welcome in Australia. The list included Russian women twenty and older, Greek men and women twenty to twenty-nine, Lebanese citizens twenty and older, Pakistanis under fifty, and people from other countries (Turkey, West Samoa, China, Croatia, Egypt, Fiji, Philippines, Romania, Vietnam, and Sri Lanka) are on this list. Citizens of those countries had been caught trying to stay in Australia after their papers expired and had joined the numbers of illegal immigrants. For example, 7 percent of Russian women twenty and older overstay their visas in Australia.

Such a discriminatory policy violates human rights. Solving the problem of criminal transportation at the expense of human rights is not acceptable. Rather, it should be a joint effort of national governments implementing policies aimed at combating criminal transportation and trafficking, and the policies should be supported by all parties involved in the process.

Trafficking in Children

Official statistics show that forty-five people in seventy-four cases were charged with trafficking of children in Russia in 1997, forty-nine people in thirty-five cases in 1998, thirty people in twenty-eight cases in 1999, and eight people in thirty-seven cases in 2000. For modern Russia, characterized by very low morals and with a number of people who are ready to make quick money, those are low numbers. At the same time, intelligence from a number of Russia's regions shows that trafficking in children has become an industry. For example, inspections carried out by the regional procurator's office in the Sverdlovsk region showed that the number of children adopted by foreign families has increased by five times. During 1999, 378 Russian children were adopted by families in Europe and the United States. According to our source in the procurator's office, the adoption process in most cases was not in accordance with existing law. All orphanages in the regions made sure that foreign families interested in adoption were told about new children in orphanages before Russian families who wanted to adopt children were told of them. The procurator's office found that directors of orphanages were in direct contact with foreign adoption centers and "took orders" to supply children. "It was trafficking in children, when foreigners would order healthy children of certain age and gender and got their order," commented a source in the procurator's office.[10]

Article 165 of Russia's Family Code regulates the adoption of Russian children by foreign citizens and people without citizenship. Obviously, if the number of children adopted by foreign families grows, the number of children available for adoption by Russian families goes down. In 1994, 2,196 children were adopted by foreigners and taken outside Russia, in 1995 this number was 1,497,[11] in 1996—3,251, in 1997—5,739,[12] in 1998—5,647,[13] in 1999—6,000.[14] The number of children adopted by Russian families is as follows: 1996—27,377, 1997—20,677, 1998—19,800, 1999—18,830. If foreign families continue to adopt Russian children, in 2004 the number of children adopted by foreigners will surpass the number of children adopted by Russian families.

Adoption of Russian children by foreign families has become common. However, according to regulations on control over adoption of children and the conditions under which they live in their new families, foreign citizens or people without citizenship can adopt Russian children only if Russian families or the children's relatives are not able to adopt them.

It is not bad that foreigners adopt Russian children. Yuri Sergeev, a judge in the Omsk region, during an interview said: "We should be grateful to foreigners who adopt our sick or dying children. There was an incident when the paper-work for adoption took too long and the child died before he was taken out of the country. Had it been done faster, the child might have survived. Foreigners take our sick children out of this poor country to help those children; they save their lives." It is true that Russian citizens tend to adopt fewer children, which indicates that the people in the country are becoming poorer.

We should support and encourage humanitarian efforts of foreign citizens while at the same time making sure that philanthropy does not become a cover for trafficking in children.

In 1997, the Russian State Duma approved a decree "On Emergency Measures to Increase Control over Adoption" aimed at preventing the negative tendencies that endanger Russia's national security through criminalization of international adoption.[15] A more recent government decree on adoption enacted in March 2000 states that every Russian child adopted by a foreigner should be registered with a Russian consulate. There are other normative acts and laws that regulate control over the lives of children adopted by foreign citizens. For example, every year consulates are required to submit lists of Russian children adopted by foreigners and registered with the consulate to Russia's Ministry of Education. They are also required to inform Russian authorities of any violation of the rights of the adopted child and of his well-being in the new family. Thus, there is legislation aimed at controlling the process of adoption of Russian children by foreign citizens. On the other hand, there are flaws and drawbacks in this control that allow various abuses, including those of a criminal nature. For example, there are still intermediaries who charge foreigners a fee for helping to find a child, which is illegal under Article 126-1 of Russia's Family Code.

It is important to address the problem of criminal transportation of children abroad. They can be taken out of the country by using the lack of control on certain borders, for example, the border between Russia and Kazakhstan. The CIS countries are often used as a staging point for criminal transportation of people. It is very easy to enter Azerbaijan (Russian citizens do not need visas to travel there) and then Iran (Azerbaijan and Iran do not require visas for their citizens to travel to the other country), and so forth. As Ludmila Guseva, an officer with the Passport and Visa service in the Omsk region notes, this creates a so-called "green corridor."

The challenge that traffickers in children face is obtaining a child. They can either buy it from the parents or from doctors in a hospital. For example, in Nizhnii Novgorod one doctor sold almost a hundred children to foster parents. In Riazan, a criminal group that specialized in trafficking in children had been active for a long time. Among its members were local government officials in charge of making decisions about adoptions and the director of a Riazan orphanage. "In a Riazan orphanage there was a well-established business of selling children to foreigners," said Viktor Golev, an officer with the Riazan police. "Olga Svetlova, the chief doctor of the orphanage; her daughter, who worked as a nurse, and her son-in-law, who worked in the same orphanage, were all involved. It was some sort of a 'family business.'"[16]

Physiological Exploitation of Minors

There are other schemes of trafficking in children that involve the use of and exploitation of a person's physiognomy. One example is the use of surrogate mothers whereby an offer is made to a woman in Russia that she be impregnated with the donor's sperm. The delivery is to take place in, for example, Israel or the United States. After the baby is born, the mother must give it up for $1,000–$2,000 dollars. Organizers of this scheme in Russia will get $10,000 and more in cash, said Mikhail Churaev, an officer with the Moscow police.

Complex investigations are required to prevent such activities. Unfortunately, in many regions—such as Omsk—no preventive measures are being taken. Possible channels used for trafficking in children have not been found and closed. Moreover, there is no legislation that regulates the criminal responsibility for intermediaries in helping foreign nationals to adopt Russian children who are criminally transported abroad.

The majority of respondents to our survey (33 percent) noted that victims are being used as organ donors. However, only 20 percent of law-enforcement officers believed that it was one of the goals of CTP. Most of them said that although such a crime may exist they personally are not aware of it. Experts can only guess that some victims of criminal exploitation become organ donors. This phenomenon can be explained in two ways: either the information on CTP for transplantation is incorrect or such cases are very latent. Evidently, both of those explanations are true. However, the fact that CTP for transplantation exists, even in very small numbers, should not be neglected.

In addition, in recent years there have been a number of cases when people with birth defects were used as beggars. Police arrested a group of Ukrainians who trafficked deaf-mutes from Ukraine, Belarus, and Moldova to European countries as tourists. The deaf-mutes were promised a decent job abroad. However, when they arrived at their destination they were placed in cheap hotels and forced to become beggars. They also had to pay $700–$1,400 a month to their traffickers. Police worked for nine months on the operation to arrest this group. It was not easy to arrest and to charge the criminals, as they were acting on behalf of a union of people with disabilities and their leader was the director of a Ukrainian association of deaf-mutes. However, not long ago forty-six members of the group, including the leader, were arrested in France. During the investigation, police found that in France alone there were more than four hundred deaf-mutes who worked for this group, bringing in about $400,000 in profits every month. Unfortunately, France was not the only country where the group was active; they also penetrated Spain, Germany, Austria, Greece, and Portugal.[17]

Last but not least, we would like to mention the criminal use of minors to transport narcotics in their bodies. This type of CTP uses victims as mules to carry drugs. Very often victims are held in bondage to drug traffickers. Materials studied show that 11.8 percent of all publications on CTP issues dealt with cases where persons were used as mules.

Determinants of Criminal Transportation of People

The major determinants in transportation of people are:

Lower moral standards of the Russian people. The use of criminal methods to implement social and economic reforms in the post-Soviet state, combined with the replacement of moral values with economic expediency, propaganda of more cynical and dissolute attitudes among young people by the mass media, and new idols of the young people that contradict moral norms and traditional values have led to the emergence of a new category of people that produces both "entrepreneurs" ready to do the dirtiest business and believe that any money is good, and victims who are ready to take part in any adventure, provided that it will provide them financial well-being.

Economic difficulties in Russia. Statistics show that 34.7 percent of Russians (50.5 million) live below poverty level. Ten percent of all Russians of employment age are unemployed. It should be noted that these are the official statistics that are often much lower than the real numbers.[18] Many Russian citizens feel neglected by their own government. The reforms have a criminal nature and so far the new regime has all of the negative effects of capitalism that were condemned in Soviet times. Living conditions are deteriorating instead of improving. Those are the criteria that shape attitudes in the Russian society. A poll taken in thirty Russian regions after the financial crisis of 1998 showed that 18 percent of Russian citizens were ready to immigrate if the economic situation continued to worsen.[19] Many representatives of the generations that grew up during reforms have neither the education nor the skills to perform certain jobs. All they are interested in is making money.

Strong economic foundation of the shadow economy. According to Luciano Violante, the former speaker of the Italian parliament, in 1996 alone profits from the shadow economy constituted 2 percent of the world's GNP, and they have almost doubled in recent years. Most of the criminal profits come from trafficking in weapons, drugs, and people. Violante believes that modern slave trade brings up to $5 billion a year in profits, and most of its victims are refugees, immigrants, and children. In his opinion, the only way to stop trafficking is to undermine its economic foundation. This is why he proposed closing offshore zones. (There are about twenty of them in the world).[20]

Economic instability in military conflict areas. Areas of military conflicts and economic instability attract criminals and become zones without law and order. Kosovo is an example of such a zone. Peter Finn reported in the *Washington Post* that from the end of 1998 through early 2000 UN troops and peacekeepers rescued fifty Moldovan, Ukrainian, Bulgarian, and Romanian women who worked in brothels in cities and towns in Kosovo.[21] Police forces and humanitarian organizations believe that hundreds of women who come to Europe to make money are kept as slaves. Police officers say women, some of them as young as fifteen, are brought from different parts of Eastern Europe to Macedonia, which shares a border with Kosovo. There they are kept in motels until they are sold at auction to pimps, most of whom are ethnic Albanians. Officials believe that the pimps work under the protection of the major criminals in Kosovo, including some who are members of the so-called Kosovo Liberation Army.

Lack of legislation and investigative units. Law-enforcement structures that specialize in combating criminal transportation of people are poorly developed. The majority (77.8 percent) of the law enforcement officers who responded to our survey noted that criminal exploitation of people is not recognized in Russia; therefore, there is no appropriate legislation on the issue.

Imperfections in using the appropriate laws and legal norms. Often, the existing legal norms and laws are used either ineffectively or not at all.

Latent nature of CTP problems. Most CTP victims are afraid of the traffickers. 48.1 percent of the experts among the respondents said that victims are afraid to come forward.

Therefore, we can conclude that we can combat criminal transportation of people only if we find solutions to a number of interwoven problems. Priority should be given to improving the legislative basis of the laws to create legal barriers that will prevent criminal transportation of potential victims.

Notes

1.   "Concept of Human Trafficking: Problems in Combating Organized Crime," Information Bulletin, Irkutsk Center for Research on Organized Crime 7 (2000), 3.
2.   Larisa Kislinskaia, "How Much Is a Russian Slave on the Chechen Market?" *Sovershenno Sekretno* 3 (1999).
3.   Vladimor Shurygin, *Caucasus* (Munich: Zavtra, 1999), 11.
4.   Russia's Ministry of the Interior Bulletin 4 (2001): 46.
5.   Evgeniy Krasinets, Elena Kubishina, and Elena Tiuriukanova, *Illegal Migration in Russia* (Moscow: Academia, 2000), 82.
6.   Federal Border Service announces "quiet expansion" of Chinese into Russia, *Lenta.Ru,* 26 June 2000, http://lenta.ru.
7.   Materials of the Center for Strategic Studies, www.csr.ru (25 April 2000).
8.   *Nezavisimaia Gazeta*, 3 November 2000.
9.   Sally Stoecker, "Organized Crime as a Factor in Increase of Human Trafficking: Organized Crime and Corruption: Surveys, Reviews, Information," *Socio-legal Almanac* 1 (2000): 57.
10.   "Sverdlovsk Region. The procurator's office is about to open 20 cases on charges in trafficking in children," Political News Agency, http://apn.ru (17 March 2000).
11.   "Family in Russia: Statistical Data/Russia's State Committee on Statistics," Moscow, 1996, 134.

12. See State Report, "On the Situation with Children in the Russian Federation in 1997" (Moscow: Synergia, 1998), 40.

13. State Annual Report, 40.

14. According to experts at the Court Department.

15. Russian State Duma Decree passed on 19 September 1997, N 1728-II GD "On Emergency Measures to Increase Control over Adoption," *Rossiiskaia Gazeta*, 10 October 1997.

16. Alexander Badanov, "Child traffickers: The Art of Possible, http://www.poptsov.ru (9 November 2000).

17. Russian News Bureau, 6 May 2000.

18. *Rossiiskaia Gazeta*, 29 August 2000.

19. Immigration News 1, "Sweet Dream" (Internet weekly publication for immigrants) INFOTEK, Inc., www.sd.and.ru (21 June 2000).

20. Lev Moskovkin, "Novosti Dnia: v Gosdume," *Russkii Zhurnal*, http://www.russ.ru (17 June 1999).

21. *Washington Post*, 25 April 2000.

Chapter 3

ক৯ক৯ক৯

Classifying the Elements of Human Trafficking Crimes

Anna Repetskaia

None of the existing definitions of "human trafficking" reflect the true meaning of this phenomenon or illustrate all of its dimensions.[1] Human trafficking is a complex phenomenon consisting of several phases and stages, the aggregate of which allows the criminal exploitation of people.

Types of Victim Acquisition

The first stage involved in human trafficking is acquiring and transporting the person who will be exploited or sold for future exploitation. First and foremost, a person needs to be acquired.[2] This can be done in a number of ways, which differ according to the purpose of future exploitation.

Classifying victim acquisition by type shows that criminal exploitation does not always involve the sale of a person. It depends on the stage at which a victim is acquired. One can speak about initial and subsequent acquisition. Initial acquisition as a rule does not involve any sale, whereas subsequent acquisition of the same victim usually occurs when ownership of a victim is transferred from one owner to another as property.

Sales of persons presuppose that victim acquisition for criminal exploitation is by purchasing a victim from a third person. In those cases, a victim is sold, given as a gift, or used as security. Initial acquisition can involve kidnapping, capture, or fraud. Fraud usually involves the use of advertisements in mass media for work abroad or for marriage, or through acquaintances who can turn out to be recruiters. Initial kidnapping and capture of a victim for further exploitation usually occurs in regions troubled by difficult political and military situations or regions of military conflict.

Types of victim acquisition can also be divided according to acquisition purpose—for future sale or for immediate exploitation. For example, in Ukraine, traffickers make between $200 and $5,000 for each woman they "recruit."[3] Their "recruitment" is by acquiring a person for future sale, or when a middleman purchases a victim to sell to a new owner.

Neither the recruiter nor the middleman in those cases exploits the victim, but they profit from selling the victim to other parties, who might either exploit the victim themselves or sell the victim. Often, a victim is transported to a destination country and then sold to a "master" who exploits them. The "master" is able to sell the victim to someone else if it would be more profitable than acquiring the profits of the victim's labor.

Usually, a victim is given advance funds for airfare and documents necessary for traveling abroad. The victim then is asked to sign a contract that describes an acceptable job. It is assumed that all the expenses will be repaid after the victim starts working. According to the Global Survival Network, recruiters in Russia and the Commonwealth of Independent States (CIS) charge $1,500–$30,000 for their "services" in helping to prepare documents, finding jobs, and providing transportation to a foreign country.[4] Very often, the victim learns on arrival that he or she will be working under different conditions and in different positions; it is almost impossible to repay the initial costs under such conditions of severe exploitation. Women, as a rule, are exploited in the sex industry.

A buyer can purchase a victim for immediate exploitation. In this case, it is those who buy the victim from a middleman who is the exploiter, and the victim becomes a prostitute or works in an industry immediately after he or she is purchased.

Classification of Transportation Types

When a victim has been acquired, the next stage is transportation to the exploitation site. Classification of transportation types is very diverse and is based on several criteria, such as crossing national borders, victim's consent to be transported, and the legality of transportation of potential victims. Victim relocation for criminal exploitation can occur with or without the victim's consent. Although criminal exploitation presupposes lack of consent by the victim, often a victim agrees to be relocated. Frequently, young women or men would like to travel abroad to accept a job they have been offered and they leave the country voluntarily, without being forced or threatened to do so.

As a rule, a person becomes a victim through acquisition. He or she is held by the recruiter through some action, including violence, or is involved in fraud. Most of the victims in this category come from marginal groups, have no place to live, and have no relatives who would be concerned about their disappearance.

If the victim is not willing to be relocated, other means of coercion, such as violence, intimidation, and threats are used to influence her. The victim can also be forced into bondage and relocated. In such cases, the victim's decision to be relocated cannot be seen as voluntary because it was made under duress. Transportation in these cases is illegal and should be considered criminal.

Once a victim is recruited, he or she is transported to the site of criminal exploitation. There are several types of transportation, and the victim may or may not have to cross the border of the country of residence. Thus, transportation can be of two types: within the country of the victim's residence and outside the country of the victim's residence.

In the first case, the victim is criminally exploited in the country where he or she resides. The victim can be a citizen, a person without citizenship, or a person with dual citizenship. Within the victim's country of residence the victim can either be taken from his/her place of residence or left in his/her original town.

Criminal exploitation within national borders presupposes that the victim will be transported from the place of his or her permanent residence and taken outside of the administrative border of the region. The current situation in southern Russia, for example, in Chechnya, is a good example of such transportation. Chechen human traffickers recruit people in other regions of Russia, mostly in the neighboring areas, or inside Chechnya. In both cases, they are transported to Chechnya or another region for further exploitation. Later they will either be used as laborers or sold to other "owners." There have been a number of cases where Russian soldiers liberated victims taken prisoners of war or bought years ago and made to work as slaves living in inhumane conditions.

If a victim is not transported from the place of residence, he or she is moved within the administrative region. Victims who work in underground sweatshops or as seasonal workers are examples of such exploitation. Russian mass media recently covered a case in one of the country's regions where a man turned his garage into a sweatshop for manufacturing underwear. He lured his potential victims by asking them to come in and have a drink. Some of the victims had spent several years in the garage, where they were not only deprived of all human rights, but were not even allowed to go outside. All of the victims had previously lived close to the garage but had no permanent housing or jobs.[5]

Acquisition and transportation of victims for criminal exploitation within national borders still takes place in states of the former Soviet Union. For the most part, victims came from marginal groups and previously had been arrested for hooliganism or other minor offenses. They were used to work in illegal goldmines. The profits from their exploitation were used to support organized crime.[6]

Although criminal exploitation within national borders does exist, it is not nearly as widespread as criminal exploitation of victims outside the country of their permanent residence. Several factors make transporting victims to a foreign country for criminal exploitation more alluring. First is the poor economic situation in the country of the victim's origin. Since most of the victims go from poorer countries to more developed countries, the market for the services they offer is larger and the demand for those services is higher in the destination country than in the country of the victim's origin. Also, it is much easier to exploit the victim in a foreign country where he or she has very few rights.

Because of the poor economic situation in a number of Eastern European countries, the CIS, and some other states, victims often leave their native countries looking for a better life, but instead become victims of criminal exploitation. These victims are different from illegal immigrants, who choose to illegally enter a foreign country looking for a better life. Unlike them, the victim might have entered a foreign country legally, but does not have the right to be employed. Illegal immigrants are ready to work in worse conditions and for lower pay. However, they are not forced to do so; they can quit their jobs any time they want. Also, illegal immigrants usually work in legal sectors of the economy, such as industry and the service sector.

At the same time, victims of criminal exploitation and illegal immigrants have a lot in common. Very often illegal immigrants become victims of human smugglers after they enter a foreign country to try to find a job. They cannot afford to pay intermediaries for helping them cross the border and they become indebted to smugglers who immediately start exploiting them. As a result, illegal immigrants are often used in criminal activities such as drug trafficking and prostitution.

When a victim is transported across a border legally, he or she enters a foreign country in compliance with the law. A victim can be transported abroad with all of the rules observed and all the necessary documents in order—in such a case, the transportation is legal. Many agencies that recruit human "commodities" help the victim to prepare documents for traveling abroad. As a rule, a victim is issued a tourist visa that in many countries (especially in Europe) is valid for three months. Also, a victim can travel to a foreign country on a visa allowing her to work in the entertainment industry. For example, in 1994 Switzerland issued 1,074 "artist" visas to women from developing countries, more than half of whom came from Eastern Europe and almost one-third (three hundred) from Russia.[7]

A victim is transported across the border illegally when he or she either cannot enter the destination country legally or there is not enough time to prepare all of the necessary documents. In that case, smugglers use fake documents, transport a victim by car, or help her walk across the border. As a result, a victim is even more vulnerable in the destination country because he or she has entered it illegally.

Corruption is a useful tool for both legal and illegal transportation. Most of the agencies involved in human trafficking have connections with state officials and consular officers who help to prepare documents necessary for traveling abroad or who prepare fake documents. According to the Global Survival Network, persons involved in human trafficking were able to buy fake passports from the officials at the Ministry of Foreign Affairs or from agencies that work with Interpol and used these documents to change names, citizenships, or ages of the victims before they were transported abroad.[8]

In cases when a victim cannot be transported to the destination country because of strict visa control and the country of origin and the country of destination do not share a common border, complex types of transportation are used. At times, victims are legally transported to a country neighboring the destination country and later taken to the destination country through "holes" in the border. There have been cases when Russian women entered Egypt on tourist visas and then were illegally transported across the border to Israel to work in the sex industry. Another example is Germany, where immigration is highly regulated but Polish nationals are not required to have visas to enter the country—many women enter Germany on fake Polish passports.[9] In such cases, transportation should be considered illegal, as the victim is transported to the destination country illegally.

Types of Criminal Exploitation

The third stage of criminal exploitation of persons is the actions aimed at criminally exploiting the victim. There are a number of exploitation types that can be distinguished according to several qualitative criteria, such as, object of exploitation, types of coercion, sector of the economy where victims are exploited, and type of labor performed.

Women tend to be exploited more often than men; in the OSCE countries only 2 percent of victims are male.[10] As a rule, men are used to perform hard physical labor, such as building houses, digging basements, or performing hard industrial tasks. Also, men can be recruited to serve in the armed forces and forced to participate in military conflicts. Most mercenaries join the army voluntarily. However, there have been cases when men who were recruited in Ukraine to work on construction projects in the Caucasus region later were involved in fighting in the Nagorno-Karabakh conflict.[11]

Children are generally exploited in the spheres that require hard physical labor, such as working on a farm, being a servant, etc. Quite often, boys are used for child pornography and prostitution.[12]

However, most victims of criminal exploitation are women. This is because of both their psycho-physiological attributes and their low social status. There are several reasons that explain this phenomenon. Usually, the unemployment rate among women is higher and many unemployed women believe that going to a richer and more developed country is the only way of finding a job. Since women are not as strong physically, it is easier for smugglers to control female victims. Also, women can be exploited in many more ways than men can.

Women and girls are exploited in services and in the porn industry. Women exploited in the sex industry constitute the majority of the victims of criminal exploitation. According to the experts' estimates, up to two million women and girls are forced into prostitution and the porn industry every year.[13] Women are also exploited in the service sector and in industries where female labor can be used. There are two types of criminal exploitation, depending on the way a victim is forced to work.

Physical Coercion

In this type of criminal exploitation, a victim is physically forced to work and might be physically hurt. A victim can be injured, beaten, or tortured. Most of the time, a code of rules that the victim will have to obey is established, and the victim is punished every time he or she breaks one of these rules. For example, a victim may be severely beaten or deprived of food when he or she refuses to work or attempts to escape. Human traffickers can force a victim to obey by using violence or by using narcotic and psychotropic substances.

When a victim is forced into obedience by using violence, it means he or she has been physically injured and there is damage to the victim's body. Also, the victim can be deprived of certain things that a human body cannot function without, such as food, water, and medical help, which leads to physical damage to the victim's body. These types of restrictions force the victim to carry out any order. At the same time, the victim's basic human needs are not satisfied and the victim suffers physically. In a study conducted in Holland, 177 of 250 trafficked women said they had been physically injured and violated by smugglers, pimps, or clients.[14]

Another way to lower a victim's resistance is to use narcotic and psychotropic substances—a method that has proven especially successful in cases of sexual exploitation. Narcotic or psychotropic substances can initially be given to the victim without his or her consent—added to food without the victim's knowledge or given to the victim as medicine. Once the victim develops an addiction, he or she will carry out any order to get more narcotics. If tranquilizers are used to control the victim's willpower, the victim becomes subject to physical exploitation. Russian television reported a story of a group of people who had no recollection of their past when they were found. The investigation suggested that these people might be victims of criminal exploitation who had been influenced by an unknown substance that erased their memories and made them incapable of resistance.

Psychological Coercion

Psychological coercion occurs when a victim is subject to psychological violence, which can be used against either the victims themselves or against their family. There are several types of psychological coercion, which are distinguished according to their nature:

Blackmail. Blackmail is a threat to make public derogatory information about the victim or the victim's family. A person is held in bondage because he or she cannot let this information be disclosed because it will lead to negative consequences for a family member or to moral suffering. As a result, a victim agrees to be exploited. For example, a woman who goes abroad hoping to find a job as a professional becomes a victim and is exploited in the sex industry. In this case, she is told that unless she continues working as a prostitute, her family will learn what she does for a living.

Also, a victim who was trafficked to the destination country illegally constantly lives in fear of being arrested and deported, and exploiters use the fear by threatening to report illegal immigrants to the local police.

Threats of Violence. Psychological coercion also includes threats to use violence, that is, to physically injure or kill the victim. Such threats do not mean a victim will necessarily be hurt, but there is a high probability of that happening. A threat to use violence can be directed not only at the victim, but also at his or her family if the victim refuses to obey. To show that the threat is real the victims might have to witness a public execution of someone who refused to carry out orders. For example, in Italy it has been reported that one prostitute is killed every month. In Istanbul, six Russian women witnessed the execution of two Ukrainian women. In Serbia, a Ukrainian woman who refused to obey was publicly decapitated.[15]

Financial Coercion. At times, the relationship between the exploiter and the victim involves financial obligation. Because the victim cannot get out of this obligation, she has to comply with demands and carry out orders. Financial means used for criminal exploitation include debt and other ways of making the victim financially dependent.

Debt is one of the most widespread ways of keeping a person in bondage. A person can become a victim of financial coercion if she borrows money or has to pay for the services provided by the exploiter. For example, to find a job in Germany, a woman might have to pay $5,500–$27,700 to have a passport prepared, buy a visa, and pay for transportation. Very few Russian women have the money to pay for these services and, therefore, have to borrow the money to be paid back with up to 60 percent—or more—in interest.[16] If the recruiter pays for the woman's transportation to the site of exploitation, she will have to work off that debt as well as pay back the buyer who purchases her in the destination country. In addition, she will have to pay basic expenses such as rent for her room and her place in the brothel, fees to the pimp, lawyer and doctor bills, and so forth. Whatever she does, chances are she will still be in debt.[17] The victim's debt grows as the owner adds interest to her initial debt and includes funds spent on the victim's needs and/or fines for her disobedience. In the end, the owner can even sell the woman and her debt to someone else with a large profit for himself.[18]

In Japan, for example, a woman who is put on the market owes the average of $35,000 and some even accrue as much as $300,000 in debt.[19] Women who owe such amounts know that they have to obey any orders, because even if they manage to escape, they or their family will be punished for the debt that has not been paid.

A victim can be held in financial bondage not only when she owes money, but also if there is a relationship between the victim and the exploiter that makes the victim financially dependent on the exploiter. When the victim has no income and she has to ask someone for shelter and other help, she will have to obey the demands of the benefactor who can use this dependency to exploit the victim.

Legal Coercion. Legal coercion exists in cases when there is a relationship such as marriage, custody, or adoption that is regulated by the legal and moral norms in the given society. There are several types of legal coercion that are determined by the legal relationship between the victim and the exploiter.

- *Legal coercion by marriage.* In such cases, one of the spouses marries the other to exploit him or her later. A wife can become dependent on her husband if she wants to stay in her husband's country or for some other reason. Such dependency usually occurs when one of the spouses is a citizen of a foreign country. Having moved to a new country, a woman is isolated and can become exploited as her legal dependency transforms into financial dependency or she is physically forced to comply. Also, the husband can threaten to deport her, as she is eligible for citizenship in her husband's country only after several years of residence in that country.

  A woman can find herself in a similar situation if she enters a pro forma marriage. Her "husband" can use the woman for some time, but later force her to work in the porn industry or sell her to be exploited in the sex industry. Laws in some countries, such as Germany and Switzerland, allow a wife who is a foreigner to work as a prostitute, although it is illegal for a woman immigrant. A woman who is transported to a foreign country to be married can become entirely dependent on her "husband," who can very well be an owner of a club or a pimp.[20]

- *Legal coercion by adoption or custody.* Children under eighteen who have been adopted or taken into custody can be exploited by their new parents or guardians. A child is dependent on these people because of its age. Recently, the number of Russian children illegally adopted and transported abroad has been growing. Sometimes these children are resold to other people to be adopted. Trafficking in children is a business that is not only very profitable, but also is a way to avoid paying taxes and to launder money. For example, the Russian adoption market is potentially a billion dollar industry, and the profits in this business are growing.[21]

- *Slavery.* Slavery is a very distinct type of criminal exploitation as well as the most dangerous. Its major characteristic is that very often it is intertwined with other types of criminal exploitation. Slavery presupposes that a victim is held in servitude to the exploiter. A victim is criminally exploited, kept in isolation, and is incapable of changing his position—the victim cannot turn to the state, police, or others for help. A victim has no rights and becomes a "commodity" for the owner.

This type of criminal exploitation is seldom found on its own, and it takes at least one of the above-mentioned types of coercion to force a victim to perform a certain type of labor. As a rule, under slavery, victims are physically hurt, threatened, or kept under the influence of substances that suppress their willpower. Thus, slavery represents the victim's entire bondage to the exploiter.

Exploitation of the Victim's Labor

In this type of exploitation, the exploiter uses the victim's labor and the victim is forced to provide services or manufacture goods. Exploitation of the victim's labor can occur in different economic sectors or spheres of human activity. The services can be provided and the goods can be manufactured in both legal and criminal sectors. Depending on the law regulating the victim's labor, we can differentiate between the following subcategories:

Exploitation of Legal Labor. In this case, the victim's labor is used in the legal sector. A victim can be exploited in a number of legal activities ranging from manufacturing industrial goods to providing services for maintenance and repair of those goods as well as providing other legal services.

Exploitation of physical labor and exploitation of intellectual labor can occur. Exploitation of physical labor is exploitation of a victim's skills and experience, physical strength, and ability to provide certain services. According to the nature of the physical work that a victim performs, one can distinguish between exploitation in the sex industry, exploitation in the services sector, or exploitation in the industrial sector.

Exploitation in the sex industry presupposes satisfaction of human sexual needs. There are certain jobs in the industry that are legal and are not punishable by law. For example, this can be working as a stripper or as a prostitute in countries where prostitution is legal, or other types of legal services that aim at satisfying human sexual needs.

Also, a victim's labor can be used in the services sector where the victim serves the exploiter or provides services to other people. Depending on whether the victim's labor will be used to satisfy the needs of the exploiter or for generating profits, one can distinguish between exploitation in the trafficker's household and exploitation in the services sector.

In the first case, the victim's labor is used in the exploiter's household—for example, working in the garden, in the fields, cleaning, cooking, and housekeeping. Here, the victim's labor is not used within the household to satisfy the personal needs of the exploiter and his family.

In the case of exploitation in the services sector, the victim's labor is used for generating profits. The victim's task is to provide services for the general public, for example, to repair industrial goods in an underground workshop. The exploiter can also force the victim into manufacturing certain goods and get profits from the victim's labor, for example, in an underground shop for manufacturing clothes or other consumer goods.

In cases of intellectual exploitation, the victim's intellect, knowledge, ability to think, and artistic skills are exploited. This kind of exploitation is used very rarely, but probably should be mentioned in the classification of exploitation types. Legal intellectual exploitation can occur when the victim is forced to provide intellectual services for the exploiter. For example, a scientist or a specialist can be made to work on improving the manufacturing process of certain goods to increase the exploiter's profits. This type of exploitation can exist in various situations and sectors.

Exploitation of Labor in the Criminal Sector. In exploitation of labor, the victim's labor is used in the criminal sector—the victim performs tasks that are illegal. Exploitation in the criminal sector is similar to exploitation in the legal sector, but there are certain differences. For example, in exploitation of physical labor, one can distinguish among:

•   Forced participation in military conflicts. As a rule, victims of this exploitation are men who are forced to participate in military conflicts, in terrorist attacks, and similar illegal activities, and whose physical abilities are exploited;

•   Exploitation of labor in the sex industry, either in the porn industry (victims are used for making pornography, for example, often girls are trafficked abroad and forced to act in porn films or pose for pornographic photos) or for sexual services (victims are forced to provide sexual services, for example, work as prostitutes);

•   Exploitation of labor for manufacturing illegal goods and providing illegal services (in this case, the victim is forced to produce certain goods that are illegal, working in underground shops for producing and processing narcotic drugs, manufacturing of unlicensed liquor, weapons, etc);

•   Exploitation of intellectual ability. In cases of illegal intellectual exploitation, a scientist can be forced to develop a formula for a new narcotic substance.

Exploitation of the Victim's Physiognomy

Apart from using the victim's labor, the exploiter can use the victim's body parts and physiological abilities. Victims can be forced to become organ donors or surrogate mothers. Transplantation is a process when an organ of one person is transplanted into the body of another person. Modern medicine is capable of performing a wide range of operations such as kidney transplants, liver transplants, eye cornea transplants, and so forth. Often, people find themselves in a difficult situation and have to sell their organs. Smugglers abuse such situations and profit from other people's misfortune. Donors who have been recruited and promised a job abroad are forced to sell their organs very cheaply (approximately 3 percent of the amount the recipient of the organ pays for it), or directly offered to sell their organs. For some poor people their organs are the only commodity they can sell to raise money to support their families.[22]

Exploitation of surrogate mothers involves using women's childbearing ability. A female body is used to bear and give birth to a child, who may later be sold for adoption or other purposes, including becoming an organ donor.

There have been cases when women were trafficked to the United States to carry and give birth to children who were later adopted. In such instances, the baby is born a U.S. citizen, which makes the adoption process much easier. However, the surrogate mother is paid very little for her "services," and most of the payment goes to "middlemen" who found the woman, prepared her papers, transported her to the destination country, and watched over her during the pregnancy and after the labor. Such practice existed in Hungary, where police discovered a network that had a business of selling unborn children to people in the United States and Canada. There are about a hundred similar cases that have been investigated, and the mechanism for trafficking future mothers abroad appears to have existed for more than three years.[23]

Problems of Legislative Regulation

The existing Russian law does not enable law-enforcement agencies to combat human trafficking. The norms existing in Russia's Criminal Code that authorize punishment for kidnapping (Article 126), illegal deprivation of freedom (Article 127), trafficking in children (Article 152), and other articles such as Articles 120, 133, 134, 135, 150, 153, 154, and 240–242, do not cover the complexity of human trafficking.

For example, if we look at Article 126 of Russia's Criminal Code, a person can be prosecuted for capturing another person openly or secretly or involving another person in fraud that leads to illegal acquisition. Most of the time, the victim consents to leave the country, even if there is a possibility of criminal exploitation.

In some cases, a woman decides to go abroad to work as a housekeeper, waitress, servant, sales assistant, or dancer, and agrees to be transported abroad. Only on arrival in the destination country does she learn that she will be forced into prostitution. Because under Articles 126 and 127 of Russia's Criminal Code this kind of activity is not a crime, not a single case of human trafficking has been prosecuted in Russia. All that exists is some operations intelligence about certain businesses suspected of being involved in recruiting and transporting persons for future exploitation.

Article 240, which authorizes criminal responsibility for forcing women into prostitution by using violence and threats of using violence, blackmail, destroying and damaging property, or through deception, does not provide for criminal responsibility for human trafficking. Smugglers do not always use violence against victims or threats of violence. Usually, smugglers use other ways—such as psychological blackmail, taking the victim's papers away, threats to report the victim to the police—to control the victim and force her to obey orders. Many women believe the police are on the same side as their exploiters and, therefore, are susceptible to this type of threat.

The major reason that smugglers cannot be prosecuted for illegal transportation and criminal exploitation of victims is that the criminal intent of the smuggler in most of the cases is only revealed outside of Russia. Hence, the result of the crimes committed in Russia is only seen outside of Russia's jurisdiction. Because Russian law does not have a statute that authorizes prosecuting people involved in recruiting victims for future exploitation and human trafficking, law-enforcement agencies ignore the existence of the problem.

Meanwhile, the state has declared that its priority is to ensure that civil rights, such as the right to life, freedom, honor, and dignity, are not violated or limited unless required by law. Because the state has undertaken the responsibility to protect human and civil rights and liberties of its citizens, it should protect the rights of women, children, and men who are exploited and who, as Russian citizens, are entitled to have their human rights protected.

The fact that many victims are illegal residents in destination countries further complicates the situation. These victims avoid contact with authorities, often refuse to cooperate (usually because they fear the wrath of smugglers), and never give the names of their recruiters.

Very often, children become victims of human trafficking. Article 152 of Russia's Criminal Code authorizes legal responsibility for trafficking in minors or any other forms of violating rights of underage citizens. Unlike grown-ups, children seem to be protected from being trafficked and exploited because there is an article that authorizes legal punishment for trafficking in children. The Commentary to the Criminal Code states that the subject of the crime "is the person who has authority and control over an underage person. It can be parents, foster parents, guardians, medical personnel and staff of child institutions."[24] The description of the person who can be prosecuted for trafficking in children under this law is very narrow. Cases where a child is sold by a smuggler who is not related to him or when a child is sold by a middleman are not taken into consideration. Therefore, Article 152 of Russia's Criminal Code does not solve the problem of trafficking in children.

Ukraine has proved that is it possible to deal with the issue of human trafficking on the state level. In 1998, Article 124[1] was added to Ukraine's Criminal Code. This article authorizes legal responsibility for human trafficking, which is described as "open or secret acquisition of a person followed by legal or illegal transportation with or without the victim's consent for the purposes of future sale or any other profitable transaction resulting in sexual exploitation, involving criminal activities, debt bondage, adoption for commercial reasons, using victims in military conflicts and exploiting the victim's labor."

There are also different levels of exploitation of labor and sexual exploitation. Sexual exploitation can be a component of exploitation of labor. Many countries include articles in their criminal codes—Belarus (Article 187), Holland (Part II, Article 250), and Germany (Part II, Article 181)—that consider recruiting for purposes of sexual and other types of exploitation through fraud schemes to be criminal activity.

Having analyzed the data on human trafficking and criminal exploitation, methods of exploitation, its possible forms, types, and manifestations that are mentioned in classifications, it appears to be very difficult to give a comprehensive definition of human trafficking. The concept itself covers only one of the stages of the phenomenon. It is necessary to determine and regulate legal responsibility for all of the existing stages of criminal exploitation.

Thus, it seems expedient to include two articles in Russia's Criminal Code that will regulate the responsibility for recruiting and trafficking, transactions in persons as commodity. As to recruiting, Article 187 in Belarus's Criminal Code seems optimal because it authorizes legal responsibility for "recruiting for purposes of sexual and other exploitation through deception."

Based on the analysis of the existing forms, types, and ways of criminal exploitation, I would like to suggest the following amendment to Article 126 of the Russian Criminal Code,[25] which would regulate criminal responsibility for human trafficking:

Article 126[1] Human Trafficking

1.   Human trafficking is a purchase/sale of a person, or any other criminal activity aimed at this person, as well as recruiting, exploiting, and controlling the person that results in profiting from his labor or for future exploitation of any type when the person had no other choice or was involved in a fraud.

2.   Same actions:

a)   aimed at two or more persons;

b)   committed on a number of occasions and as a pattern;

c)   that involved using psychological and physical violence, or threats to use it;

d)   committed by an organized group as part of a criminal scheme;

e)   committed by an official or a state employee who abused the power given by his office;

f)   resulting in financial or other dependency of the victim;

g)   involving the victim's illegal transportation across the border of the Russian Federation;

h)   involving taking the victim's organs and tissues for transplantation;

i)   resulting in using the victim as a surrogate mother;

3.   Activities described in Parts 1 and 2 of the article that resulted in death of the victim or other severe consequences to the victim's health.

Ensuring that criminal charges can be brought against a person for activity that endangers society will give law-enforcement agencies a real tool to combat human trafficking and criminal exploitation.

Notes

1. See, for example, "Trafficking of Migrants," IOM Policy and Responses, March 1999, 4–5; Protocol to Prevent, Suppress and Punish Human Trafficking, especially Women and Children, Supplementing the UN Convention against Transnational Organized Crime, November 2000, A/55/383; The Hague Ministry Declaration on European Recommendations for Preventing Trafficking in Women and Their Sexual Exploitation, 24–26 April 1997.
2. I use the word "acquisition" as opposed to "recruitment" because in English, recruitment usually connotes agreement on the part of the person acquired for a trafficking scheme. Since a person can be kidnapped and forced into exploitation against one's will, the term "acquisition" is more appropriate.
3. "Ukrainian Women—Victims of Sex Industry," Itar-TASS, 30 June 1998.
4. "Crime and Slavery," Global Survival Network Report, Washington, D.C., 1997, 17.
5. See *Komsomolskaia Pravda*, 25 March 1997.
6. G. Podlesskikh and A. Tereshonok, *Vory v zakone: brosok k vlasti* (Moscow: Khudozhestvennaia literatura, 1994).
7. See "Human Trafficking and Prostitution: Growing Exploitation of Women-Immigrants from Central and Eastern Europe," IOM, Budapest, Hungary, May 1995.
8. "Crime and Slavery," 52.
9. "Crime and Slavery," 19.
10. "Trafficking in Human Beings: Implications for the OSCE," Warsaw, 1999, 11.
11. "Dikie Gusi Sbivaiutsia v Staiu," *Trud*, 2 March 2000.
12. "Country Reports on Human Rights Practices for 1997, U.S. Department of State, Washington, D.C., 30 January 1998," *Trends in Organized Crime* 3, no. 4 (Summer 1998.): 36–39.
13. Donna M. Hughes, "Transnational Shadow Market of Trafficking Women," *Journal of International Affairs* (Spring 2000); "Progress on Legislation to Help Foreign Women and Children Forced into Sex Industry," Associated Press, Washington, D.C., May 2000.
14. "One Year of La Strada: Results of the First Central and Eastern European Program on Prevention of Trafficking Women," STV/La Strada Program, September 1996, 21.
15. Donna M. Hughes, "The 'Natasha' Trade: The Transnational Shadow Market of Trafficking in Women," *Journal of International Affairs* (Spring 2000).
16. E. Volkova, "Seks Torgovlia," *Chto pochem*, 11 January 2000.
17. "International Organization for Migration, Informational Campaign against Trafficking in Women: Research in Ukraine," Geneva, IOM, July 1998.
18. Human Trafficking: OSCE Platform, 1999, September, ODIHR Reference Material 1999, 3.
19. "Crime and Slavery," 26.

20. Louise Shelley, "Criminal Kaleidoscope: The Diversification and Adaptation of Criminal Activities in the Soviet Successor States," *European Journal of Crime, Criminal Law and Criminal Justice* 3 (1996): 248–52.

21. "Market of Unwanted Children," *Itogi* 20 (1997): 60–67; "Profitable Children," *Kommersant Daily*, 15 April 1997, 14.

22. "A Trap for the Credulous," *Trud*, 20 March 2000.

23. "Motherhood for Sale," *Rossiiskaia gazeta*, 26 September 1997, 27.

24. *Commentary to the Criminal Code of the Russian Federation*, 2nd edition with changes and additions (Moscow: M. NORMA-INFA. M, 1998), 325.

25. Criminal Code of the Russian Federation, 15 January 2004 (Moscow: Kodeks), 50-51.

Chapter 4

◈◈◈

Russian and Chinese Trafficking:
A Comparative Perspective

Louise Shelley

Massive illegal movement of people from Russia and China occurred in the 1990s after the collapse of the Soviet Union and the loosening of state controls in China. With the introduction of markets, Russia and China no longer guarantee the economic security of their citizens; this transition resulted in economic dislocations for many. The declining border controls provided the opportunity to leave, and the demand for cheap labor and sexual services provided a market for people to migrate illegally to more developed countries. The combined forces of organized crime and governmental corruption facilitated the mass movement of people, which often violates national laws and the national sovereignty of the countries to which Russians and Chinese are moved illegally.

The Russian trade consists almost exclusively of the trafficking of women and minors for sexual exploitation, whereas the Chinese trade combines trafficking of women with large-scale illegal smuggling of men from Fujian province. Both of these trades are consequences of the difficult transition away from the communist system. The ill-conceived Russian transition wiped out both positive and negative aspects of Russian society. The investment in women's education and the ideological commitment to women's advancement were undermined by an economic transition that denied social benefits to women and transferred property almost exclusively to former *nomenklatura* (party bureaucrats) and members of organized crime groups who were overwhelmingly male. In China, income inequality has increased with development. Standards of living are significantly higher in urban areas than in the rural areas from which the trafficking occurs.[1]

Louise Shelley

The "business" of smuggling and trafficking people differs dramatically between Russia and China although both have emerged from communist states. The Chinese, who have always been great traders, run their smuggling operations as integrated business operations, maximizing profits from start to finish. Chinese organized crime views trafficking as a means of generating capital for development at home. The Russians, who historically have been sellers of natural resources rather than traders, treat their trafficking business as a commodity market. The human resource of women is plundered like the precious metals, oil, and gas of the former Soviet Union with no thought to the investment of the profit of this trade in the domestic economy.

Both human smuggling and trafficking involve serious violations of human rights. However, although organized crime views the trade in human beings as an ongoing business that must be sustained, there are fewer gross violations of human rights of Chinese than there are of Russians. Therefore, most smuggled Chinese will survive to help pay for their next family member who will be moved by the smugglers; Russian traffickers are not concerned with women's survival once they have been sold to brothel owners abroad. There is no long-term financial incentive to ensure the women's health or well-being because there is no relationship between the women being trafficked and those who will follow. The present pool of trafficked Russian women is not related or known to those who were earlier trafficked, unlike the Chinese where migration occurs within extended families.

In both countries, the illegitimate trade mirrors the legitimate. In China, organized crime groups trade human beings as a tool for economic development. In Russia, organized crime has a "raider" mentality toward its own resources. Although China looks to foreign investment and repatriation of capital as a means of fueling economic development, Russia receives limited foreign investment from legitimate sources or from the trafficking of human beings. The demographic situation of China permits the loss of human capital through smuggling whereas Russia, where births are far below the replacement level, cannot afford the trafficking of women of childbearing years. The human trade for China is part of its overall economic growth; for Russia, it is a further drain on its resources.

The Comparative Transition Process

For much of the twentieth century, both Russia and China had an ideological commitment to communist ideology. Under communism, the state assumed responsibility for development, placed all production under state ownership, and emphasized strong central controls at the expense of individual freedom and initiative. The formerly closed communist societies of Russia and China once controlled internal migration and prevented exodus from the countries through strict border controls.

In the past decade, both Russia and China have moved away from the communist system. Diminution of ideological control has resulted in profound change in the economic and social systems of both countries. In both states, there are fewer social protections and sharp economic differentiation among regions and citizens of the country. Since the Soviet system collapsed, Russia has disbanded many of the controls over citizens that existed for seventy years. Although a communist government still exists in China, the changes are no less profound than in Russia, which has officially abandoned communism. In both countries, there is lessened state control, a consequence of the declining authority of the central state and the corruption of the control apparatus.

The abandonment of the Soviet ideological commitment to the equality of women has led to the feminization of poverty. The economic transition in Russia removed women's social safety net without providing them with any possibility of acquiring and maintaining property. The privatization of state property resulted in the mass transfer of wealth, primarily to men. Women were left with neither capital nor the nonwage supports that allowed them to survive. Billions of dollars in natural resources and state budgetary resources were transferred overseas; taxes were not paid. As a consequence, salaries and pensions could not be paid.[2]

In the Soviet period, there was an ideological commitment to full employment, and employment for women was a societal right. Sustaining this legacy of full employment for women was difficult in the economic crisis of post-Soviet society. Women were disproportionately unemployed in Russia; as many as 73 percent of the unemployed in impoverished parts of the Russian Far East were women.[3]

Many women turned to prostitution to survive. The rise of prostitution was not only a result of economic necessity, but also was a rejection of the socialist ideology in which prostitution was suppressed—even the criminal code did not acknowledge its existence. During the final years of the Soviet Union, the "emancipation from the desexualization of life under communism" meant that for many there was glorification of the erotic and idealization of the prostitute as an individual breaking barriers.[4] This accounted for some of the attraction to prostitution.

In China, the economic transition has resulted in a boom for those who had the skills to survive in a rapidly developing economy. But those from the poor agricultural and fishing communities of the south are left behind. With limited land to farm, many in Fujian and Guangdong provinces are left with no legitimate opportunities for advancement in a country where many are benefiting from rapid economic growth. It is the disparities of economic opportunity in China, rather than the collapse of the economy as in Russia, that lie at the base of the illegal population movement.

In both countries, strong crime groups with links to the communist power structures have stepped in to fill the power vacuum of the political and economic transition. Many of those groups cannot be defined as traditional organized crime, but represent some amalgam of traditional organized crime—individuals from the same region, corrupt government officials, and members of the diaspora community. Members of the security apparatus, the FSB (security police), in Russia and of the Public Security Bureau of Fujian are involved. In China, as in Russia, the collusion of government officials is central to the capacity of smugglers to operate.[5] These groups operate on a global scale, work with corrupt officials in other countries, and cooperate with international crime groups as necessary.[6] The trade in human beings from China and Russia owes much to the legacy of corrupted party power structures and their international ties.

State controls are less pronounced in areas distant from the nations' capitals. In the southern regions of China and the Far East of Russia operations of crime groups are least controlled by the central state. Trafficking and smuggling activities are especially acute in these regions but by no means confined to those areas.

Smuggling versus Trafficking

According to the United Nations protocol, "Smuggling of migrants shall mean the procurement, in order to obtain, directly or indirectly, a financial or other material benefit, of the illegal entry of a person into a State Party of which the person is not a national or permanent resident."[7] This protocol was meant to address the burgeoning trade of illegal immigration facilitated by criminals specializing in the illegal movement of people.

Smuggling and trafficking both result in the mistreatment of individuals being moved across borders, but there is a fundamental difference between the two. In smuggling, a voluntary relationship is entered into by the individual who wants to be moved across borders. "Smuggling is sometimes called 'facilitated migration,' which more accurately reflects the process" from the point of view of the person being smuggled.[8] The potential migrant contracts with the smuggler to be moved to his intended destination abroad. The smuggler may subject the individual to much worse conditions that he anticipated at the time of the agreement. Or the smuggler may change the terms of the contract, demanding more money or a longer period of service until the "debt has been paid." At the outset, there is a consensual relationship between the smuggler and the person seeking to leave the country.

Significant violations of human rights may occur even though the smuggling process began with a consensual relationship. Smugglers may physically abuse the humans they move, subject them to overcrowding, or deprive them of food or water or needed medical care. One of the most egregious examples of this was a case in 2000 in which fifty-eight Chinese men and women perished after being crammed into a truck with no ventilation to cross the English channel on a ferry from Belgium to Great Britian.[9] Another notorious example was the Golden Venture in which ten people died of hypothermia or drowning in 1993 off the coast of Queens, New York.[10]

Trafficking involves deception, coercion, abduction, fraud, debt bondage, and abuse of power. According to the United Nations Protocol definition, exploitation includes sexual exploitation, forced labor or services, slavery or practices similar to slavery, servitude, or the removal of organs.[11] The trafficker—through deception, threats of violence, or actual use of violence—forces the individual to work in conditions of forced labor, servitude, or debt bondage. "A person who hires a 'smuggler' or travels for a job promised by a 'recruiter' does not realize that this person is actually a trafficker who will place him in these unanticipated conditions." Some traffickers do not move individuals internationally. Therefore, it is a crime against the individual and only in the international context is it a violation of state sovereignty.[12] There are different degrees of deception among Russian trafficked women. Some Russian analysts estimate that as many as 50 percent of the women have been coerced or duped into the sex trade. A second group received some information on what they would do at their intended destination but lacked a full picture. Many signed phony contracts expecting to be paid high wages that never were provided. Instead, the women were made to work off a significant debt. They had no alternative because their passports had been confiscated at the time of arrival at their foreign destination. Another group agreed to go with traffickers but were not aware that they would be subjected to significant physical abuse by those who trafficked them or by those to whom they would be "sold."

Research Methodology

My research draws on a wide variety of sources, including newspaper reports on cases that have been initiated and investigated, human rights reports, and materials prepared by multinational organizations such as the United Nations and the International Organization for Migration. Scholarly literature was used but even now, with a rise in interest in the topic, there is limited material available.[13]

Analysis of the Russian trafficking situation was facilitated by research conducted in conjunction with two grants received by the Transnational Crime and Corruption Center at American University. The first grant permitted hiring a team of interdisciplinary researchers across Russia and Ukraine to investigate human trafficking. These specialists were sometimes given access to police records and were able to conduct interviews with individuals who had been trafficked and those who were involved in recruiting women to be trafficked. The second grant, for training to combat trafficking, gave us access to Western law enforcement investigators and prosecutors who have conducted investigations of cases of human trafficking in the United States. Interviews were conducted with law enforcement officers in England, Belgium, Italy, the Netherlands, and Germany to understand more about the dynamics of trafficking and smuggling in those countries.[14]

The analysis of Chinese organized crime is based on a variety of law enforcement and academic sources and the case materials of prosecuted cases. Materials of actual investigations of the business side of Chinese organized crime were made available, including economic analyses of the crime based on materials of criminal investigations. In addition, information was obtained from Interpol's organized crime division that is now analyzing the relationship of Chinese trafficking organizations operating in Europe.[15]

Demographics of Those Being Trafficked and Smuggled

In both Russia and China, there are significant numbers of citizens who are ready to seek employment or a new life abroad. Russian and Chinese initiatives to emigrate or work abroad reflect, in part, the realization that citizens cannot depend on the state to provide for them and their families—a rude awakening for citizens accustomed to the minimum protections of the socialist system of the past decades. Population controls, the barriers to residence and immigration in many countries of the world, mean that desperate individuals cannot legally move to other countries. The impoverished residents of Fujian province and the women of Russia lack the financial resources to emigrate legally, and many prosperous regions of the world will not permit them to enter. Therefore, they are vulnerable to the services of traffickers who move individuals illegally around the world and extract payments through subsequent employment in sweatshops, as laborers, or as providers of sexual services.

Chinese gangs traffic women for prostitution, but their largest trade may be the smuggling of males for labor abroad. There is also significant trafficking of women for domestic prostitution and the number of women working as prostitutes is in the millions.[16] Many of those who are trafficked come from poor homes and are sold into prostitution by their families.

Chinese smugglers draw primarily on the male population of Fujian province who are able to engage in the hard physical work that is required to pay back their debt. American law enforcement officials reported in interviews that demographic analyses of ships' ledgers, confiscated from the traffickers, indicated that at least 95 percent of those smuggled were male, almost entirely youthful males who could survive the arduous conditions of the trip. According to their observations, only a small percentage of those smuggled were women, who went into prostitution; this point also was made by Ko-lin Chin in *Smuggled Chinese*.[17] In the southern regions of China, such as Fujian and Guangdong provinces where young men do not have the education or skills to survive, there has been an impetus to emigrate.[18] Because they are unskilled, those smuggled have no possibility of legally obtaining entry permits. The generations who follow those who originally emigrated are not part of a nuclear family. Therefore, immigration laws of most countries do not recognize them for favorable treatment. Migration must be by irregular means because the structure of relationships and the financing of migration are outside the immigration framework of the Western societies to which they seek to move.[19]

Whereas Chinese smugglers draw from low economic and educational strata, Russian traffickers recruit different strata of women. Research by law enforcement officials in the St. Petersburg area revealed that they could not profile trafficking victims because the women recruited did not differ from the general demographics of women in the eighteen to twenty-five age bracket. Some of the trafficked women are more enterprising and seek work abroad, even in the sex trade, as an alternative to their limited economic horizons. In one notable case, an educated Vladivostok woman, trafficked to Macao, returned home only to be killed with her boyfriend, a distinguished Hong Kong lawyer, who came to Vladivostok to buy her out of prostitution.[20]

Traffickers recruit Russian women from all regions of the country, especially from impoverished regions with limited economic alternatives. Some are single mothers with no means of providing for their children in communities where work for women is low paying or almost nonexistent. Particular targets for the traffickers are women from the Russian Far East, but they also come from poverty-stricken parts of the Urals and Siberia.[21] Interviews with women from the Far East reveal that many had high school educations but went into prostitution because of their limited prospects and their boredom with the impoverished lives of their communities.[22]

A significant number of young female prostitutes come from the lowest tier of post-Soviet society. These are the homeless, children of alcoholic and abusive parents, and the hundreds of thousands of abandoned and orphaned children and youth confined to children's homes, all of whom are natural sources for the traffickers. The homes where children live for years in abusive conditions give them little preparation for life after they leave the institutions. The decline in expenditures on these homes has left the hundreds of thousands of residents in egregious conditions.

Another likely target for the traffickers is women subjected to domestic violence and spousal abuse. Violence against women has a long history in Russian society, but the collapse of the USSR and the accompanying economic crisis in many families has contributed to a rise in domestic and sexual violence, a problem that is not addressed by the totally inadequate social and law enforcement resources.[23]

Trafficking and smuggling are also tied to the sense of familial responsibility. In China, male children assume the role of guarantor of the family's well-being. In Russia, in contrast, women are the pillars of support of society. The disproportionate number of male children born in China is because of the parental desire to have sons to take care of them in their old age.[24] In the Chinese transition, without guarantees of state support in old age, family members rely on each other, particularly on male family members. Therefore, many go overseas to support their families when their domestic environment cannot guarantee their well-being.

Women, even in prerevolutionary society and its literature, were glorified as the maintainers of Russia; mother and the homeland are equated. Russian women in the post-Soviet period face an enormous reversal in both their status and their ability to support their families. Middle-aged women cannot support family members in their teens and twenties. Young women, many of them already single mothers, feel a strong responsibility to support both children and parents. Under these conditions, women are vulnerable to the financial offers of traffickers.

Where Are They Trafficked?

Russian and Chinese who are trafficked often have little control over where they will be moved. This is the case with those who are trafficked more than with those who are smuggled. Chinese women from the coastal regions of Guangdong, Fujian, and Shanghai are trafficked to Australia, Canada, Japan, Myanmar, Taiwan, and the United States for prostitution.[25] Russian women are trafficked for sexual exploitation throughout Asia, Europe, and the United States, and even as far as Latin America. The vast majority of Russians trafficked are sent to Western Europe; estimates of the number of women trafficked there range from tens of thousands to hundreds of thousands.

Groups in the Russian Far East work with Japanese and Korean organized crime to transport women to China, Japan, Korea, Thailand, and other destinations of the Pacific Rim. These ties are particularly important for Russian organized crime as Japanese groups have years of experience in this area. Groups in the Caucasus work with traffickers in Turkey to move women to brothels in Turkey, Cyprus, and elsewhere in the Middle East. Women from Kazakhstan are trafficked to Bahrain, where the Moslem links of the traffickers provide women for this free-trade zone.[26]

In Asia, the largest number of Russian women are trafficked to China,[27] followed in frequency by South Korea and Japan. The latter two are less frequent because of the higher costs of transport and of obtaining entry documents for the women. Among those working under registered businesses, the figures are different. According to the internal affairs department of the Khabarovsk region, in 2000, there were twenty-seven firms specializing in finding foreign employment in show business, usually a cover for female trafficking. In six months in 2000, more than 400 people left under trips arranged by these show business firms. Among those trafficked, 240 went to South Korea, 160 to Japan, and 5 to China.[28] But many more women went to China under different terms because border crossings are less regulated between Russia and China than other Asian countries.

Traffickers move large numbers of Slavic women to Belgium, Italy, the Netherlands, and Germany, where there is a large demand for attractive blondes. Traffickers have used violence against competitors and trafficked women to gain a foothold in the lucrative prostitution markets of Western Europe.[29] Dutch researchers suggest that approximately one-third of the women illegally engaged in prostitution in the Netherlands are from Ukraine, and that the countries of the former USSR have overtaken all other countries in providing the preponderance of women engaged in unauthorized prostitution in the Netherlands.[30] The problem is not unique to the Netherlands; the patterns that their researchers have identified are common throughout Western Europe.

Chinese human smugglers move their "clients" to the United States and Canada, Western Europe, Latin America, Japan, Taiwan, and Australia. They are transported by plane and, increasingly in the 1990s, by boat.[31] The most desired destination is the United States because of the possibilities of making much money and of eventually obtaining legal status. Yet the presence of overseas

Chinese in many other parts of the world provides a diaspora community that can help the traffickers and aid in integrating those who are smuggled there.[32] For example, Italian authorities estimate that there are now 30,000 Chinese who have been smuggled into Italy, whereas hundreds of thousands of illegal Chinese reside in the United States and Canada. Yet the movement to Europe is less desirable because there is much less chance of obtaining a legal right to stay in most European countries.

Crime Groups That Move Human Beings

The crime groups that smuggle and traffic people out of China and Russia are quite different. The Chinese groups more closely resemble traditional crime groups; those in Russia are not based on familial or community relationships. Yet both rely on their links with political power structures and the security apparatus that permit them to operate without restraint in many areas. Relationships are central to their activities in both countries.[33]

In China, human traffickers, often referred to as "snakeheads," have emerged from a variety of sources, including traditional Chinese organized criminal structures that continue in Hong Kong, Taiwan, Macao, and other parts of southern China. Also included are individuals who are not part of these groups, but who are linked by language or lineage. The groups benefit from their links with Hong Kong and the central role that the island plays in the regional and international economy.[34] Extensive shipping and transportation links permit the hiding of the illicit along with the significant legitimate trade from the region. Therefore, the crime groups combine traditional structures with the advantages of a high-tech economy.

Communist officials in Beijing crack down on southern officials for corruption but there have been few similar reprisals against the crime groups that continue to acquire wealth and influence in that region. According to recent analyses by Interpol, based on tracking the communications of the traffickers, these are not smaller disparate groups operating across Europe, but networks that link back to a single larger boss in China.[35] High-level protection must exist for these groups to operate on such a large scale.

Russian trafficking organizations range from small-scale operations that traffic a limited number of women each year to significant criminal organizations that use trafficking in women as a major revenue source of their criminal activity.[36] Some of the larger groups are the gangster element of organized crime that emerged visibly in the early 1990s with the division of state property. They have now moved into the international trade in women and drugs. They could not operate internationally without employing present and former security personnel. The FSB's ability to monitor telephone communications, e-mail, and traffic over websites allows its personnel an ideal advantage to participate in trafficking and profit from its continued existence. They also have experience in the international arena and their skills as money launderers allow them to move the significant profits of the traffickers.

The international links of the Russian and Chinese groups allow them to "enforce contracts" across borders. Although the contracts are not legitimate in the destination countries, individuals cannot run away from their "contracts" because the crime groups can retaliate against family members at home. In a case in Chinatown in New York, a smuggled woman was killed when family members in China did not make required payments to the smugglers at home. In a Canadian case, two Chinese in Canada were kidnapped and were freed only after Canadian and American law enforcement traced phone calls back to the crime group in China.[37]

The ability of post-Soviet crime groups to intimidate the women under their control and to threaten retaliation against family members at home makes women particularly vulnerable. In a New York case, a Russian woman rescued from forced prostitution in New York by a Wall Street executive found that not only was her life at risk, but also the lives of her parents at home in St. Petersburg, where her father was a former high-ranking military official.[38] Because of the ability to communicate by telephone and other rapid forms of communication, individuals are subject to the "laws" of the smugglers and the traffickers even though they are in direct contradiction to national laws and international legal conventions.

The illegal status of the immigrants compounds their dilemma and increases the control of the traffickers. Until the 2000 antitrafficking legislation, the Victims of Trafficking and Violence Protection Act, was passed in the United States, women who had been trafficked there had no protection from deportation under the law and were treated as criminals. In many countries, victims of trafficking have the same legal status as the traffickers. Therefore, those trafficked can expect no protection from the country to which they are trafficked.

The Business of Trafficking

The business of trafficking is growing because the profits are high and the risks of detection are low. Even for those who are caught, the penalties are lower than in other areas of organized crime. Furthermore, in many countries there are no provisions to confiscate the profits of human trafficking and smuggling such as there are in drug cases.

Smuggled and trafficked individuals are considered to be "commodities" that are especially lucrative for international organized crime because they are a renewable resource. They can constantly generate profits for the crime groups because they can be exploited repeatedly, unlike the one-time profits in a drug delivery.

A large-scale American investigation into a group of Chinese human smugglers permitted law enforcement personnel to gain enormous insight into the financial operations of the criminals. The confiscated records contained information from the recruitment stage through to the money laundering at the end of the operation. They revealed that this group of traffickers made a 90 percent profit on the "business." The largest expenses of the traffickers were the costs of corruption in both the transit countries and the United States, their final point of destination.[39]

The corruption consisted of payments to government officials along the way to ignore the movement of the people. The largest expense of one group of smugglers was their payments to an American lawyer who subsequently was indicted in American courts as an accomplice of this group.[40] He not only filed false asylum claims, but also paid bribes to bail bondsmen to get the smuggled individuals out of jail. The profits from this trade were sent to China through wire transfers. After the arrest of the lawyer in this case, the smugglers returned to the system of underground banking that is the traditional money laundering technique of Chinese organized crime.

The large amounts of capital returned to China are not unique to this case. In a French investigation that ended in 2000, the police estimated that in the eighteen months of the investigation £500,000 (approximately $750,000) was paid to the group at the center of the investigation every day and a total of £170 million or $250 million was laundered through two bureaux de change.[41]

Post-Soviet trafficking in women differs from that committed by Chinese organized crime groups. The Chinese run an integrated business operation. Chinese traffickers control the recruitment of individuals and the same or related groups run the brothels to which they transport the women, or they control the labor in restaurants or sweatshops in the country of destination.

In the post-Soviet case, women are more often sold into prostitution to brothel owners and pimps of different nationalities. Although post-Soviet groups control the sex trade in Israel[42] and, to a smaller extent, run some sex services in the United States and Europe, the women are traded as a commodity such as drugs and arms. They are not used as a continual source of financial profit as is the case in the people-smuggling trade out of China or the prostitution rings procuring women for the brothels of India or Thailand.

Chinese trafficking operates as a business, integrated from start to finish. The control of the smuggling from recruitment through employment or debt bondage in the recipient country allows for long-term profits. Much of the profits is repatriated and fuels the development of Fujian province. In contrast, Russian traffickers, even if they are part of larger criminal organizations, do not operate as integrated businesses. They sell the women at relatively low prices to other crime groups at the first opportunity, often in countries of Eastern Europe. Therefore, their profits are smaller than those of the Chinese.

Both trafficking and smuggling represent gross violations of human rights, but the degree of violations is dependent on the structure of the business. Although some Chinese smugglers severely abuse those who are moved, individuals are able to maintain contact with their families and must survive so that new individuals can be recruited. Russian women sold to pimps and brothel owners of other nationalities often are severely abused and cannot maintain contact with their families. The greater abuse of the women is not just the result of coercion and deception. Russian traffickers do not depend on the women they presently control to obtain subsequent trafficking victims. In contrast, Chinese smugglers cannot stay in business if their abuses are too great because they are dependent on individuals agreeing to conclude "contracts" with the traffickers. Chinese who contract to be smuggled rationally calculate their decision based on the experience of their compatriots.

Conclusion

Smuggling and trafficking out of China and Russia are both consequences of the difficult transitions away from centrally controlled and planned economies dominated by rigid communist parties. Millions have suffered in this transition to market economies where the central state no longer assumes responsibility for all of its citizens. Trafficking and smuggling groups have flourished with the decline of police controls and the complicity of past and present Communist Party officials and security personnel. Corruption at home, in transit countries, and in recipient countries is also central to the success of the traffickers and smugglers.

The rise of international organized crime has coincided with the collapse of the Soviet system and the profound changes in the Chinese state and society. The crime groups emerging from these communist states are among the most prominent of global international crime groups. Both groups have capitalized on the desire to leave transitional states and the demand for cheap physical and sexual labor in developed countries. Unlike many international crime groups that focus almost exclusively on the drug trade, Chinese and Russian crime groups have made the illegal movement of people a central focus.

Beyond the obvious similarities in the Chinese and Russian trade in humans, there are important differences. The international Chinese trade is primarily in males who pay to be moved and become laborers in Western Europe and North America. The Russians traffickers in women and youths recruit all over the country for the sex trade. The fates of those moved illegally differ significantly. Most smuggled Chinese eventually buy themselves out of debt and pay for their next family member to emigrate, helping to perpetuate the business. Russian women who are trafficked can rarely leave the world of prostitution and do not personally profit from their exploitation.

The trade in human beings resembles the prerevolutionary commerce of the two socialist states. The traditional Chinese trader mentality has survived the communist period. Chinese organized crime operates human trade as a business, keeping ledgers, investing profits, and planning for the future. Profits from human smuggling are invested in the community by funding housing, small restaurants, and some small businesses. Russian traffickers operate like prerevolutionary fur traders who kept few records, had a short-term time frame, and had no concern for the survival of their product. Russian traffickers, moreover, do not reinvest or repatriate their profits. The Chinese trade contributes to growth in a society with population to spare, whereas the Russian trade contributes to economic decline and a loss of women in childbearing years in a country that is severely underpopulated for its large land mass.[43]

Chinese trafficking facilitates the growth of both the Chinese legitimate and illicit economies, whereas the post-Soviet trade mirrors the overall downward development of the post-Soviet economies. Human beings may be used as commodities in both situations but the economic and demographic outcomes for the countries are very different.

Notes

An earlier version of this chapter appeared as "Post-Communist Transitions and the Illegal Movement of Peoples: Chinese Smuggling and Russian Trafficking in Women" in *Annals of Scholarship* 14, no. 2 (Fall 2000, released in 2002): 71–84. Reprinted by permission.

1.   Zhao Manhua, "The Income Gap in China: Rural Areas Need a Lift," *Transition Newsletter* (February–March 2001): 13–14.

2.   Alexander Boulatov, "Capital Flight from Russia" (paper presented at Kennan Institute, Washington, D.C., 4 June 2001).

3.   Liudmila D. Erokhina, "Seksualnaia ekspluatatsiia zhenshchin i detei v rossii" (research paper, January 2001, for TraCCC [Transnational Crime and Corruption Center] grant on Sexual Exploitation of Women and Children, funded by USIA).

4.   Erokhina, "Seksualnaia ekspluatatsiia zhenshchin i detei v rossii."

5.   Ko-lin Chin, *Smuggled Chinese Clandestine Immigration to the United States* (Philadelphia: Temple University Press), 44–45.

6.   Chin, *Smuggled Chinese*, 41–42; "Transnational Ethnic Chinese Organized Crime: A Global Challenge to the Security of the United States, Analysis and Recommendations," testimony of Willard Myers, Senate Committee on Foreign Affairs, Subcommittee on Terrorism, Narcotics and International Operations, 21 April 1994.

7.   "Protocol against the Smuggling of Migrants by Land, Sea and Air, Supplementing the United Nations Convention against Transnational Organized Crime," United Nations 2000.

8.   Human Rights Caucus, website www.hrlawgroup.org/siteprograms/traffic/No3.htm (25 June 2002).

9.   "China," Country Reports on Human Rights Practices 2000, United States Department of State, 56. www.state.gov/g/drl/rls/hrrpt/2000/eap/index.cfm?docid=684 (20 June 2002).

10.   "Criminal Practice: Conviction/Sentencing Regarding Growing Trade in Illegal Immigration is Upheld, U.S. appelle v Lee Peng Fei," *New York Law Journal*, 27 September 2000, 25.

11.   "Protocol to Prevent, Suppress and Punish Trafficking in Persons, Especially Women and Children, Supplementing the United Nations Convention against Transnational Organized Crime," United Nations 2000.

12.   Human Rights Caucus, website www.hrlawgroup.org/siteprograms/traffic/No3.htm (25 June 2002).

13. Among the notable exceptions are the books by Paul Smith, ed., *Human Smuggling* (Washington, D.C.: Center for Strategic and International Studies, 1997); Chin, *Smuggled Chinese*; Kevin Bales, *Disposable People: New Slavery in the Global Economy* (Berkeley: University of California Press, 1999); Ronald Weitzer, *Sex for Sale: Prostitution and the Sex Industry* (New York: Routledge, 2000); Pasuk Phongpaichit, Sungsidh Piyarasnasan, and Nualnoi Treerat, *Guns, Girls, Gambling, and Ganja: Thailand's Illegal Economy and Public Policy* (Chiang Mai: Silkworm Books, 1998); David Kyle and Rey Koslowski, eds., *Global Human Smuggling* (Baltimore, Md.: Johns Hopkins University Press, 2001); Peter Andreas and Timothy Snyder, eds., *The Wall around the West: State Border and Immigration Controls in North America and Europe* (Lanham, Md.: Rowman & Littlefield, 2000); Phil Williams, ed., "Illegal Immigration and Commercial Sex: The New Slave Trade," *Transnational Organized Crime* 4, no. 4 (Winter 1997) (Special issue); Alexis Aronowitz, "Smuggling and Trafficking in Human Beings: The Phenomenon, the Markets That Drive It and the Organizations That Promote It," *European Journal on Criminal Policy and Research* 9, no. 2 (Summer 2001): 163–95.

14. One grant was provided by the United States Information Agency of the U.S. State Department and supported interdisciplinary research on trafficking, and the other was to prepare training material for the Bureau of International Law Enforcement.

15. Presentation of Gwen McClure at "Corruption within Security Forces: A Threat to National Security," conference sponsored by the George Marshall Center, Federal Bureau of Investigation and the Bundeskriminalamt, Garmisch-Partenkirchen, 18–21 May 2001.

16. "China," Country Report on Human Rights, 55.

17. Chin, *Smuggled Chinese,* 124–25.

18. Zheng Wang, "Ocean-Going Smuggling of Illegal Chinese Immigrants: Operation, Causation, and Policy Implications," *Transnational Organized Crime* 2, no. 1 (Spring 1996): 59.

19. Willard H. Myers III, "Of qinqing, qinshu. Guanxi, and heiyu: The Dynamic Elements of Chinese Irregular Population Movement," excerpted in *Trends in Organized Crime* 2, no. 2 (Winter 1996): 44–47.

20. For a fuller discussion of this case, see Steven R. Galster, testimony on "The Sex Trade: Trafficking of Women and Children in Europe and the United States," Hearing before the Commission on Security and Cooperation in Europe, 28 June 1999, 14.

21. The nongovernmental organization Miramed has worked extensively to combat trafficking in areas with the most severe problems.

22. Erokhina, "Seksualnaia ekspluatatsiia zhenshchin i detei v rossii."

23. Igor Kon and James Riordan, eds., *Sex and Russian Society* (Bloomington: Indiana University Press, 1993), 6.

24. Scientific technology is now being used to identify female fetuses for abortion. See John Pomfret, "Tipping China's Sex Balance: The Use of Ultrasound, Boys Take Big Lead in Births," *Washington Post,* 30 May 2001, 24.

25. "China," 56; Laura Lederer, *Human Rights Report on Trafficking of Women and Children* (Washington, D.C.: Johns Hopkins School of Advanced International Studies, 2001), 95.

26. Gaukhar Isaeva, *Kazakhstan: Reket, moshennichestvo, suternerstvo* (Almaty: Al-Farabi, 1995).

27. Victims of Trafficking and Violence Protection Act 2000, Trafficking in Person Report, U.S. State Department, July 2001.

28. Erokhina, "Seksualnaia ekspluatatsiia zhenshchin i detei v rossii."

29.   Cyrille Fijnaut, Frank Bovenkerk, Gerben Bruinsma, and Henk van de Brunt, *Organized Crime in the Netherlands* (The Hague: Kluwer, 1998), 138.

30.   Gerben Bruinsma and Guus Meershoek, "Organized Crime and Trafficking in Women from Western Europe in the Netherlands, *Transnational Organized Crime* 3, no. 4 (Winter 1997): 105–118.

31.   Wang, "Ocean-Going Smuggling of Illegal Chinese Immigrants," 49.

32.   Chin, *Smuggled Chinese*, 26–27.

33.   For Chinese this is *guanxi*, whereas Russians refer to it as *znakomstvo i sviazi*. Willard H. Myers III, "Of qinging, qinshu. guanxi, and shetou: The Dynamic Elements of Chinese Irregular Population Movement," in *Human Smuggling*, ed. Paul Smith (Washington, D.C.: Center for Strategic and International Studies), 93–133.

34.   Roy Godson, "Criminal Threats to U.S. Interests in Hong Kong and China," testimony before the U.S. Senate Committee on Foreign Relations, East Asian and Pacific Affairs Subcommittee, Washington, D.C., 10 April 1997, 1–15, reprinted in *Trends in Organized Crime* 3, no.1 (Fall 1997): 43-47.

35.   Similar analysis has been done in the United States; see, for example, James Harder, "Mother of All Snakeheads," *Insight on the News*, 5 February 2001, 18.

36.   See Steven R. Galster testimony.

37.   Interview with John Beasley, assistant U.S. attorney, transnational crime branch, Washington, D.C., September 2000.

38.   Daniel Jeffreys, "Beauty and the Banker," *Moscow Times,* 18 September 1999.

39.   Based on extensive interviews in 2000 with law enforcement officers investigating the case.

40.   Mark Hamblett, "Government Outlines Case against Porges," *New York Law Journal*, 27 September 2000, 1.

41.   Harry de Quetteville, "International Smuggling Gang Is Smashed," *Daily Telegraph*, 15 July 2000, 15.

42.   Menachem Amir, "Organized Crime in Israel," in *Organized Crime: Uncertainties and Dilemmas*, ed. S. Einstein and M. Amir (Chicago: Office of International Criminal Justice, 1999), 239–40.

43.   The Russian birth rate is still declining precipitously and is now at the level of 1.17, far below the replacement level. Murray Feshbach, "What Is Happening to Russia's Human Capital," www.ceip.org/files/programs/russia/tenyears/transcript9.htm?#MF (10 October 2002).

Chapter 5

෯෯෯

Trafficking in Women in the Russian Far East: A Real or Imaginary Phenomenon?

Liudmila Erokhina

Trafficking of women in Primor'e? No, for us it is not serious. It is there, in the West it's a problem. But here it is not—just occasional cases. And it is the women's fault anyway. They know why they are going abroad.
—Tatiana Filimonova[1]

Trade of women (trafficking) as a sociocriminological phenomenon elicits many controversial and radical attitudes—from direct acknowledgment of the problem and calls for fighting it, mainly from representatives of public organizations, to complete denial of "trade of humans" by a number of governmental organizations, including law enforcement agencies. Meanwhile, trade of women has reached a level so threatening that it resulted in implementation of a number of international legal documents. The preamble of the 1949 UN convention "On trade of humans and exploitation of prostitution by the third parties" emphasizes that "prostitution and trade of humans for prostitution are not acceptable from the human rights perspective and threaten the well-being of people, families, and society."[2] The articles of the convention listed the following activities as criminal offenses: procurement, enforcement into prostitution by the third party (even with consent), exploitation of prostitution by the third party, keeping brothels, and so forth. The general ideology of the convention is against sexual exploitation of women.

Russia, unfortunately, is not one of the countries taking an active role in efforts to curb human trafficking, although this process is clearly progressing. There is a complacent attitude toward the phenomenon of human smuggling because transnational trade of women is considered to be a new type of crime for Russia and the other Newly Independent State (NIS) countries. Russians encountered this crime for the first time at the end of the 1980s, a period of rapid political change that affected international migration, trade, and tourism. The "Iron Curtain," which for decades separated the USSR from the world, isolated Soviet citizens from the international community, finally fell, and people were permitted to move freely across borders. However, freedom of movement was given to criminal groups as well as to regular citizens, and the criminal groups quickly figured out the demand and supply in the international market for goods and services. The western and then the southeastern sex industry turned out to be very attractive markets for the supply of "human chattel," the term used for trafficked Russian, Asian, and Latin American women. This commercial exchange was conducted with minimal risk and costs for the seller and the buyer. Criminal organizations' annual profits from the sale of women from Russia and NIS countries amount to $7 billion.[3]

The fight against trafficking of women in Russia faces difficulties, mainly because of the lack of legislation dealing with the problem. Three factors prevent the resolution of this problem. First, there is a lack of objective information. Research on this issue has been conducted in Russia for only a few years, mainly by international nongovernmental organizations (NGOs), but did not attract much attention from the academic community.

Second, sex trafficking continues to be a latent problem for law enforcement agencies, agencies for the social protection of the population, and governmental organizations overseeing the travel of Russian citizens abroad. There are two reasons for this: the lack of statutes in criminal legislation of the Russian Federation that define the term "human trafficking" and provide for criminal punishment for such activities; and the patriarchal ideology—the traditional opinion that the responsibility for engaging in prostitution lies with the women themselves—of civilians who work in administrative governmental agencies responsible for combating human trafficking.

Agency officials do not look at the problem of trade of women as a problem of governmental and national security. Although international treaties look at prostitution and illegal smuggling of people as a human rights violation, in Russia prostitution and "trade under agreement" are viewed as private occurrences on all levels of government.

Third, the public consciousness is not ready to accept the victims of trafficking in women as victims of the activities of criminal traffickers. Many law enforcement officials place the blame for sex trafficking on victims themselves. Public opinion about trafficking of women is that no one made them leave the country; they left on their own, looking for an easy and beautiful life. In some countries of the world—Israel and Turkey, for example—the flow of women from Russia and other countries of the former USSR is so massive that these women are now referred to as "Natashas."[4]

Because of the lack of counteraction to slave trade, the scale of trafficking has become so large that government representatives are now forced to recognize not only the fact of its existence, but the existence of organized crime in this sphere.

According to Victor Iliukhin, former chairman of the Committee on Security of the State Duma,

> Russian post-Soviet truth for the first time encountered such a shameful phenome-non, as massive illegal export of women and children abroad and their use for sex-ual and other degrading activities. We have encountered the disguised facts about purchase and resale of people and their exploitation, the savage occurrences of the slave-holding system. We also note that a lucrative criminal business has formed inside the country, a business of brothel-keeping, pimping, open prostitution and enticement of minors into prostitution.[5]

But, as a member of the Russian Duma stressed at a meeting of a roundtable on the problem of trade of humans, "this type of criminal activity has a very secre-tive character."[6]

That is probably why the Ministry of Internal Affairs and other law enforce-ment organs tend to address the problem of trafficking only when it is tied to other criminal activities: contraband, murder, illegal migration, and so forth. However, it is obvious that such an approach is now obsolete. The statistics and practices of organized crime groups show that trafficking is a crime on its own. In addition to the contraband of humans, other types of crime associated with trafficking are car-ried out by national and international organized crime networks: purchase and sale of drugs and weapons, import and export of precious metals, automobile businesses, corrupting officials, and so forth. Forcing women to engage in prostitution is asso-ciated with a low risk for the traffickers, while the profits are very high. At the same time, the revenues from these activities go into the "shadow economy" and then are laundered legally through trade networks, banks, and so forth.

Trafficking of people is a less risky activity for criminals than, for example, trafficking of drugs and automobiles. In Russia and Central European countries, the laws on drug trade have become stricter and the methods of decreasing the number of car thefts have become more sophisticated. At the same time, the punishment for trade of humans in many countries is much softer than for illegal sale of drugs, and in Russia it is completely absent. Even if the country has laws on punishment for trafficking of humans, such crimes are very difficult to prove and prosecute, and only a few women agree to testify in court. Therefore, those who exploit foreign women and force them to engage in prostitution have almost nothing to fear.

Some high-ranking officials of the Ministry of Foreign Affairs (MFA) of the Russian Federation expressed concern about the growing trade of women. Official data from the MFA show that from 1994 to 1997 several hundred organized crime groups engaged in recruitment of Russian citizens for prostitution in the countries of Eastern and Western Europe, the Middle East, North America, and Asia were un-covered. Those groups were mainly in Moscow, St. Petersburg, Kaliningrad, Ekaterinburg, and Buriatiia. They were exporting women to the countries of West-ern Europe, China, and Turkey, using fake passports, visas, and invitations. In 1996 alone, 4,500 women and more than 5,000 children who tried to migrate to other countries were not allowed to cross the border.[7]

In 1997, employees of the Administration of Internal Affairs of Kaliningrad region, in a joint operation with the Russian Bureau of Interpol and German police, managed to uncover and arrest an international criminal group that used media sources to find women who wanted to work in Germany as administrative assistants or housekeepers. Members of this criminal organization used fake passports to send the women abroad. Once abroad, they passed the women on to their partners, who were citizens of Turkey, and the deceived Russian women ended up in Turkish quarters where they were forced to engage in prostitution.[8]

At hearings of the Commission on Security and Cooperation in Europe, it was noted that during the last decades trade of women flourished in the countries of Southeast Asia, but currently the most vigorous rise in trade of people, especially women and children, is in the former republics of USSR.[9] Official German criminal statistics show that women from NIS constitute the majority of those engaged in prostitution in Germany; women from Poland are in second place; and women from Thailand—who formerly were among the most frequently exploited—are now in seventh place.[10] The number of Slavic women trafficked into Belgium, the Netherlands, Poland, and Switzerland has exceeded the number of traditionally trafficked African, South American, and Asian women.

All regions of Russia are involved in the international network of organized trade, and one of the most problematic regions is the Far East, because of its proximity to countries of Southeastern Asia. Prostitution in both regions is closely connected with the slave trade of women and their transport for sexual exploitation to neighboring countries, primarily China, South Korea, and Japan.[11]

According to Konstantin Chaika, deputy general prosecutor of Russia in the Far East federal district, the "Russian Far East is now more under the heavy pressure of the criminal clans in neighboring countries."[12] Chaika stressed that the Primorskii region is the most attractive for Russian and Chinese criminal groups.[13]

Methods of Recruitment and Transportation in Primor'e

There are common methods of recruiting women and girls for prostitution and sex industries in foreign countries. The first method of recruitment for local and international prostitution is conducted through "Help Wanted" newspaper ads, offering women aged eighteen to thirty high-paying and safe jobs as maids, strippers, dancers in nightclubs and recreational firms, or in other areas of "low-qualified workers." The newspaper *Dal'press* places twenty to forty ads of this type in each issue.[14] Such advertisements promise government contracts, high and stable earnings (U.S. $500–800), flexible work schedules, and safety. Transportation to the place of work and residence is paid by the firms.

The list of countries offering such "prestigious" jobs is diverse: Japan, South Korea, China, Italy, United Arab Emirates, and others. At the same time, the advertisements do not clarify the standard of living in those countries—all of the money earned often goes toward food, clothing, other everyday expenses, and countless fines. Additional money can be earned only by prostitution. However, the firms placing the inviting ads refuse to admit the potential and real danger of working through them. They assure the naive and uneducated young women and their parents of the legality and safety of working through these firms, which have licenses for providing employment. Their main argument is the availability of so-called government contracts. That is nothing more than a lie. Employees of the migration service of the Primorskii krai reported that during the ten years of the service there has only been one request from Germany, inviting nurses for work in the hospitals. There have been requests from Japan, Korea, and China for construction workers, low-qualified workers, or artists, as well as hostesses, disco dancers, and other professions. Russian migration services do not have information about any quotas on professions in these countries. Thus, women who turn to firms that publish "Help Wanted" advertisements and guarantee safety end up as deceived and powerless victims.

Another popular method of recruiting has been named "the second wave," and occurs when the women who had been sold come home to recruit other women. When women are sold into slavery or lured into the sex industry they have almost no choice—to free themselves from violence they go back home and hire new victims, thus turning into pimps. Many women interviewed admit that they went abroad following the advice of friends who told them about the wonders of an easy life.

The third method of recruitment is through public events such as photography competitions and beauty pageants. This process is usually complex, with well-thought-out deception, intended to ensure women that the possibility of receiving employment is real. Almost 20 percent of the women sold are recruited by advertisements about competitions.

The fourth method of recruitment is an open announcement about hiring for prostitution. For example: "A group of attractive young women is needed for working abroad. Salary is up to $1,000. Housing and food provided by the company."[15] "Work for women in South Korea." "Commercial firm announces the availability of vacancies. Up to 33 years of age."[16] It is important to note that this particular category of women is the most vulnerable with respect to being legally and morally unprotected, despite the fact that they have experience in the sex industry and a clear understanding of the nature of the job offered. From the legal perspective, they are "illegals," because they know that prostitution is forbidden in most southeastern countries; however, they entrust their life to pimps, who use them as bait. According to the owners of the service firms, pimps, agents, and other individuals who were interviewed, every woman sold as a prostitute abroad brings two to three times more profit to the Russian owner than they would bring in Russia. The yearly profit from one prostitute to a firm in Vladivostok is $6,000–$7,000.

The fifth method of recruitment is "marriage agencies," which are sometimes referred to as "mail order bride" agencies. Such firms offer services both as a marriage agency and as an employment agency. Although they charge a large fee for their services (up to $520), these firms in no way guarantee the results of the matches, nor do they guarantee safety of the rendezvous trips, accommodations of the meeting places, and so forth. The head of the migration service of Primorskii krai, C. G. Pushkarev, stated that approximately 90 percent of the agencies involved in setting up marriages with foreigners are swindlers. The absence of licenses for this type of activity and requirement of immediate payment should alert the potential brides.[17]

Analysis of Travel and Employment Agencies

Because expenditures for exporting women for prostitution are very small and it is very difficult to prove legally the purpose of the export, the chain of transporting women includes numerous organizations, from recreational firms and small travel agencies to governmental agencies. To test this hypothesis two types of organizations were chosen—firms offering "prestigious jobs" and travel agencies. Their methods of work were studied during a period of several months.

Employment agencies in the Russian Far East have a few common characteristics. To a large degree, they work in Southeast Asia instead of European countries because Moldovan, Ukrainian, Moscow, and St. Petersburg agencies, which are closer to Europe, are more competitive; also, in the Far East, white (Caucasian) women are considered "exotic" and there is great demand for them in Japan, Korea, and China. The agencies offer employment to young women aged eighteen to thirty-five, whose looks match those requested by the Chinese, Japanese, or Koreans. The middlemen who answer phone calls and meet with job candidates are not particularly interested in whether the candidates have experience or know a foreign language. They are more interested in their height (not taller than 170 cm), weight (only slim are accepted), and eye and hair color. Those chosen are offered jobs abroad, fast document processing, high salaries, and security, but without official registration with the police on arrival at the employment destination. They are assured—deceitfully—that the work will be given on legal terms.

In twenty-one of twenty-eight cases we observed, firms offering jobs abroad cannot show a license for providing employment services, cannot guarantee that activities of the foreign partner firm are legal, and cannot name people responsible for the employment procedure. Most of the firms (eighteen) present themselves as branches of a Moscow or St. Petersburg firm, whose names are a deep secret. As of 1 July 2001, only fifty firms in the Primorskii region had the legal right to find employment for people abroad; there are many others that avoid the required licensing procedure and engage in employment services illegally. However, even those that have licenses present documents that do not pass the basic requirements.

For example, we analyzed documents of the Primorskii committee on employment of the population concerning firms involved in recruiting women for work as dancers at clubs and bars in South Korea. Among the documents was a copy of an employment contract signed by the dancer and the employer. It includes the following rules: "The employee is forbidden to have personal business contacts without the employer's approval." "The employee does not have the right to break the contract without the employer's approval, regardless of the situation." "The employer is spared from any obligation to the employee in the following cases: a) if the employer loses his license for this type of activity due to the actions of the employee, b) if the employee stops working by the schedule without the agreement of the employee." There is no explanation of what type of activities the employee must perform and what responsibility they have according to the "schedule." This and many other aspects of the contract show that women can be used in any way and one can do anything he wants with them. Any slip can be considered a violation of the "schedule." The women are forced to engage in any activities assigned by the employer. Otherwise, according to the contract, if they violate certain points, the employees have to pay a fine of $2,000.

It is very difficult to punish those involved in exporting "human chattel" from Russia. First, there are almost no complaints from the victims, and there are many people willing to live abroad. For example, young women in search of jobs come to Vladivostok, the largest city in Primor'e, from Khabarovsk, Irkutsk, Novosibirsk, Krasnoiarsk, Sakhalin, Kamchatka, and so forth. Vladivostok is basically the "acceptor-distributor" of the cheap labor force en route to the West and the East. Without complaints it is difficult to determine who is engaged in transporting the victims abroad.

Second, and most important, under the existing procedure of controlling activities of private firms by the government law enforcement and inspecting agencies, it is difficult to stop the criminal activity of these firms. It is not clear from the licensing materials whether firms caught with violations linked to exporting and employing Russian citizens abroad can continue their activities or have their licenses revoked. In a number of cases it was difficult to determine whether the firms that do not pass the licensing procedure give up the illicit activity of finding employment for citizens abroad. According to the data of the Primorskii Committee on Tourism, two hundred firms have permission to engage in tourism business; however, in actuality, many more are engaged in it. Many firms apply for licenses after already working in the business, and if they are rejected, simply continue to operate without any legal foundation. A number of Primorskii tourism firms engaged in illegal transportation of tourists (primarily women) abroad are examples of this.

In July 2000, the passport and visa department of the Ministry of Internal Affairs of the Primorskii region received a request from the Administration of the Border Troops to check the activities of nine tourism firms in Vladivostok that send Russian citizens abroad without proper permission. The request indicated that these firms—with cooperation of travel agencies "Sputnik," "Primorintourist," and "Anna"—arranged for travel documents for a group of thirty women who left for China in 2000 and still have not returned. The term of their stay expired long ago, and now they are in China illegally. Nothing is known about the fate of these women and the request of the Border Troops is still pending. The cases, which in this situation can certainly be classified as slave trade, are not viewed as such by the prosecuting, administrative, and other agencies. That is why many "merchants" are able to escape the responsibility.[18]

Employees of the department on visas and passports of the city of Nakhodka have stated that there is a direct link between the activities of firms transporting citizens abroad and some of the employees of their organization. Many women who would have been denied a visa or a passport by official channels because of a previous deportation or of being underage can easily get them, avoiding the official channels. The conclusion that can be drawn from this is that many high level structures have an interest in the illicit activities of the tourist firms.

The activities of a number of firms providing employment for citizens also show the corruption in the tourism business. For example, in 1999 the license of the Vladivostok firm "Elite Planning" was revoked because blank international passports were discovered in their office. It is not known how many of the passports had already been used. It is likely that the firm violated laws on issuing and receiving international passports and that, during the period of its activity, it sent a number of Russian citizens abroad illegally. This also indicates corruption in the visa and passport issuing agencies and the participation of organized crime in transporting women from the Primorskii region abroad.

The situation in the Khabarovsk region is no less difficult. According to statements of the employees of regional special services there, employment firms are closely watched and it is more difficult to transport women abroad though fraudulent channels. But even here opportunities for their transport still exist. The activities of the International Association of Children's Funds, which assisted women going to China, provoked much criticism from the visa and passport issuing agency, the deputy director of the Khabarovsk regional border control point, the migration agency, the Ministry of Foreign Affairs, and tourist agencies. It is interesting to note that that association stopped operating in 1998. Its headquarters were in Moscow and there was a branch named International Children's Fund Family Excursion in Khabarovsk. One of the employees of the Khabarovsk branch hid a few hundred blank documents during the time of her work there. After the Moscow headquarters closed, she continued to work in Khabarovsk under fake documents, without a license to issue tourist visas. She was selling the old blank forms to tourist firms that young women used to go to South Korea and China.

An unpublished report prepared by the deputy director of the Khabarovsk regional border control point to the director of the department overseeing the activities of law enforcement agencies of the Khabarovsk region administration indicates that there are currently thirty-six firms in Khabarovsk engaged in providing employment search services abroad for Russian citizens. Twenty-seven of them operate in the entertainment business. In six months (January–June) in 2000, 857 people left the Khabarovsk region seeking employment; 407 of them were planning to work in the entertainment business. The report notes that representatives of the migration and law enforcement agencies have not received any complaints about the activities of firms providing employment services officially. Everyone who left under the contracts of those firms is alive and well and is working according to the provisions of the employment contract.

The report also indicates that despite the fact that there is only one firm in the

Khabarovsk region that offers employment for Russian citizens in China, in six months of 2000, five people went there. China is the primary country providing employment in the prostitution business. According to the documents of the Khabarovsk regional border patrol checkpoint, 150 groups left for China with and without visas. Only fifty-one of them returned on time. In 1999, twenty-seven Russian women were deported from China because instead of passports they had only ID's; in the first half of 2000 there were sixteen such cases. Border guards suspect that their passports were taken from them by their employees, and they were probably working illegally because the length of their stay had expired. Seventy-two women were deported from South Korea, but the reasons have not been indicated.

Trafficking Routes

Most individuals smuggled from Primor'e go to China. Their points of destination vary from those bordering Primor'e's northern Chinese provinces Sun'fuikhe and Dalian' to southern provinces. The largest and the most prestigious regions are considered to be Shanghai, Harbin, and Macao. The channels of transporting persons abroad are carefully worked out. Transportation to the border regions is by the cheapest method, buses; and to the most distant regions (Harbin and Beijing), by trains and airplanes. They go either alone or as part of groups making shopping or tourist trips. In the first case, the women travel at their own risk; in the second, the group is accompanied by a middleman who receives his share of the profit from the seller and the buyer.

Individuals who recruit the workers usually receive $100 or more for each woman transported. Individuals who order the women are responsible for the costs associated with transporting them to China. When they arrive at Harbin, Beijing, or other destination points, the groups are met by these individuals or their representatives, they are placed in hotels, and their documents are taken away. During the next few days, the women are distributed to the owners of brothels and other entertainment establishments throughout China. After their purchase and the confiscation of their documents, the women become completely dependent on their owners. According to the statements by women who returned from China, the conditions of payments are not followed, the scheduling of their time and transportation is determined by pimps, and the women who do not obey them are punished physically. In 1999, deaths of two prostitutes in China were reported: in the province Sichuan' (killed with an ashtray) and in the town Shanchzan' in southern China (died from drug overdose).[19] The Primorskii administration of the border troops states that in 1999, 162 women who were returning from China through Primor'e officially declared that they had been in slavery.[20] Resale of women is also practiced. After a certain period of work, when women lose their "marketable appearance," they become less valuable to the brothel owners. They are simply thrown out onto the streets, often without money or documents, or are given only a small amount of money and sent back to Russia. Cases of women returning without the proper documents for crossing the border are often reported at the border checkpoints of the Khabarovsk and Primorskii regions.

South Korea is second in the number of women "imported" from Russia, and Japan is third. The methods of transporting women to those countries are more varied, and also more expensive. Vessels leaving the ports of Vladivostok and Nakhodka or airplanes are most frequently used. Tourist visas (analogous to the Chinese version), temporary work contracts, guest invitations, and other means are used in these situations.

In addition to being employed in long-term jobs as dancers, maids, and hostesses, women are also sold temporarily, for short periods of time. In those cases, the women are registered on the ship headed to Japan as waitresses, housekeepers, or as regular passengers on tourist visas. As soon as the ship docks, the dancers and waitresses turn into prostitutes. On shore, they are met by the "buyers"—owners of massage parlors, bars, and other establishments of this type. The women are taken away for a week or ten days—the period of the ship's stay in the port—and are returned by the time of its departure.

Law Enforcement Response in the Far East

Attitudes of law enforcement agencies toward the problem of trafficking in regions of the Far East differ considerably. From February 2000 until October 2001 a number of interviews were conducted with employees of law enforcement agencies in the Primorskii region and with organizations that control the migration of the Russian citizens abroad. The purpose of the interviews was to determine their attitudes on the problem of prostitution and migration of Russian women abroad. Thirty-two employees were interviewed (six women and twenty-six men). Among the many questions, the following was particularly stressed: "In what lies, in your opinion, the cause for prostitution?" All of the interviewees put the rapid decrease in the standard of living first. There was less agreement on the other causes:

- Lack of proper legislation for punishing those involved in prostitution (24);
- Lack of control over children in families, which leads to their involvement in prostitution during teenage years or when reaching adulthood (15);
- Unwillingness of young people to engage in socially productive activities (15);
- Advertisement of prostitution in the mass media as a profitable business (11);
- Psychological disorders (1).

As can be seen from the answers, the officials see the worsening of the economic situation in Russia as the main reason for prostitution; they would like the main efforts of the law enforcement system not to be against individuals luring women into prostitution, but against the women themselves. Even women occupying official positions in law enforcement agencies believe that the laws should be directed not at prostitution as a phenomenon, but at the prostitutes. It is obvious that with such an approach prostitution will not disappear as a social phenomenon. That conclusion is supported by answers to the question "Do you believe that prostitution is something that can be rooted out from the society?" All thirty-two respondents answered "No," because: (1) a particular category of women has always been involved in this activity to make a living and there will always be those willing to engage in this activity; (2) there are no laws punishing prostitution.

Although they placed the responsibility for prostitution on the women, none of the interviewees mentioned anything about the consumers of prostitution—men. Stereotypes of men who use a woman's body without punishment are very strong in the Russian consciousness. The following answers were received to the question "Should the men carry criminal or any other type of responsibility for using the services of a prostitute?"

- Only if it involves minors (32);
- When prostitutes have experienced severe physical trauma, threatening to their life (24);
- The customer does not carry criminal responsibility for using the services of a prostitute, because it is a mutual business agreement (10).

Some respondents provided clarifications to their answers, attempting to "smooth over" their position with respect to punishment for prostitution: "consumers of prostitution should be subject to administrative responsibilities involving large fines" (8); "the cases of forceful engagement in prostitution are so rare and difficult to prove that the issue of responsibility can only be discussed in theory" (10).

The attitudes of representatives of law enforcement and administrative agencies in Primorskii krai who were interviewed serve as evidence of the existing stereotype about prostitution—that it is a phenomenon created and maintained by the women themselves. Almost all of those interviewed declared that "fighting prostitution is a waste of time because prostitutes like their work." By having such an attitude, the law enforcement agencies in Primor'e practically assist the trade of women as a commodity.

The lack of interest among the officials in solving the problems of women's involvement in prostitution and their transportation abroad with the purpose of sexual exploitation is based on the common administrative and legislative philosophy that when Russian women end up in slavery abroad it is their personal problem, created because of their own frivolousness or because of other obvious reasons. Among the thirty-two individuals interviewed, almost half stated that there are already so many serious unresolved problems in Primor'e that the problem of exporting Russian citizens abroad for sexual exploitation cannot be considered one of the most important. Only five respondents believed that it was a serious problem that should be resolved on the governmental level. In general, the officials and law enforcement agencies view the problem as citizens' private matter.

In contrast to Primor'e, in the Khabarovsk region law enforcement agencies realize the importance and the scale of this problem. In my opinion, there are a few
reasons for this. First, the accumulated experience of fighting prostitution in the
Khabarovsk region has shown its danger to the order and health of the society. One
of the primary dangers is the spread of sexually transmitted diseases. In 1999, the
Khabarovskii Express reported that for the first time a professional prostitute in-
fected with AIDS was discovered in Khabarovsk.[21] The question of how many clients she had had is left to the imagination. In addition, prostitution is linked directly
and indirectly to other criminal structures and is the breeding ground for them.

Second, transportation of women abroad is one of the channels of illegal export
of hard currency and import of goods that are tax-exempt or subject to preferential
duty. Therefore, law-enforcement personnel must solve the problem of trafficking to
solve the problem of contraband trade and ensure collection of proper taxes on the
goods imported. For example, a person is eligible to import a car and pay preferential duty on it if she spent six months abroad. Criminal groups have been taking
advantage of this regulation. They provide women with money and force them to
bring cars and expensive goods into Russia. Border control officers and officers of
the Regional Directorate for Combatting Organized Crime say that most of the
women who return to Russia are controlled by organized criminal groups. These
groups rob women of their earnings and belongings. As a result, border control officers in Khabarovskii krai work to ensure protection of Russian citizens coming back
into the country.

Third, the number of reports of missing wives, daughters, or relatives who have
gone abroad has been growing. According to the Department for Missing People of
the Khabarovskii krai Directorate of Internal Affairs (UVD), from 1998 to 2000,
there were eight reports of women reported missing after they went to work in
China.[22] After investigation of the reports, five out of six women were found and
brought back with the help of UVD, the Ministry of the Interior, and the National
Interpol Office. According to an Interpol officer, fifteen women were reported missing from 1998 to 2000. All of them had disappeared in China. Of the fifteen, eight
returned to Russia.

In comparison, in Primorskii krai, the first missing persons report was investigated in November 2000. On the TV show "Mestnoe Vremya" on 18 December
2000, the deputy head of the Primor'e Department of the Interior reported that Primor'e law-enforcement officials, in collaboration with the Chinese police, worked
on the case of three women who had been sold first in China and then resold in
Burma. As a result of the investigation, a businesswoman has been charged with
recruiting women for employment abroad. In October 2001, the Primorskii krai
UVD and the Ministry of the Interior office in Primorskii krai received a second
report about a young woman who had been missing since September 2000, when
she had left to work in China.

Apart from the Department of the Interior and Interpol, the Khabarovsk office
of Russia's Ministry of the Interior received ten missing persons reports from families asking to find women who had disappeared in China. A memo from the Minis-

try of the Interior to the region administration shows that all missing persons are young women between eighteen and twenty-five years of age who went to China either without a visa, or as part of a tour group or as individuals with tourists visas. In both cases, they planned on working in China. The memo states, "In all cases, they went to China having no job offers, and without work visas." Therefore, from the very beginning they were illegally employed in the destination country. The memo further states, "Many of them agreed, some others were forced, to become prostitutes in China." It further states that "according to the Embassy of the Russian Federation in China, there are a number of young Russian women in China. Many of them have already been arrested for prostitution. This year, the number of such arrests has increased dramatically. According to the reports of Chinese police, at the end of March 2001, there were about 15,000 Russian women held as slaves in China."[23]

In studying the cases of missing women who disappeared in China, it is evident that all of them went to China not as part of official travel agencies' tours but with the help of individual recruiters. The recruiters were usually close acquaintances who promised them high earnings in China. The story of Olga Sh. (UVD officers insisted on keeping the victim's last name secret) is a typical example of how the scheme works. On 7 November 1999, Olga and three other women entered China on work visas to work as waitresses in Harbin. A friend who had traveled to China for business and said she had established business contacts there convinced the women to go to China. On their arrival in Harbin, the women discovered that their friend owed a considerable amount of money to the restaurant's owner. To pay off her debt, she brought a group of women to the restaurant, left them there, and went back to Russia. Shortly after, she left Khabarovsk and had been wanted ever since. The restaurant owner sold the women. Olga found herself in the hotel "Sinhua Bright Pearl" in the Putyen District, somewhere between the cities of Tunzyan and Saman. There she was kept prisoner and was forced to work as a prostitute. Eventually, she was able to convince Russian tourists to take a letter back to her husband, whom she asked for help.

In 1999, there were two cases of transporting young women who had contracts to work in Harbin, but were taken to Beijing and found it very difficult to return to Russia. A number of individuals suspected in recruiting women for work abroad are on file at the Border Control Service in Khabarovskii krai.

Very often, Chinese recruiters come to Khabarovsk and other cities in the region. They meet with women in specially prepared apartments and appraise the "human commodity." On 4 July 2000, Khabarovsk law-enforcement officers arrested a Chinese citizen who recruited four women to work as hostesses, dancers, striptease dancers, and prostitutes. From 1999 to early 2000, fifteen recruiters were deported from the region. On 8 August 2000, in his report to the director of the Department for Coordination of Activities of Law-Enforcement in Khabarovskii krai, the head of the Border Patrol Unit in Khabarovsk pointed out, "Chinese police officers do participate in trafficking of Russian prostitutes. Almost all brothels are under their secret control. There have been instances when women ran away from their owners and turned to police for help. Police officers would find out the name of the place the woman escaped from and returned her there or would sell her to another brothel."[24]

The report also mentioned another very disturbing fact. It states, "Recently, young Russian girls have been in high demand in China. Recruiters help young girls to acquire fake papers that allow them to travel abroad." Officers of the Visa and Passport Services agency in Khabarovskii krai confirmed that they worked with cases where strangers came to receive passports for young girls. Minor prostitutes who had been deported try to get a new passport under a different name. Border patrol officers detained a number of young girls trying to enter China on fake passports.

Because the number of Russian women entering Asian-Pacific states is increasing, the governments of those states have introduced preventive measures. Mr. V.A. Chernov, head of the Khabarovsk Region Tourism Department, said that Japan and South Korea made it more difficult for Russian women to travel to those countries. The Japanese consulate no longer allows Japanese businesses to sign work contracts with Khabarovsk businesses that work in show business. Chernov believes that this is a blow to legal employment: "We had no early control over Russian citizens' employment in the entertainment business abroad and could not guarantee their security and appropriate work conditions. Now it has become very difficult, almost impossible."[25] Just as many people still go to work abroad, but most potential employees use letters of invitation, questionable acquaintances, and personal contacts. People still leave the country, but on tourist visas that do not allow employment. Japan also raised the age limit for women who go to work in Japan. As a result, there is a booming industry of services to provide young women with invitations to study and do research. In addition, the visa fee has gone up to $300, which an average Russian woman cannot possibly afford. Therefore, recruiters offer to lend women the money, which they can pay back by working abroad. The women then become prostitutes to pay off the debt.

Khabarovskii krai has introduced a number of measures aimed at combating human trafficking. According to the region's Migration Service, from 1998 to 2000, fifteen businesses and individuals who worked without licenses and three firms issuing licenses were closed down. In 2000, eight businesses were denied licenses because they did not have employment contracts.

On 11 August 2000, Victor Ivanovich Ishaev, governor of the Khabarovskii krai, signed Decree 585, "On Organizing a Working Group for Preparing a Set of Measures Aimed at Preventing Young Women from Becoming Prostitutes in Cities and Towns in Khabarovsk region." A working group was formed under this decree consisting of leaders of all relevant agencies—deputy director of the Department for Coordination of Activities of Law-Enforcement Agencies, deputy head of UVD, head of the Criminal Investigation Department, head of the Mass Media Department, head of the Immigration Department, deputy head of the Federal Border Patrol Department, Council from the Ministry of the Interior, representatives of FSB, and head of the Tourism Department.

During its first meeting, the group agreed on a program of thirteen points aimed at preventing transportation of women abroad for future exploitation. The measures included investigation, providing information, licensing, education, and other types of activities. In October 2000, Ishaev signed the decree "On Preventing Involvement in Prostitution of the Citizens of Khabarovsk region Traveling Abroad." This decree emphasizes the danger of illegal transportation of women for sexual exploitation. In addition, the law enforcement agencies were ordered to start cooperating with their counterparts in the region as well as in the neighboring countries "to combat prostitution and protect constitutional rights of the Russian women who travel abroad."

To sum up the findings of our research, compared to Primorskii krai, Khabarovskii krai is much further ahead in understanding the importance of combating human trafficking. The people of Khabarovsk have shown a state approach to the problem of human trafficking. The universal philosophy of the agencies involved can be defined as "Any Russian citizen is a citizen of Russia in any situation. Therefore, the task of the Russian state is to protect its citizens from violence, no matter how difficult this task can be."

Notes

1.   Excerpt from an interview with Tatiana Filimonova, an employee of the regional administration of Primor'e.

2.   "On trade of humans and exploitation of prostitution by the third parties. Prevention and eradication of exploitation of women." International legislation. Kyiv, 1999, 11.

3.   C. Ling, "Global Survival Network. Rights Activists Rap Ex-Soviet States on Sex-Trade," Reuters, 6 November 1997.

4.   William H. Webster, *Russian Organized Crime—Project of Global Organized Crime* (Washington, D.C.: Center for Strategic International Research, 1997), 26–32.

5.   Webster, from a speech by the chairman of the Committee on Security of the State Duma, Victor I. Iliukhin.

6.   Webster, *Russian Organized Crime.*

7.   Information site of the Russian State Duma, http://www.akdi.ru/GD/safety/p09-10/r09-10.htm.

8.   "International cooperation in the fight against illegal export and exploitation abroad of women and children: Verbatim report of the round table," State meeting, Parliament of the Russian Federation, State Duma, Moscow, 9–10 October 1997, *Trends in Organized Crime* 4 (1998): 39–40.

9.   "The Sex Trade: Trafficking of Women and Children in Europe and the US." Testimony of Anita Botti, deputy director for International Women's Initiative. Hearing before the Commission on Security and Cooperation of Europe, Washington, D.C., 29 June 1999.

10.   Sally Stoecker, "Trade of Humans: A Form of Expression of Organized Crime," *Transnational Organized Crime: Definitions and Realities*, ed. Vitalii Nomokonov (Vladivostok: Far Eastern State University Press, 2001), 189.

11.   A. Iliukhov and A. Rasputnyi, "Slaves Are Mute," *Ocean Avenue*, 6–16 April 2001.

12.   Deputy General Prosecutor of Russia in the Far East federal district Konstantin Chaika, at the international conference "Contemporary Problems of Fighting Prostitution in

the Asia-Pacific Region," Khabarovsk, March 2001.

13. *Dal'press*, no. 5, 2000.

14. *Babylon* 14 (1999).

15. Vladivostok television advertisement, 10–16 February 2002.

16. *Babylon* 23 (1999).

17. "Can't Wait to Get Married," *Komsomolskaia Pravda na Dal'nem Vostoke*, 14 July 2000.

18. "Illegal Business Became a Problem for Diplomats," *Tikhookeanskaia zvezda*, Vladivostok, 4 September 2001; interview with the head of the passport and visa service of the Ministry of Internal Affairs of the Russian Federation, Yuri Sharagorov, in a television program on NTV, "Morning News," 20 May 2000.

19. "The Chinese Get Down to the "Night Butterflies," *Zolotoi Rog* (The Golden Horn), 25 May 2000.

20. "Russian Sex Slaves in China," *Izvestiia* (Primorskii edition), 16 June 2000.

21. *Khabarovskii Express,* June 1999 (issue #271).

22. Statistical data from the Khabarovsk Regional Directorate of Internal Affairs, 2001.

23. Official correspondence of the head of the Khabarovsk Regional Border Point to the governor of Khabarovsk krai, 18 September 2000.

24. Oleg Zhunusov, "Russian Concubines in China," *Izvestiia*, Primorksii edition, 16 June 2000.

25. Interview by the author, 6 August 2001.

Chapter 6

<ঞ><ঞ><ঞ>

Female Labor Migration Trends and Human Trafficking: Policy Recommendations

Elena Tiuriukanova

The Russian Federation became actively involved in the international migration process in the second half of the 1980s. Free migration in Russia began with the passage of the Russian Federal Law "On Entry to and Exit from the Russian Federation," adopted in 1993 (revised in 1996). During the last decade, the country changed from an isolated, closed society to a large world center for the entry and exit of migrants. Without a doubt, an open society is an important component of Russia's democratization. However, numerous social problems and challenges have accompanied the new opportunities. In the last quarter of the twentieth century, a global migration process developed in which different countries and regions of the world played strictly defined roles. The main trends and contradictions that shape the reality of contemporary migration now apply to Russia—an important participant in the globalization process. Russia has gradually evolved into a "gender migration" regime shaped in the past several decades. The basis of a gender migration regime is the division of labor resulting from national gender segregation of workers in postindustrial societies. In such a division of labor, women-migrants are assigned roles as cheap service providers, including "marginal" or demeaning services. The emergence of Russia and other postcommunist countries on the international migration scene has altered Western service and entertainment markets, including the sex industry. In this chapter, I discuss some of the results of Russian integration into the global migration process from the perspective of new opportunities and challenges facing women-migrants.

Challenges of Globalization

The relationship between migration and global socioeconomic changes is filled
with complexities and contradictions. On one hand, global changes are accompanied by the intensification of international migration. On the other, it is acknowledged that "people are less mobile than money, goods or ideas: people
always belong to a state, are dependent on passports, visas, residence permits
and the labor market."[1] The movement of goods and finances occurs on a much
larger scale than the movement of people. In 1996, the export of goods worldwide constituted 29 percent of the world's GDP, while foreign direct investment
constituted about 6 percent of the total investment worldwide.[2] At the same
time, global labor migration was 120 million people—only 2.3 percent of the
world's population.[3]

There are several reasons why it is imperative that Russia respond to the
challenges of the global migration regime today. First, the growing polarization
of the world into poor and wealthy countries provokes unprecedented migration
pressures from poor and highly populated nations and those that are less populated and highly advanced. Second, "migration management" is in crisis. Countries have lost control over migration processes and in many cases are unable to
track the scale and location of many immigrants—including temporary laborers
and students—within their borders. This has translated into an enormous illegal
movement of persons and the criminalization of migration relations. Third, the
creation of a global division of labor based on discriminatory practices of national and gender segregation among workers in international labor markets
must be addressed. Such segregation and discrimination has resulted in depen-
dence of the developed nations on an enormous and uninterrupted flow of migrants. Fourth, there is a need to resolve the contradictions between the concept
of human rights as a basis of contemporary liberalism and national interests—
the contradiction between the rights of a person and the rights of a citizen. All of
those processes require attention and analysis to understand the role of Russia in
contemporary migration and to search for effective migration policies that will
counteract the marginalization of migrants.

Today, the contradictions between receiving and sending countries are becoming more pronounced because international migration policy is based on
competing principles. On one hand, there is a strict division into "desirable" and
"undesirable" migrants from the perspective of national interests; on the other,
there is the declared principle of respecting migrants' rights and freedoms.
Those contradictions result in conflicts and discriminatory practices with respect
to certain groups of migrants (especially women) in certain countries. The inability of states to manage migration flows is becoming more and more apparent. The ineffectiveness of the contemporary model of international migration is
evidenced by large-scale illegal migration composed of a cheap, largely female,
labor force lacking in rights. It is doubtful that any country can claim to have
developed effective mechanisms to combat illegal immigration.

The scale of illegal movement may be considered an immanent quality of the contemporary phase of migration development. Every year, millions of people become involved in an illegitimate human flow "managed" by a well-organized global network that has transformed migration into a profitable business. There are official, semi-official, shadow, and openly criminal organizations receiving enormous profits from trafficking people and serving as middlemen in the employment of migrants. Trafficking in persons has become an international organized business.

International Labor Migration at the Turn of the Twenty-First Century: The Gender Perspective

The reality of migration today has been shaped by the processes of the second half of the twentieth century when the nature and structure of interstate movement underwent significant change. The following brief review of current processes is essential to understand today's reality and the extent to which we can manage migration flows.

The internationalization of economies and the uneven development of countries have resulted in labor migration becoming much more economically, socially, and politically significant than before. Labor migration has turned into a truly global phenomenon. At present, almost all countries are involved in labor migration exchange. According to United Nations (UN) and International Labor Organization (ILO) estimates, there are 120–200 million legal labor migrants in the world today compared to 75 million in 1965.[4] The difference in the standard of living and economic opportunities among different countries is the main moving force for such migration. Hourly wages in the manufacturing industry are $0.25 in India and China, $0.60 in Russia, and $2.09 in Poland, compared to $17.20 in the United States, $23.66 in Japan, and $31.88 in Germany.[5]

Steady labor migration during the last several decades has resulted in the segmentation of labor markets in developed countries. Job sectors filled by migrants are mostly nonprestigious and do not require special skills; they have difficult working conditions and low wages. They are also the most discriminatory, informal, or illegal employment segments. Women-migrants are employed mostly in the entertainment industry (dancers, strippers, sex workers), in the service industry (low-end hotel, bar, and fitness center personnel) and as domestic helpers (nannies, maids, and caregivers of children, the elderly, and the ill). Male migrants work in the construction industry, on the low-end of heavy industry, and in other low-skill and difficult jobs.

The national and gender segregation of workers in the labor markets of industrially developed countries resulted in a division of labor in which women-migrants play a specific role. The division of labor between national workers and migrants, as well as among the migrants themselves based on gender, has become more significant than the mere existence of certain economic niches for migrants of different nationalities in labor markets of the receiving countries. It is turning into an economic order on which developed countries build their economies. Moreover, the economic and social prosperity of those countries is becoming more and more dependent on migrant labor, and a similar process of migrant labor niches is developing in Russia. Eventually, the Russian economy will become as dependent on migrant labor as economies of developed countries. Considering Russia's demographic trends and the estimated reduction of the working age population after 2005, this scenario seems plausible.

The feminization of migration (the increasing percentage of women in the migrant population), is recognized by experts as characteristic of a new stage in the development of international labor migration.[6] In large part, this is related to structural changes in the world economy accompanying the globalization processes: relative reduction of the industrial sector in the postwar period and the growth of the service sector, also called the "service economy."[7] The dominance of the service sector in the employment sphere resulted in a growing demand of developed nations for women-migrants for employment in unskilled jobs.[8]

Women-migrants have long been performing the role of cheap service providers (mainly sexual services) in the international migration industry, thus filling marginal niches in the labor markets of receiving countries. According to IOM, almost half a million foreign prostitutes are trafficked to Europe every year. In Germany, three out of four prostitutes are foreign, and in the Netherlands every second prostitute is from overseas.[9] The sex industry and sex tourism in the metropolitan centers of industrial countries, being an integral part of the global "service economy," form an extremely profitable, transnational organized business of trafficking women across countries for the purpose of sexual exploitation.

Today, the sphere of sexual and quasi-sexual services (jobs often entailing sex services such as dance shows, striptease, escort services, modeling, and so forth) represents significant migration opportunities for women from donor countries. The wave of "Russian" (including women from other post-Soviet states) prostitution in the West that is widely discussed in Western media simply demonstrates the "entry" of Russian women into the world migration scene. The Russian "wave" arrived after similar waves of prostitutes from the Philippines, China, Columbia, and Nigeria (1960s–1970s), and then from Poland, the Czech Republic, and Romania (second half of the 1980s). In 1997, 175,000 women and girls from Eastern and Central Europe, including Russia and the CIS countries, were sold into the sex markets of developed countries of Europe and America.[10] The end of isolation for Central and Eastern Europe, including the former USSR, has provoked the restructuring of the world sex markets.

Although the phenomenon of trafficking in persons has existed since the beginning of the twentieth century (International Agreement on White Slave Trade of 1904), modern globalization gives it a new form, which today is considered to be slavery and a gross violation of basic human rights. With the increase in population mobility (along with the mobility of goods, finances, and information), it is necessary for national states and federal governments to improve the mechanisms for managing the contradiction between globalizing processes and institutes, on one hand, and national concepts for managing those processes and institutes, on the other. This contradiction is represented by a so-called management crisis. Just as governments are losing millions of tax dollars as a result of the internationalization of manufacturing and the increasing number of international financial transactions, estimated at hundreds of millions of dollars daily,[11] controlling population movements is becoming problematic for government authorities. The result is the growth of illegal migration. According to U.S. Immigration and Naturalization Service estimates, there were between 4.6 and 5.4 million illegal migrants in the United States in 1996.[12] In Russia, there are about 4 million illegal labor migrants.[13] Women are concentrated in this illegal pool of migration for reasons discussed below.

Steady migration flows eventually give rise to migration networks that connect immigrants in receiving countries with their home countries. Those networks reduce the expenses and risks related to migration and support the migration flow even when the objective reasons for it are no longer acute, or when new factors contravening migration appear (for example, when the immigration policy of receiving countries becomes more strict). The networks often acquire a criminal character and limit the ability of governments to manage migration flows.

Another important characteristic of the latest period in the development of migration is that migration problems are now being discussed in the context of human rights, which influenced government policies in this field, although these changes seem to be of a declarative character. Discriminatory practices toward migrants still persist in countries with developed democratic traditions, but are now being criticized by human rights organizations and liberal political movements. The migration issue is becoming a trump card in political games of the powerful. For example, right-wing parties often play the migration card using the unfavorable attitudes of some groups of the population toward immigrants.

Marginalization of Female Migration

The reasons for the marginalization of female migration are found in the nature of jobs that women-migrants perform and in their role in the economic structures of society. Women-migrants are employed in the most discriminatory, unregulated, and corrupt sectors of migrant employment. Jobs in the service industry, where most women-migrants are employed, have particular features that make workers more vulnerable and less socially protected than workers in other sectors. Jobs in the service industry (in both the private and public sectors), traditionally were not recognized and still are not recognized de facto as socially and economically equal to other types of labor. That is especially the case with so-called "domestic services."

The paltry wages paid to women-migrants confirms that they are employed in the least prestigious employment sectors. A study conducted by the Institute for the Socio-Economic Problems of the Population under the Russian Academy of Sciences among Russian citizens going for work abroad shows that the proportion of women to men in the group of poorly paid labor migrants (less than $500 per month) is 3:1; in the group of highly paid migrants (over $1,000 per month) that proportion is reversed to 1:3.[14] Apart from an objective economic aspect, the low status of migrant labor has a subjective manifestation. Based on the fact that women are usually employed in nonprestigious, often socially demeaning jobs, the society forms a negative, stigmatized image of women-migrants. Specific features of female labor migration are related not only to the existence of typical employment sectors for women-migrants and the nonprestigious nature of jobs in those sectors, but also to the flexibility of women's labor, which is difficult to regulate in contracts and is individual by nature. In addition, the socio-demographic characteristics of migrants tend to be young age, a low level of education, and motives such as marriage and emigration.[15]

For these reasons, female labor migration in Russia during the last ten years has turned into a "zone" of heightened risk and mass human rights violations. This is especially the case with risky and marginal jobs, which include sex jobs and so-called quasi-sexual jobs. In 2000, a survey was administered to women who intended to go abroad for temporary jobs. One of the purposes was to find the attitude of potential women migrants toward different types of jobs that are in demand on Western markets. The survey was published in the newspaper *Inostranets*, which specializes in migration issues.[16] One hundred sixty-five completed surveys were received by mail from almost all regions of Russia, from Irkutsk to Tver oblasts (Baikalsk, Ufa, Volgodonsk, Kazan, Samara, Voronezh, Kirovo-Chepetsk, Sochi, Perm, Tula, Novokuznetsk, Saint Petersburg, and so forth). Ten percent of respondents already had options for departure, about half were looking for such jobs at the time, and the rest intended to start looking for jobs. Results of the survey demonstrate that during the last decade of free migration from Russia a population group of so-called "potential migrants," including women, was formed. These people have certain conceptions about labor migration and have certain migration preferences. Because Russian labor migration processes started from scratch, it is interesting to note that today, ten years after the official birth of labor migration in 1993, Russian women have experienced new employment opportunities and new threats wrought by labor migration.

The respondents were asked to choose from several types of jobs, and their preferences among those jobs were distributed as shown in table 6.1.

Table 6.1 Job Preferences of Potential Migrants (percentages)

Service industry (hotel personnel, restaurant personnel, small trade, etc.)	51
Domestic services (nannies, maids, caregivers, etc.)	56
Entertainment industry (dancers, models, strippers, etc.)	5
Health-fitness services (fitness clubs, massage salons, etc.)	5
Seasonal agricultural jobs	16
Any jobs with good working conditions	44
Other	30

The most popular jobs are in the service industry and domestic services. Forty-four percent of the respondents would take any job if they were satisfied with the conditions (they do not have preferences regarding employment sectors). That indicates the flexibility of the labor supply from Russia as a donor country and the readiness to adjust to the demand for labor in the receiving countries. Thus, further segregation of workers in the labor markets of developed industrial countries may increase in the future.

Table 6.2 demonstrates the attitude of potential women-migrants toward specific jobs. The majority of respondents consider jobs as maids, nannies, caregivers for older people, fashion models, and photo models acceptable and "normal." Such jobs are in the high-risk category because they are mostly in the informal labor market.

There are lively debates in the West about social recognition of housework, including care work that employs mostly women. There is no common opinion as to what form this recognition should take. Nevertheless, it is clear that the results of the debates and the consequent possible changes in social policy will have a strong impact on the development of female migration.

As for the sexual services, only 4 percent consider this job "normal." Almost a quarter of respondents think that prostitution should be prohibited. At the same time, a large number of women consider a job as a stripper to be normal. Employment in a bar to sit down near a customer and entice them to order more alcohol and other types of exploitation in the entertainment industry are also considered to be normal, although by a slightly smaller number of women. However, those jobs have an image similar to prostitution in the public eye. According to the survey, 26 percent of respondents think those types of jobs are practically the same as prostitution and sexual exploitation (table 6.3).

Almost none of the women who responded would easily agree to work in the sex industry or to combine "normal" jobs with sex work. Eighty-four percent of respondents rule out the option of working in the sex industry; 7 percent consider such a job "undesirable," and only 2 percent checked the option "It depends on how much it pays" (5 percent did not answer).

Another question allowed us to estimate how many potential women-migrants would work in the sex industry abroad. When asked what job option they would prefer, 90 percent answered "Where the pay is less but sexual services are excluded"; 5 percent "Where the pay is higher but sexual services are not excluded"; and 5 percent did not respond. However, if one analyzes the distribution of answers to this question according to age of the respondents, the result will be that in groups of young (under 30) and very young (under 20) women up to 25 percent prefer the variant "Where the pay is higher but sexual services are not excluded."

It is also interesting to analyze how potential migrants, the majority of whom do not want to work in the sex industry, evaluate their chances of finding a job abroad that does not involve sexual services. In response to the question "Is it easy to find a job abroad that does not involve sexual services for a

Table 6.2 Attitude of Respondents toward Types of Jobs (percentages)

	Normal	Shameful	For those who can do nothing else	Socially harmful
Dancers in entertainment establishments, stripper	35	23	35	4
Enticing bar clients to buy alcohol	17	17	46	16
Sex services	4	35	33	23
Model or fashion model	79	–	14	2
Nannies or caregivers	84	–	14	–
Maids	79	4	14	2

Table 6.3 Responses to Questions on Job Options (percentages)

How often do job offers as dancers, etc. mean sexual services?	
Always	26
Often	53
Sometimes	18
Never	-
Don't know	3

young woman from Russia without higher education?" 12 percent thought it was very difficult, almost impossible; 49 percent, difficult but possible if one acts actively; 21 percent, not difficult if one is not demanding; and 18 percent, it is easy to find a normal job for all who want it.

Twelve percent of respondents think that practically all jobs abroad for young women involve sexual services. If a woman does not accept work in the sex industry, her options for leaving the country are very limited. At present, all employment sectors listed above, including domestic services and service industry jobs, are high-risk because of labor relations in those sectors and because legal channels for labor migration for mass professions are almost nonexistent.

Migration Legislation and Services

Until 1993, opportunities for going abroad for work were very limited, selective, and elitist. There were almost no opportunities for average citizens to leave Russia. There was no legal basis and no institutional support for free labor migration. After 1993, migration legislation was liberalized and the legal basis as well as institutional support for labor migration began to develop. Mass media regularly provided information about opportunities for employment abroad. At the same time, the Federal Migration Service (FMS) was created as the main state

Table 6.4. Dynamics of Russian Labor Migrants (thousands of persons)

Year	Number of labor migrants		
	Total	Men	Women
1994	8.1		
1995	11.2		
1996	12.3	11.1	1.2
1997	21.1	19.6	1.5
1998	32.5	29.6	2.9
1999	32.7	29.8	2.9
2000	45.8	40	5.8

body making decisions on labor migration. Its powers were transferred to the Ministry of the Federation, National and Migration Policy of Russia in 2000. In 2001, those powers were transferred to the Ministry for Internal Affairs (MVD). In 1993, a Law on Entry and Exit was adopted (revised in 1996). This law gave a legal right to Russian citizens to move freely and to select their place of residence and work abroad; it also abolished exit visas.

Russia began to cooperate actively with several international organizations that work on migration issues and develop international documents on the status, rights, social protection of labor migrants, and so forth (IOM, ILO). Some private organizations started to legally employ Russian citizens abroad after obtaining the relevant license issued by the FMS. Russia concluded several intergovernmental agreements on the exchange of workforces with Germany, Finland, Switzerland, China, Poland, Vietnam, and other countries. Foreign employers and their agents began to advertise job opportunities in Russia.

As a result of those activities, labor migration is losing its elitist nature and becoming more common and accessible to people from different social and professional groups. Workers now have an opportunity to work abroad as construction workers, drivers, medical personnel, teachers, scientists, and workers in the service industry. Development of the legal basis and institutional infrastructure for temporary labor migration from Russia is not yet complete. Nonetheless, the basis for temporary labor migration is expanding.

The official channel for labor migration from Russia is through firms that find employment for Russian citizens abroad. These firms have licenses issued by the Ministry of the Federation of Russia that are based on intergovernmental agreements. In 2001, 45,800 persons left Russia through these channels. Only 7,500 of them were women, which is 16.4 percent of the total number of labor migrants. Along with the growing number of labor migrants, the proportion of women among them is also increasing, but it remains quite low. This is because most persons employed abroad since Soviet times were sailors and workers in the maritime industry.

My estimate, based on research and surveys, is that the official statistics of female labor outmigration is no more than 5 percent of the real total outflow of female labor migration from the country, which means that the number of women leaving the country through unofficial channels of labor migration is twenty times the official statistics. This includes women finding employment through personal contacts and through intermediaries operating illegally (without a license). However, exiting through official channels does not guarantee the legality of migration. Up to 90 percent of the operating licensed firms provide women with visitor or tourist visas that do not give them the right to work abroad. Such migration for labor purposes, therefore, is not legal. In Russia, informal and shadow relations penetrate formal institutions and structures and operate using the legal status but ignore the necessary official procedures.[17] In addition, companies that operate under the license of FMS use shadow and illicit mechanisms for organizing migration for their customers. Moreover, shadow and unofficial structures often work more efficiently than cumbersome legal mechanisms. If all illegal exit channels and all semi-legal relations were cut off, we would return to the situation of ten years ago behind the "Iron Curtain."

The Potential of Labor Migration from Russia

With the growth of migration flows out of the country, the number of people who intend to migrate also increases. Two surveys of working age people were conducted in Moscow enterprises and organizations in 1996 and 2000 to identify the potential for labor migration and its role in the adjustment of Russian citizens to the market economy.[18] The survey plan, its instruments, and selection parameters ensure that the data are representative. The goal was to identify and measure migration tendencies among populations. The selected samples were 404 and 465 persons respectively. A representative sample of persons of working age in Moscow was chosen based on age, gender, education, and profession. The results of these surveys are discussed below.

In the working age population of Russia, 87.7 percent of permanent and temporary labor migrants are men, and only 12.5 percent are women. Women who migrate hope to change their social status, improve their financial situation, and in some cases, change their lifestyle. Migration can be both a "strategy for survival" and a "strategy for success." In either case, labor migration provides women with a better selection of possible life strategies that would help them adjust to and improve their unfavorable socioeconomic reality. Tendencies toward labor migration among men and women are practically the same. A tendency for temporary labor migration abroad among women is seven times higher than the tendency for emigration for permanent residency.

The roles of both temporary labor migration and permanent emigration have become stronger in the adjustment strategies of the population, especially for women, as a comparison of the survey data in a five-year interval reveals: 14 percent in 1996 to 20 percent in 2000 (see table 6.5).

Specific migration tendencies among women and men that characterize the potential for temporary labor migration from Russia differ significantly. In 1996, 2–5 percent of the working age population of Moscow could be considered

Table 6.5 Do You Intend to Actively Seek Methods of Migration in the Next 1–2 Years? (responses in percentages)

Tendency	1996		2000	
	Men	Women	Men	Women
Yes	7	2	13	4
Very likely	6	4	5	1
Maybe	28	24	25	25
No	59	70	57	60

active potential labor migrants. In 2000, this number was 4–8 percent, while 10–15 percent was considered the passive or "sleeping" potential of migrants. However, it is necessary to take into account that the migration tendencies of the population in Moscow are traditionally higher than in other regions of the country.

More than half of the potential women-migrants intend to migrate abroad to work for a period of up to one year. About 20 percent of potential migrants intend to migrate for a period of up to three months, which means that they want to make some money quickly and return home. Knowing the preferences of people is important in forming policy in this area. Based on such preferences, one could recommend that countries that historically have cooperated in migration strategies should introduce pilot projects on legal short-term labor migration that would involve a quota of work visas specifically for women. Russia, a country with a great interest in such projects, should take the initiative. It is unlikely that a receiving country would take the initiative to propose such a quota, although receiving countries are committed to developing means of reducing illegal migration.

The following three processes are occurring: increases in actual migration flows, the development of legal and institutional infrastructures supporting labor migration, and increases in migratory tendencies among populations. Currently, the legal basis and institutional infrastructure for labor migration is underdeveloped and, as a result, shadow structures facilitate migration without any state control or monitoring, which in turn causes marginalization of migrants—especially for women-migrants.

Linkage between Female Migration and Trafficking in Persons

Because sex and quasi-sex work provide the majority of migration opportunities for young women, most female labor migration is in the marginal area of labor relations. Human rights violations in this field are numerous and are not limited to sex work. A quarter of women respondents believe that all jobs abroad are high risk. In addition, 43 percent sense some kind of danger associated with work abroad. Fewer than 5 percent of respondents feel protected on leaving for work abroad, and almost 60 percent said they feel completely unprotected. More than 40 percent of respondents agree that many women who left to work abroad find themselves in slavery-like conditions. Approximately the same number believes that is an overstatement. Only 5 percent of respondents did not agree with the statement. Because of the attention of the mass media on human trafficking schemes and crimes, many potential women-migrants are well aware of the dangers awaiting labor migrants (table 6.6).

If conflicts arise in the receiving country, most potential migrants (about 70 percent) would rely on the assistance of the Russian consulate there. Half of the respondents would rely on the police and other state structures of the receiving country. Thirty percent know about NGOs in receiving countries and would rely on those; 30 percent rely on friends, relatives, and acquaintances; 23 percent rely on lawyers; and 18 percent rely on their future employer. When analyzing this data, it is important to take into account that respondents were readers of a newspaper that regularly publishes information on labor migrants, including descriptions of conflict situations and ways to resolve them.

As one can see, even such "advanced" respondents still rely on traditional law-enforcement structures. Significantly fewer respondents rely on NGOs and even fewer rely on human rights institutions. In reality, however, the real assistance to women-migrants in crisis situations comes from NGOs and international organizations whose mandate of protecting human rights comes before protecting national interests. Police, migration agencies, and even Russian consulates base their decisions and actions on a narrow-minded administrative perspective in which the lack of legal status is justification for refusing to protect the rights of a migrant.

However, the answers to the question "Who would you consult (or already consulted) with before choosing options for working abroad?" demonstrate that civilized forms of migratory behavior are starting to develop in Russia. Forty percent of respondents consulted with their parents, husbands, or other relatives; 43 percent consulted with their friends; and 36 percent (this is not a low number even considering the characteristics of the selection sample) consulted with lawyers or other specialists outside the firm that facilitated their employment.

In contemporary Russia, the problem of trafficking in human beings and the term itself translated from English were given legal status on a state level in 1997.[19] In 2000, Russia signed the UN Convention on Transnational Organized

Table 6.6 Potential Women-Migrants' Awareness of Possible Human Rights Violations in Labor Migration (percentages)

Type of violation	Well aware	Heard something	Not aware
Removal of a passport	11	84	5
Limiting freedom of movement	14	64	14
Violation of conditions of contract (underpayment, longer hours, etc.)	25	66	2
Debt bondage	9	61	20
Forcing into sex work	5	82	5
Threats, violence	5	66	18

Crime and its Protocol to Prevent, Suppress and Punish Trafficking in Persons, Especially Women and Children. Trafficking in women is considered one of the main types of transnational organized crime, along with arms trade and drug trafficking. This Protocol defines trafficking in human beings as:

> "Trafficking in persons" shall mean the recruitment, transportation, transfer, harboring or receipt of persons, by means of the threat or use of force or other forms of coercion, of abduction, of fraud, of deception, of the abuse of power or of a position of vulnerability, or of the giving or receiving of payments or benefits to achieve the consent of a person having control over another person, for the purpose of exploitation. Exploitation shall include, at a minimum, the exploitation of the prostitution of others or other forms of sexual exploitation, involuntary labour or services, slavery or practices similar to slavery, servitude.[20]

Although the problem of trafficking in persons is closely related to illegal migration and human smuggling, it is necessary to differentiate these concepts. In principle, trafficking in persons may take place through legal migration channels from the perspective of entry to and stay in the receiving countries. Moreover, criminal groups often use legal channels and instruments. Such instruments may involve visa regimes used in some countries. For example, in an effort to attract women-migrants into the entertainment industry, the Japanese embassy in the Philippines introduced a so-called "entertainer visa" in the early 1980s. This practice spread to other countries and essentially created a legal basis for sex-migration. Today, such visas are also issued to Russians to work in Japan and Switzerland. Another legal visa instrument used by traffickers to ensure the "legality" of their businesses is a "fiancée visa" common for many countries. Enticement of women as mail-order brides is another method for trafficking in women. In many cases, brides are selected for specific economic functions, for example, to work on a farm or to take care of the elderly parents of a groom or of the disabled. False marriages can be a way to recruit women for illegal jobs in the sex industry.

A narrower interpretation of trafficking equates it to involuntary prostitution. In international documents, trafficking in humans is defined in broader terms than just sexual exploitation. It defines trafficking as exploitation of any form of labor that violates human rights. The following forms of trafficking in human beings may be identified:

- Involuntary labor, including sweatshop labor
- Sex trade
- "Civil" prostitution
- Military prostitution
- Sex tourism
- Domestic servitude
- Forced marriages, including marriages through mail-order-bride system
- Forced reproductive functions, including giving birth to a child

- Forced donors (trade in persons for organ transplants)
- Involuntary adoption

It should be noted that trafficking in persons might involve not only women, but also children and men of working age. However, the scale of trafficking in women for profit is much higher. According to CIA data, only 2 percent of trafficking in persons involves men.[21]

The main issues that arise when defining trafficking in persons include recruitment, deception, and the *exploitation* of trafficked persons. It is not yet agreed as to what defines exploitation of labor, where it starts, and where it ends. If a woman is paying thousands of dollars to be transported abroad and obtain employment there, can she be considered a victim of exploitation? For many, these questions seem absurd because the criterion for considering a certain act as an act of trafficking is whether there is the use of force, violence, or deception. Specific forms of human rights violations that explain the term exploitation include:

- Use of physical or psychological force and/or threats
- Removal of identity documents
- Debt bondage
- Involuntary labor
- Limiting the freedom of movement
- Deception

Several years ago, before the provisions of Protocol became commonly known and accepted, it was considered important to differentiate between migrants who were sold into involuntary labor and those who voluntarily agreed to engage in certain types of activities, such as sex work abroad. The latter commonly were not considered as victims of trafficking. Today, migrants who travel abroad voluntarily and continue to work there voluntarily can also be classified as victims of trafficking in persons and human rights violations if it can be proven they are exploited or abused in keeping with the protocol. The definition from the Protocol to Prevent, Suppress and Punish Trafficking in Persons, Especially Women and Children, supplementing the United Nations Convention against Transnational Organized Crime, does not cover forced migration or labor (Article 3, b). It states: The consent of a victim of trafficking in persons to the intended exploitation set forth in subparagraph (a) of this article shall be irrelevant where any of the means set forth in subparagraph (a) have been used.

It is necessary to differentiate between the criminal-procedural definition, the general understanding of trafficking in persons, and the social aspects of the problem. When looking at migration of women to high-risk employment sectors as a social problem—not through the prism of criminal liability but through the prism of social policy—one cannot use the principle of "involuntariness" and only look at facts of violence, the latter being a traditional mandate of law enforcement agencies. First, forcing a person into prostitution is an essential component in defining trafficking in persons;[22] however, it turns this problem into crime and is devoid of its social context. The purpose of looking at the social context is to find social reasons that are the root cause of sex work and to form social policy that could limit this phenomenon.

Second, very often, for example in the entertainment industry, the "voluntary" nature of the provision of sexual services by women is a relative concept. In many cases, this is "forced volunteerism"[23] dictated by the established regime of this employment sector—making a choice when there is no other choice. Third, using the "principle of involuntariness" narrows the strata of women migrants who need special mechanisms to protect the rights of those migrants who were literally forced into prostitution. At the same time, because of the weak legal basis and shadow structures in this area, women-migrants voluntarily working in the sex industry need protection no less than do women physically forced into prostitution. There are additional arguments for not limiting the problem to cases of forced exploitation: Traffickers receive profits from selling "voluntary" workers equal to profits from those that are kept by force and forced to work, and there are many more "volunteers" than there are victims of direct violence. Perhaps human rights violations among voluntary migrants are not as grave, but they are more numerous.[24]

The Roles of Various Actors in Combating the Trafficking of Persons

Combating the trafficking in persons is on the agenda of numerous organizations on the national and international levels. The main directions, called the "Three Ps" (prevention, protection, prosecution), are: (1) creation of a legislative and law enforcement basis for effective protection of victims; identification and punishment of criminals involved in trafficking in persons; (2) conduct of a comprehensive informational campaign for women in the risk group and other population groups (society, parents, teachers, etc.); and (3) assistance to and rehabilitation of trafficking victims. Combating trafficking in persons, especially in the sex trade, is impossible without creating a *partnership of social forces* that would unite various structures and institutes of the society. The following institutions could participate in such a partnership:

- National state/government bodies
- Public organizations (women's, human rights groups, etc.)
- Mass media
- Professional associations (educational, medical, and scientific organizations)
- Businesses
- International organizations

At present, such a partnership is being formed in Russia. Each member of the partnership has specific functions directed toward achieving a common goal: to combat trafficking in persons and the sexual exploitation of women.

Until 2000, combating trafficking in women was limited to the work of the nongovernmental sector. After Russia signed the UN Convention against Transnational Organized Crime and the Protocol on Trafficking in Persons, the attention of several Russian federal ministries was drawn to the problem of trafficking, especially to trafficking in women for sexual exploitation. The international community has played an active role in this process, with the Russian Ministry for Foreign Affairs playing the role of a catalyst. In April 2001, the problem of preventing trafficking for sexual exploitation of women and girls was discussed at a meeting of the Commission on Improvement of Status of Women under the auspices of the Russian president. That meeting resulted in a "Program of Action" on the prevention of sexual exploitation of women and girls. The Program of Action assigned tasks to various departments and defined a reporting mechanism on its implementation.

Functions of state bodies include the development of national legislation against trafficking and ensuring its effective application. This activity, stipulated in the convention, "Trafficking in Persons," was not identified as a crime in Russian criminal law. Consequently, the Roman legal concept used in such cases is "if there is no punishment, there is no crime." That might explain why only a small percentage of crimes involving sexual exploitation and trafficking in persons is reported and investigated. The Ministry for Internal Affairs developed draft amendments and addenda to the Criminal Code of the Russian Federation to criminalize trafficking in human beings. Russia also needs a law on witness and victim protection.

Apart from adopting legislative measures, receiving and sending countries need to actively cooperate to combat trafficking in persons and marginalization of female migration. In the last decade, there was a trend toward stricter immigration policies in the main receiving countries. Reasons for such policies are understandable, as states are trying to protect national labor markets from the influx of "undesired" migrants. It is unlikely that receiving countries will soften their immigration policies. Thus, an initiative by a sending country (in this case Russia) is necessary. Such an initiative should be undertaken at a high level and should include an active negotiation process with receiving countries. The goal of such negotiations would be to eliminate discriminatory immigration policies and practices that violate human rights. It is necessary for sending and receiving countries to actively discuss migration related issues to expand the legitimate zone for labor migration.

Until recently, Russia had taken a passive stand on this issue. Only in 2001 did the Russian Ministry of Foreign Affairs begin to give priority to addressing the discriminatory policies of receiving countries toward migrants from Russia by placing the topic on its diplomatic agenda. The official Russian Foreign Ministry position on this issue was announced at the intergovernmental conference "Europe against Trafficking in Persons" organized by the German Foreign Ministry and the Organization for Cooperation and Security in Europe's Office of Democracy and International Human Rights (OSCE/ODIHR), which took place in Berlin on 15–16 October 2001. This position consists of three main theses: (1) promotion of the principle of equal responsibility of countries of origin, transit, and destination for the consequences of trafficking in persons; (2) countering discriminatory policies (specifically visa policies) of receiving countries toward migrants from Russia that are practiced under the guise of combating trafficking in persons; and (3) readiness for close cooperation with international organizations, in particular with OSCE, on this issue.

In addition to the Russian government's enhanced focus on combating trafficking in persons, the main actors at the national level have been nongovernmental organizations (NGOs) actively supported by international organizations and foundations. Currently, there are several dozen NGOs working against trafficking in persons, including trafficking for the purposes of sexual exploitation. This work is made possible mainly by grants from international organizations and foundations. NGOs provide psychological, legal, and social assistance to victims of trafficking and to women who are at risk of becoming victims. In general, NGOs are effective in achieving their goals. However, effective cooperation with government agencies is lacking because authorities are not aware of the problem (the leading principle here is "if there are no statistics, there is no problem"); all so-called women's problems are considered "of secondary importance" and are viewed as "individual cases" by the authorities; conservatism and hypocrisy of authorities when it comes to problems of sexual violence and sexual exploitation; scornful attitudes of authorities toward public organizations; corruption of some government representatives and their participation in the profitable sex business; and bureaucratic inertia.

The mass media play a great role in the partnership of social forces that combat trafficking in women. However, the role of mass media in dealing with subjects related to sexual exploitation of women is sometimes controversial. Along with dissemination of necessary information about the problem, mass media are also a powerful tool in spreading undesired stereotypes on sexual exploitation and trafficking in persons, speculating on piquant details and the image of a woman as a sex commodity. In this regard, it is necessary to create joint projects between mass media and NGOs to combat trafficking in persons and stop the spread of stereotypes that are humiliating to women.

International organizations such as the United Nations Development Program Fund for Women, IOM, ILO, and OSCE are active participants and organizers of antitrafficking campaigns and projects. These organizations have done a lot for the development of antitrafficking programs in Russia. However, the authority and potential influence of international organizations is not adequately used to effect migration-related discussions between receiving and sending countries. Such influence could be used to achieve détente in those relations and facilitate less discriminatory migration policies that would foster expansion of the legitimate migration zone and, consequently, decrease illegal and criminal migration activities.

Changing the international migration policy is a difficult task, especially on a global level, and it will take a lot of time. Yet, without a new policy, combating trafficking in persons and exploitation of migrant labor will continue to grow, no matter how many resources the international community allocates to the problem.

The problems associated with female labor migration should not obscure the positive and important aspects of migration. Migration expands social opportunities for women and helps them to become successful and achieve their goals. The "marginality" of women migrants is a social construct that reflects overall social gender inequality—low social status of women, unequal status in the family, and lower paid employment sectors. It is crucial that states undertake appropriate measures in their social, economic, and migration policies to improve the labor opportunities of their citizens working abroad.

Notes

1.   P. Hirst and G. Thompson, "Globalization and the Future of the Nation State," *Economy and Society* 24, no. 3 (August 1995): 408–42.

2.   *Global Development Finance* (Washington, D.C.: World Bank, 1998).

3.   Peter Stalker, *Workers without Frontiers: The Impact of Globalization on International Migration* (Boulder, Colo.: Lynne Rienner; Geneva: ILO, 2000), 1.

4.   "Labor Migration," in *International Migration Policies* (New York: UN Dept. of Economic and Social Affairs: Population Division, 1998), 87–172.

5.   Stalker, *Workers without Frontiers.*

6.   Stephen Castles and Mark J. Miller, *The Age of Migration: International Population Movements in the Modern World* (London: Guilford Press, 1993).

7.   See, for example, Saskia Sassen, *Transnational Economies and National Migration Policies* (Amsterdam: Institute for Migration and Ethnic Studies, University of Amsterdam, 1996); Jonathan Gershuny and Ian Miles, *The New Service Economy: The Transformation of Employment in Industrial Societies* (New York: Praeger, 1983).

8.   Marina Malysheva and Elena Tiuriukanova, "Zhenshchiny v mezhdunarodnoi trudovoi migratsii," *Narodonaselenie* 2 (Spring 2000): 91–101.

9.   "Prestuplenie i poraboshchenie: Razoblachenie seks-torgovli zhenshchinami iz stran byvshego SSSR," Global Survival Network, 1997.

10.   "Traffic in Human Beings: Implications for the OSCE," ODIHR Background Paper 1999/3, OSCE Review Conference, Warsaw, Poland, September 1999.

11.   Nora Hamilton and Norma Chinchilla, "Global Economic Restructuring and International Migration," *International Migration* 34, no. 2 (1996).

12.   "Population in Europe and North America on the Eve of the Millennium: Dynamic and Policy Responses," Regional Population Meeting, 7–9 December 1998, Budapest, Hungary, UN, New York and Geneva, 1999, 18.

13.   Evgeny Krasinets, Elena Kubishin, and Elena Tiuriukanova, *Nelegalnaia Migratsiia v Rossiiu* (Moscow: Academia, 2000), 82.

14.   Marina Malysheva and Elena Tiuriukanova, *Zhenshina. Migratsiya. Gosudarstvo* (Moscow: Akademiia, 2001), 36.

15. For more details on the characteristics of female labor migration from Russia see Elena Tuiruikanova, "Women in Search of Work Abroad: Labor Migration of Women from Russia," Materials of the 1st Summer School on Gender Studies/Moscow Center of Gender Studies (Moscow, 1997), 110–20.

16. "Da. Net. Smotra, Skolko Za Eto Zaplatiat," *Inostranets* 20 (Spring 2000).

17. Igor Kliamkin and Lev Timofeev, *Shadow Russia* (Moscow: Russian State Humanitarian University, 2001), 11.

18. The surveys were conducted with the support of the John D. and Catherine T. Macarthur Foundation and the Russian Humanitarian Scientific Fund (grant #00-02-00105a).

19. Gillian Caldwell, Steven Galster, and Nadia Stenzor, "Crime and Servitude: An Exposé of the Traffic in Women for Prostitution from the Newly Independent States." Global Survival Network, Moscow, 3-5 November 1997.

20. Protocol to Prevent, Suppress and Punish Trafficking in Persons, Especially Women and Children, supplementing the United Nations Convention against Transnational Organized Crime, UN, 2000.

21. Fedor Sinitsyn, *Mezhdunarodnoe zakonodatel'stvo po probleme torgovli liudmi* (Perm: Perm Center Against Violence and Human Trafficking, 2000).

22. "Traffic in Human Beings."

23. Malysheva and Tuiruikanova, "Zhenshiny v mezhdunarodnoi trudovoi migratsii."

24. For a detailed review of theoretical and practical approaches to trafficking in women see Elena Tuiruikanova, *Zhenshiny v mezhdunarodnoi trudovoi migratsii, Genderniy Kaleidoskop: Kurs Lektsii*, ed. Marina Malysheva (Moscow: Academia, 2001).

Chapter 7

❧❧❧

An Evaluation of Ukrainian Legislation to Counter and Criminalize Human Trafficking

Olga Pyshchulina

One of the areas of the world where trafficking is growing fastest is the former Soviet Union.[1] Human trafficking from Ukraine, especially for sex work, is a serious and increasing problem for the country.[2] Evidence exists from a wide variety of sources, including police, NGOs, healthcare providers, prosecutors, and international organizations, of the widespread and worsening nature of the problem.[3] Following a recent study by the International Organization for Migration (IOM),[4] some 420,000 women were estimated to have been trafficked out of the country in the last few years alone.[5] In 1998, the Ukrainian legislature adopted a criminal law (Article 124-1 in the Criminal Code of Ukraine) against trafficking in people, making Ukraine one of the first countries in Europe to formally criminalize this offense by adopting a discrete trafficking statute. Because most Western countries have imposed strict limits on the numbers of legal migrants who can enter their territories, many women are forced to accept the service of traffickers if they wish to migrate. Most forms of labor migration are severely restricted; however, one available and legal work option for migrant women is work in the entertainment sector as "artists" or "dancers." In practice this type of work is frequently linked to work in the sex industry.

Contemporary population movements are characterized by increasing pressures by individuals seeking, through migration, either to escape war, persecution, poverty, or human rights violations, or simply to find better economic opportunities.[6] Women from Ukraine also have a strong economic incentive to seek employment in Central Europe, where living standards are higher than in the countries of transition. There are several other reasons that Ukrainian women want to go to abroad. First, liberalization of laws has enabled international travel both to Ukraine and to the European Union.

Second, with the introduction of a free market economy, and the resulting closing of many state enterprises, unemployment has for the first time affected the nation, and primarily women, both economically and psychologically. Unemployment figures remain extraordinarily high. Although registered youth unemployment figures dropped from 30.5 percent in 1999 to 25.6 percent in 2002, unregistered youth unemployment is estimated to be as high as 40 percent. Women were the first to lose their jobs, and the possibilities of finding a new position are, to say the least, not promising, especially outside the big cities. Migration is especially popular among young women from small, underdeveloped cities and the countryside, where jobs are very scarce. In those areas, women cannot find positions in their own professions, as salespersons, teachers, or nurses, for example. Even if they do, those occupations are very low paid and cannot assure economic independence.

A third and related motivation for Ukrainian women to migrate to the West is the disappearance of the state social security system, which has had dramatic results.[7] The transition to a market economy without appropriate infrastructures has resulted in an economy that plunged to drastic lows, and a collapse in the social safety net. In fact, a recent survey indicated that two-thirds of young, Ukrainian women live on or below the poverty line.[8] According to the 2002 UNDP Human Development Report, 26 percent of the population lives below the poverty line.[9] The closing of many state enterprises has caused large-scale unemployment, which coupled with unreasonable taxation has resulted in many citizens seeking opportunities for work and a better life abroad, even at the risk of being trafficked.

Finally, the myth of an easy and affluent life in the West and the tradition of migrant workers also contribute to the phenomenon. Given this context, it is not surprising that many young women are keen to find employment in the West and to travel to countries that for years have been inaccessible to them. The economic and political reform process in Ukraine has been slow compared to some other former Soviet countries. Today, whereas some former Soviet Union countries are showing remarkable political, social, and economic progress toward stability and democracy, Ukraine is lagging behind in its transition process. The most notable reason for that is the issue of governance. Ukraine has been hesitant to embark on the political, economic, and social reforms essential to democratization. The prolonged political and socioeconomic transition has had severe implications, including the marginalization and, to some extent, exclusion of some groups from the social and political forefront. One of those groups is women.

The growth of shadow economies and transnational criminal networks in the newly independent states has compounded the vulnerability of Ukrainian women. Members of Ukrainian and post-Soviet crime rings establish contacts with willing collaborators in communities throughout the world to promote the trafficking of women. Migration from Ukraine and the Soviet successor states, which has accompanied globalization and the growth of transnational crime, has helped to establish an international network of criminal associations, particularly in Western and Eastern Europe. Increased migration also serves as a cover for traffickers in transporting women to destination countries. It is difficult to reduce or eliminate the trafficking web, as it involves not only organized crime circles that have found a profitable source of income second only to drug and arms trafficking, but also a whole network of intermediaries who subtly work between family and friends.

Ukrainian Government Response

Trafficking in human beings and human smuggling cannot totally be prevented by developing antitrafficking laws and developing enforcement strategies. A multidisciplinary approach is required, including appropriate social and economic measures that address the root causes of trafficking such as poverty, economic disparities, and unemployment. Collective efforts by origin, transit, and destination countries are also necessary. Ukraine has tried a variety of measures, including education, prevention campaigns, and economic programs. In this chapter, I focus on the legal measures used to address the problem.

Among the strategies employed by the Ukraine government, significant attention has been paid to the legal framework. The government of Ukraine has adopted several international instruments that put Ukraine at the forefront of criminalization of human trafficking in Europe. The latest international instrument—the "Protocol to Prevent, Suppress, and Punish Trafficking in Persons, Especially Women and Children, Supplementing the United Nations Conventions against Transnational Organized Crime"—was signed by Ukraine on 15 November 2001 and has been being ratified by the Ukrainian legislature.

When reviewing and considering legal measures to counter a particular societal problem, the legal and social contexts in which these measures will function are crucial. This is especially important when penal measures are considered. Criminal law is one of the most intrusive instruments in the hands of state authorities with respect to private citizens. The question is, first and foremost, whether a law promotes the rule of law.[10] Moreover, it is important to distinguish between the law on the books and the law in practice. Preventive measures for human trafficking should primarily aim at strengthening the position of women and other vulnerable groups. The protection of the human rights of trafficked persons should be at the core of any antitrafficking policies.[11]

Ukraine may be considered a country in transition from a communist totalitarian state to a democratic society, which is governed by the rule of law. One of the major problems in this process is widespread corruption, which affects all levels of society, including police, prosecutors, and judges. Ineffective privatization, the lack of law enforcement, lack of rule of law, the professionalization of organized crime, and the absence of a legal culture have allowed organized crime to flourish from human trafficking.

In September 2001, the new criminal code of Ukraine came into force, which constitutes a radical departure from the previous one, essentially based on the Soviet criminal code. Article 149 of the new code makes human trafficking a crime. As stipulated by the law, a person who is found guilty of involvement in direct or indirect, open or hidden trafficking in human beings with the intent to sell them for sexual exploitation, pornographic business, or use in military conflict, as well as any person who adopts children for commercial purposes, will face criminal charges and will be punished by imprisonment for a period of three to eight years, with confiscation of property. A person who is involved in the sale of children or an official who abuses his or her position in relation to trafficking will be punished by imprisonment for a period of five to ten years. In situations where the trafficking has led to serious consequences, is managed by a criminal organization, or is intended for the transplantation of human organs, the punishment increases to eight to fifteen years. This new article is more in accordance with the international standards stipulated in the UN Protocol[12] than the one found in the old criminal code;[13] however, Ukraine still has to reform its national legislation and is currently drafting such a proposal.

Critiques of the Ukrainian Antitrafficking Law

Article 124-1 has been criticized on the basis that elements of the crime were not defined, and so police and prosecutors were unclear as to how to apply its provisions in practice. New terms such as "debt bondage," "sexual exploitation," and "exploitation of work" were used with no guidance as to their definition. No official commentaries were provided concerning implementation of the law, and although these commentaries are not binding, courts generally rely on them in interpreting the law. Also, law enforcement officers were not provided with any new procedures in relation to trafficking, as is normally the case in connection with the enforcement of new crimes. The overall effect of these inadequacies has been to discourage police from investigating allegations of trafficking, and prosecutors have also been reluctant to initiate new cases. Until now, more than 250 trafficking cases have been filed, and many other cases are under active investigation.[14] (Unfortunately, the data regarding the number of criminal cases is controversial. For example, according to information provided by the Committee Against Torture at its twenty-seventh session, 12–23 November 2001, only thirty criminal cases on human trafficking were filed since the adoption of Article 124-1 in 1998 till the start of 2001, and thirty-seven such cases were filed in 2001.)[15] In any case, the number of prosecuted cases is steadily growing.

However, because of the difficulty in proving such cases, the lack of jurisprudential precedents, and the lack of experience of law enforcement and judicial agencies in regard to trafficking, a number of cases are only being prosecuted under related crime definitions and not as cases of "trafficking."[16] Nevertheless, as public awareness is raised and law enforcement bodies and the judiciary receive training, a greater number of cases are being prosecuted under the "trafficking" statute (see table 7.1).

As I mentioned before, a new article was meant to correspond with international standards and to prevent the commitment of human trafficking crimes. Nevertheless, this new article is deeply rooted in Article 124[1] of the earlier Criminal Code. The same terminology described above is used without further definition, and it is not clear whether new procedures will be issued to the police for their guidance in investigating crimes of trafficking. One aspect of the new law that worsens the position of trafficked women is the requirement that the person be trafficked across an international border. But according to international standards, human trafficking does not necessarily have to be international in nature, nor do the victims have to have been exploited.[17] Many of the women trafficked in Ukraine are only moved from one region to another and do not leave the country. The traffickers of such individuals could not be prosecuted under Article 149 of the Criminal Code.

As for the definition of the crime, it is noteworthy that Ukraine already uses a broad definition of trafficking, including purposes for which human beings are trafficked. However, in general the terms in the criminal code are insufficiently clear to be used in practice; for example, elements such as "coercion," "border crossing," "consent,"[18] "systematic,"[19] and "organized group" are vague. Absolutely unclear is whether or not coercion is a constitutive element in cases of sexual exploitation. Is any facilitation of migration for sex work punishable as human trafficking, or only if there is an element of coercion or deception? And does all work in the sex industry constitute sexual exploitation per se, or does only sex work under exploitative and coercive conditions qualify as "sexual exploitation"? Furthermore, many important actors on the international level consider the use of the term "sexual exploitation" as inadequate and propose to abolish the term.[20] "In order to highlight the commonality between the different purpose for which people are trafficked, the focus should be on the forced, exploitative, or slavery-like conditions of the work or relationship and whether those conditions were freely and knowingly consented to by the person."[21]

Table 7.1 Number of Criminal Cases Filed in Ukraine under Article 124 of the Old Ukrainian Criminal Code and under Article 149 of the New Criminal Code of Ukraine

Year	Number of Cases
1998	2
1999	11
2000	42
2001	91
2002	107
Total	253

In a country in which the judicial system cannot be said to be entirely incorruptible, ambiguous crimes definitions open the possibility for corruption, not only at the level of law enforcement officers and prosecutors, but also at the level of judges, as it gives them too much discretionary power. Another concern is that the principal route of trafficking in women lies through employment agencies, which legalize this activity. Article 149 of the Criminal Code does not provide any efficient mechanisms that could make it possible to prove that the activities of such agencies are for the "purpose of further sale" or other criminal purposes.

When it comes to investigation, in practice it appears to be difficult for the police to get a trafficking case opened by the prosecutor. One of the reasons is the fear among prosecutors of losing a case because of too little evidence, because the victim or witness refuses to testify in court. Prosecutors can be disciplined for losing a case, which severely affects their independence. As trafficking cases are complex, time-consuming, and carry a high risk of failure, there is disinterest among prosecutors for this kind of case at all levels in prosecutors' offices.

A special problem in bringing cases of trafficking to court is the reluctance of victims to report to the police and subsequently testify in court. Although not required by law, a request by the victim is seen as indispensable. Many reasons can be mentioned to explain the reluctance of the victims. One is absence of witness protection and procedural safeguards for victims or witnesses during criminal proceedings, especially with regard to the protection of the privacy and safety of the victim.

The Ukrainian government has undertaken various approaches to fighting human trafficking. In February 1999, the Licensing Chamber of Ukraine, the State Employment Center of Ukraine, and the Ministry of Labor and Social Policy issued an order authorizing the suspension of licenses for businesses that arrange for work abroad when the committee inspecting those businesses found violations of Ukrainian law. The order, however, targets employment agencies only. A certain number of licenses were subsequently suspended, but none of those seems to have been on the grounds of their connection with trafficking. The order has not been considered effective in addressing trafficking, because it merely prompted criminal groups to disguise themselves as tourist agencies rather than employment agencies, as they did before.

Travel agencies or "tourist firms" are often fronts for traffickers and have little trouble obtaining passports and visas for victims in much less time than is generally required. The connection of such businesses with corrupt officials is therefore open to question. The committee responsible for inspecting registered travel agencies suspects some of them of involvement with the trafficking business, but it is not empowered to suspend such licenses. All it can do is recommend that licenses are relinquished. Furthermore, many suspicious travel agencies operate without licenses.[22] The government, however, has not conducted any investigation into the practices of these firms.

The government of Ukraine created a National Coordination Council for Prevention of Trafficking in People, headed by the parliamentary ombudsman. Also, on 25 September 1999, the Cabinet of Ministers of Ukraine adopted a comprehensive national Program for Prevention of Trafficking in Women and Children by Decree 1768. This program is to be financed from the state budget funds, and its implementation is to be supervised by the State Committee for Youth and Family Affairs. However, the government's commitment to this program is questionable. First, no funding has been provided for the program by the government.[23] Funding provided by the European Commission and U.S. Agency for International Development allowed accomplishing certain countertrafficking initiatives in Ukraine, which in fact implemented several aspects of the national program.[24] However, in the absence of these funds no governmental countertrafficking activities would exist. Second, following governmental reforms, the State Committee for Youth and Family Affairs, responsible for the implementation of the national program, was disbanded and it remains unclear which governmental body takes responsibility for the supervision of the implementation of the national program in its place.

Conclusion and Recommendations

Trafficking in women and girls for the purposes of sexual exploitation, forced marriage, and domestic servitude is a serious and growing problem in Ukraine. Although the government has taken certain legislative and policy measures to address the issue, it appears that there is little political commitment to tackle the problem. I recommend that the government amend Article 149 of the Criminal Code to make trafficking that takes place within the borders of Ukraine a crime.[25] I also recommend that interpretative commentaries for judges and other officials as well as comprehensive procedural guidelines for police and immigration officers on prevention and prosecution of trafficking offenses are developed.

Measures to encourage victims of trafficking to identify traffickers and act as witnesses in criminal prosecutions should also be explored. These might include witness protection measures and restrictions on deportation of victims who are prepared to act as witnesses.[26] Victims of trafficking should have access to legal, psychological, and medical assistance. They should be awarded compensation through criminal compensation schemes, which could be financed through the confiscated criminal revenue of traffickers.

Intergovernmental agreements to guarantee the voluntary and safe return of women and ensure that protection and support is provided to trafficked women awaiting repatriation proceedings should be elaborated. The human rights of victims should be assured, and steps should be taken to ensure that they are not criminalized or imprisoned. Bilateral agreements that require cooperation between local immigration officials and consulates to assist trafficked women should be developed and publicized. Measures to guarantee the voluntary and safe return of trafficked women should be established, and barriers for trafficked women to return to their countries, with or without passports or identification documents, should be eliminated.

Broad efforts to strengthen training and public awareness of civil servants dealing with migration, particularly those at embassies and consulates and those in charge of the delivery of visas, should be increased, and governments should train law enforcement officials at all levels with respect to trafficking, violence against women, and recognition of trafficking situations, including identification of front companies and groups. Broad-based, ongoing educational and aware-ness-raising campaigns, including media efforts, to combat domestic and international trafficking should be introduced nationally, regionally, and internationally. Vulnerable groups should be particularly targeted and community-based strategies employed. Relevant cases and evidence should be collected and shared, and the modus operandi of traffickers should be exposed so as to provide a concrete basis for legal and policy change.

By all means, strategies aimed at eliminating trafficking should focus on the criminal nature of the activity and those who carry it out, rather than on the victims, whose human rights should be assured.

Notes

An earlier version of this chapter appeared in *Demokratizatsiya* 11, no. 3 (Spring 2003): 403–11. Copyright 2003 by the Helen Dwight Reid Educational Foundation. Reprinted by permission.

1.   Commission on Security and Cooperation in Europe (the Helsinki Commission), *Sex Trade: Trafficking of Women and Children in Europe and the United States*, report given by L. Shelley, 28 June 1999, available at <http://www.american.edu/tracec/ Pdfs/ HTMLs/testimony699.htm>.

2.   Ukraine is recognized as a supplier of "human stock" to Yugoslavia, Hungary, Czech Republic, Italy, Cyprus, Greece, Turkey, Israel, the United States, United Arab Emirates, and other countries. According to the Embassy of Ukraine in Greece, there are three thousand young Ukrainian women working in legal or illegal sex businesses in Athens and Saloniki, and five thousand such women are in Turkey. See: O. V. Druz' and O. O. Hryshynska, *Trafficking in Young Women: Observation of Women's Human Rights and Relevant Tasks of Law Enforcement Bodies in Ukraine*, ed. University of the Interior of Ukraine and International Women's Human Rights Protection Center (Kharkiv-Kyiv: La Strada Ukraine, 1999), 88.

3.   Minnesota Advocates Group, "Trafficking in Women: Moldova and Ukraine," December 2000, 16. The International Helsinki Federation for Human Rights, in its "Women 2000" report, cites the figure of one hundred thousand having been transported across the border illegally since 1991 from the Ukraine. Current estimates appear much higher, however.

4.   IOM, "Information Campaign against Trafficking in Women from Ukraine: Research Report," 1998, 16.

5.   Nina Karpachova, parliamentary ombudsman for human rights in Ukraine, has also been reported as referring to this number of women trafficked from Ukraine. However, these figures appear somewhat exaggerated and thus dubious to experts in sociology. Still, Ukraine has no published official statistics on the magnitude of the problem,

and unofficial estimates of the numbers of persons being trafficked out of the country differ.

6.   Vanessa von Struensee, "Globalized, Wired Sex Trafficking in Women and Children: A Worldwide, Dehumanising, Epidemic of Poverty, Disease, Corruption, Collaboration, Crime, Violence, Murder, Slavery, and the Valuing of Unprecedented Profits at the Expense of Human Dignity, Decency, and the Rule of Law," available at http://www. uri.edu/artci.

7.   Ukraine now has marginalized women who have been largely excluded from the development of democratic processes through discriminatory policies practiced by political parties, governments, and individual employers. Recent studies and discussions in Ukraine on the subject of women's situation confirm that the past political and economic changes have not been gender neutral. Women make up 54 percent of the population of Ukraine and 45 percent of its labor force. Over 60 percent of all Ukrainian women have higher education (college level and above). However, the unemployment rate of women is very high compared to men with the same educational background (80 percent of all unemployed in Ukraine are women), not to mention the extensive hidden unemployment among women.

8.   "First Annual Report of the Ukrainian Parliament Commissioner for Human Rights," http://www.ombudsman.kiev.ua.

9.   UN Development Programme, *Human Development Report 2002* (New York: Oxford University Press, 2002).

10.   The term "rule of law" embodies the basic principles of equal treatment of all people before the law, fairness, and both constitutional and actual guarantees of basic human rights. A predictable legal system with fair, transparent, and effective judicial institutions is essential to the protection of citizens against the arbitrary use of state authority and lawless acts of both organizations and individuals. Unfortunately in Ukraine, where the democratic tradition is weak and judicial independence is compromised, individual rights are not truly guaranteed.

11.   Ukraine is a member of the United Nations and has committed to adhering to internationally recognized human rights standards. Specifically, Ukraine ratified the Convention on the Elimination of All Forms of Discrimination against Women with a Decree of the Presidium of the Supreme Council of the Ukrainian Soviet Socialist Republic in 1981.

12.   United Nations, Protocol to Prevent, Suppress, and Punish Trafficking in Persons, Especially Women and Children. Supplementing the United Nations Conventions against Transnational Organized Crime.

13.   Criminal Code of Ukraine (old), Article 124.

14.   S. Cook and F. Larson, "Combating Trafficking in Women in Ukraine, Belarus and Moldova," paper presented at the European Conference on Preventing and Combating Trafficking in Human Beings: Global Challenge for the 21st Century, European Parliament, Brussels, 18–20 September 2002.

15.   These figures are cited in World Organization Against Torture (OMCT), "Violence against Women in Ukraine: Mainstreaming the Human Rights of Women," report presented at the 27th Session of the Committee Against Torture, 12–23 November 2001, New York City.

16.   OMCT, "Violence against Women in Ukraine."

17.   United Nations, Protocol to Prevent, Suppress, and Punish Trafficking in Persons, Especially Women and Children, Supplementing the United Nations Conventions against Transnational Organized Crime.

18.   Criminal Code of Ukraine (new), Article 149.

19. Criminal Code of Ukraine (new), Article 303.

20. Roelof Haveman and Marjan Wijers, *Review of the Law on Trafficking in Persons in Ukraine* (Brussels: IOM, 2001).

21. Haveman and Wijers, *Law on Trafficking*, 9.

22. OMCT, *Violence against Women in Ukraine*.

23. Information obtained from La Strada, a women's rights NGO affiliated with the Dutch organization of the same name, which has operated in Ukraine since 1997. Minnesota Advocates Group, "Trafficking in Women: Moldova and Ukraine," December 2000, 29, also reports that resources are yet to be dedicated to the program to counter trafficking.

24. IOM Kyiv reports that it is working with an interministerial coordination group to implement a European Committee project on countertrafficking, which includes implementing the relevant aspects of the national program.

25. This recommendation was made in the alternative report prepared by the Analytical and Research Group of Kharkiv Center for Women Studies, Kharkiv, Ukraine.

26. Government agencies in Europe and North America are taking steps to use a temporary resident permit in schemes to protect trafficking victims and successfully prosecute traffickers. The U.S. government has announced that the Department of Justice will soon start issuing T visas to protect the victims of severe forms of human trafficking. The visa will allow the victims to remain in the United States and assist federal authorities in the investigation and prosecution of human trafficking cases. For details, see "Temporary Resident Permits: A New Way to Protect Trafficking Victims?" *Trafficking in Migrants*, IOM Quarterly Bulletin 25 (Spring 2002).

Chapter 8

⸙⸙⸙

Legal Cases Prosecuted under the Victims of Trafficking and Violence Protection Act of 2000

Beatrix Siman Zakhari

In this chapter, I examine the Victims of Trafficking and Violence Protection Act of 2000 (hereafter, the Act or TVPA) and three recent cases brought against traffickers of Russian-speaking women from Eastern Europe, the Russian Federation, and Newly Independent States to the United States—*United States v. Virchenko, United States v. Gasanov,* and *United States v. Trakhtenberg.* The cases illustrate how prosecutions of traffickers of victims from those areas have proceeded under the Act. The different outcomes and sanctions help to outline potential problem areas.

Prostitution and trafficking in human beings are a $6 billion a year business for Russian organized crime (ROC).[1] New York, New Jersey, and Pennsylvania have historically been destinations of choice for Russian émigrés, and thus can provide venues and environments in which ROC can flourish.[2] However, as shown by two of the cases discussed in this chapter, the *Virchenko* and *Gasanov* cases, this criminal activity exists throughout the United States and, indeed, the world.

Walter Zalisko, founder of PMC International, a law enforcement consulting firm, reports that currently there are about thirty ROC syndicates operating in the United States, many of which have strong ties to organized crime groups in Russia and Ukraine. The fastest growing international trafficking business is trade in women. Penalties for trafficking and selling humans have been relatively minor compared with those for other criminal activities. Therefore, trafficking in people is often more profitable and less risky to criminals than trafficking in drugs and guns.[3]

Trafficking from countries of the former Soviet Union is particularly hard to eradicate because of the environment from which the victims come and the often similar backgrounds of Russian émigrés in the United States. Having lived in a society ruled by an oppressive government, the émigrés tend to be distrustful of government and are more reluctant than most other émigré groups to speak with or seek assistance from law enforcement officials. This has hindered investigation and prosecution of trafficking crimes.[4] The TVPA is designed to protect the victims of trafficking, eliminate its sources, and eradicate its practice worldwide.

The TVPA prohibits recruiting, enticing, harboring, transporting, or obtaining any person by force, fraud, or coercion to engage in commercial sex or forced labor. Violations of the Act also include the destruction or concealment of any document that would prevent or restrict another person's liberty to travel in order to maintain the labor or services of that person. In other words, a person violates the TVPA both for actual trafficking of persons and for using documents to aid trafficking or to enable it to continue for longer periods.[5] The criminalization of the use of documents to aid trafficking significantly broadens the reach of prosecution of trafficking cases. The TVPA also provides for assistance to other countries to help them end trafficking and for actions against governments failing to do so.[6]

In summary, the TVPA requires annual reports on human rights practices from countries receiving financial or security assistance from the United States. It establishes an interagency Task Force on Trafficking to provide protection and assistance for victims of trafficking, sets standards for other countries to eliminate trafficking, provides criminal punishments for significant traffickers in persons, and increases the criminal punishments for all traffickers.[7] Foreign countries that fail to comply with the TVPA requirement that they take action to combat trafficking face serious sanctions, including withholding of non-humanitarian, nontrade related assistance.[8]

Background

Legislation and law enforcement in the United States prior to the enactment of the TVPA was inadequate to deter trafficking and bring traffickers to justice. Until the nearly unanimous passage of the TVPA in 2000, after a bipartisan initiative, no comprehensive law existed in the United States that penalized the range of offenses involving trafficking. The Mann Act was enacted in 1910 to combat interstate and international sex trade by punishing deliberate transportation of any woman or girl for purposes of prostitution or debauchery, or with the intent to induce any woman or girl to become a prostitute or engage in debauchery.[9] The restriction of the Mann Act's focus exclusively on females was removed in 1986, when Congress recognized that men could also be transported for immoral purposes.[10] The maximum penalty imposed by the Mann Act was a fine of not more than $5,000 and imprisonment of not more than ten years (fifteen years for trafficking of victims under age eighteen) for convicted traffickers.

Because the Mann Act failed to recognize trafficking as a criminal enterprise, the seriousness of trafficking and its components were not reflected in sentencing guidelines. It also did not address the critical need to prevent trafficking. The broad-based, coordinated approach necessary to identify and eradicate the underlying causes of trafficking was lacking in this earlier legislation. In addition, many trafficked persons were not informed of their rights as victims, were not recognized as having rights, and were ultimately deported. The traffickers typically escaped punishment because there were no victims to testify against them. The Mann Act not only failed to protect victims of trafficking, but it often punished the victims who were illegal immigrants more harshly than it punished their traffickers. If not immediately deported, many victims of trafficking were detained in far less than optimal conditions, unable to work or support themselves, unable or unwilling to testify against their traffickers, and lacking the incentive to do so.

The Mann Act essentially criminalized the behavior of the trafficked victims rather than the acts of the traffickers.[11] The TVPA instead "focuses on the protection of victims of trafficking in addition to ensuring just and effective punishment of traffickers."[12] The Mann Act frequently was used for political purposes to prosecute unpopular persons or individuals who could not be prosecuted for other criminal charges. Violations of the Mann Act were not viewed or recognized as enslavements, but as violations of morality or accepted sexual behavior. As a result, individuals whose morality was perceived as different from that of the mainstream frequently found themselves targeted under the Mann Act. A classic case is *Mortenson v. United States*, 322 U.S. 369 (1944). In this case, two Nebraska brothel owners were prosecuted and convicted for violating the Mann Act because they had taken two employees across state lines for a vacation in Nevada, even though the transportation was not for an immoral purpose. Although the Supreme Court reversed the conviction of the brothel owners, this case illustrates the type of actions taken under the Mann Act and the way it was used. The legal system did not yet recognize trafficking as a serious criminal enterprise or identify it as slavery.

Although the Mann Act was designed to deter what was often referred to as the "white slave trade"—the lawmakers' perception of sexual trafficking—it did not provide the tools for investigating or prosecuting traffickers. For example, it did not prohibit psychological coercion and trickery or seizure of government identification and travel documents, nor did it provide protection for the victims. Until the later emphasis on human rights, lawmakers and jurists, as well as the public, failed to recognize trafficking for what it is.

In the United States—where much of the modern human rights movement began—the lack of effective legislation and reliance on outmoded law was especially troubling. Since the late eighteenth century, nations all over the world have relied on the U.S. Declaration of Independence and Constitution to establish recognition of inalienable human rights. It was not until after the U.S. Civil War and the passage of the Thirteenth, Fourteenth, and Fifteenth Amendments to the Constitution, however, that the United States specifically outlawed all

forms of slavery. Since then, the right of all persons to be free from slavery and
involuntary servitude has been developing. Because it so often involves women,
children, and migrant workers in marginal or "hidden" industries—who are often outside the purview of legal norms—the legal system has had limited protection of human rights. All too often, those persons have been marginalized by
labor status or relationship to property. They have been viewed as commodities,
not persons with full human rights.

In many areas, international law has been ahead of state law, including the
federal law of the United States, in constructing a broad, inclusive conceptualization of human rights as including the rights of all persons, including those who
have traditionally been marginalized or ignored. The 1948 Universal Declaration
of Human Rights adopted by the UN General Assembly recognizes broad human rights for all human beings.[13] Article 4 prohibits slavery in all forms, and
the remaining articles provide full equality for all persons. The 1998 Rome Statute of the International Criminal Court, to which the United States is not a signatory, identifies rights of humanity and criminalizes violations of those rights.[14]
The statute specifically defines enslavement, sexual slavery, sexual violence,
forcible transfer, and any "other inhumane acts of similar character intentionally
causing great suffering, or serious injury to body or to mental or physical
health," as crimes against humanity.[15] These crimes clearly include trafficking, a
contemporary manifestation of slavery. The 2000 United Nations Protocol to
Prevent, Suppress and Punish Trafficking in Persons, Especially Women and
Children provides that countries must adopt laws to criminalize trafficking, protect victims, and cooperate with other countries to prevent trafficking.[16] Unfortunately, although countries are encouraged to share this information, they are
not required to do so.[17]

With the passage of the TVPA in October 2000, U.S. law also fully identified
trafficking as slavery and committed to ending trafficking in all its guises by
ensuring more effective prosecution, punishment, and international cooperation
to end international trafficking. The TVPA also provides such serious sanctions—in the form of abrogation of all nonhumanitarian aid from the United
States—against countries that fail to work to end trafficking and which fail to
recognize international human rights and the requirements of TVPA that the
U.S. has now once again put itself in the forefront of human rights development.
The United States also acknowledged the critical work of the international legal
community to abolish slavery in all its forms. Section 102(b)(23) of the Act
states:

> The United States and the international community agree that trafficking in
> persons involves grave violations of human rights and is a matter of pressing
> international concern. The international community has repeatedly condemned
> slavery and involuntary servitude, violence against women, and other elements
> of trafficking, through declarations, treaties, and United Nations resolutions and
> reports, including the Universal Declaration of Human Rights; the 1956 Sup-
> plementary Convention on the Abolition of Slavery, the Slave Trade, and Insti-
> tutions and Practices Similar to Slavery; the 1948 American Declaration on the

Rights and Duties of Man; the 1957 Abolition of Forced Labor Convention; the International Covenant on Civil and Political Rights; the Convention Against Torture and Other Cruel, Inhuman or Degrading Treatment or Punishment; United Nations General Assembly Resolutions 50/167, 51/66, and 52/98; the Final Report of the World Congress against Sexual Exploitation of Children (Stockholm, 1996); the Fourth World Conference on Women (Beijing, 1995); and the 1991 Moscow Document of the Organization for Security and Cooperation in Europe.

Development of Legislation

The TVPA originated in concern expressed in several quarters in Congress throughout the last half of the 1990s. Representative Christopher Smith (R-NJ), with Representative Marcy Kaptur (D-OH) and twenty-five other bipartisan cosponsors, proposed H.R. 1356, "Freedom from Sexual Trafficking Act," on 25 March 1999. The House International Relations Committee considered it on 15 September 1999. Senator Paul Wellstone (D-MN) began working on his own version of an antitrafficking bill in 1997 after he and his wife spoke with Ukrainian women trafficked from their homes to work in brothels in the United States and Western Europe.[18] Senator Wellstone introduced S. 600, "The International Trafficking of Women and Children Victim Protection Act of 1999," on 11 March 1999; the bill was cosponsored on 23 March 1999 by Representative Louise Slaughter (D-NY) as H.R. 1238. This proposed legislation was broader than Representative Smith's original bill and recognized both sexual trafficking and other trafficking violations. On 11 November 1999, Representative Smith, with thirty-seven bipartisan cosponsors, proposed H.R. 3244, "To Combat Trafficking in persons, especially into the sex trade, slavery and slavery like conditions in the United States and countries around the world through prevention, through prosecution and enforcement against traffickers and through protection and assistance to victims of trafficking." Senator Sam Brownback (R-KS), working with Senator Wellstone, proposed S. 2449 on 13 April 2000 as a companion to H.R. 3244. Senator Brownback stated in the *Congressional Record*:

[T]oday, I am introducing legislation entitled the International Anti-Trafficking Act of 2000 which combats the insidious practice of trafficking of persons worldwide. As we begin the 21st Century, the degrading institution of slavery continues throughout the world. Sex trafficking is a modern day form of slavery, and it is the largest manifestation of slavery in the world today. . . . Presently, no comprehensive legislation has been adopted, yet, which holistically challenges the practice of trafficking and assists the victims. I am introducing this legislation . . . as a companion to the legislation introduced by Congressman Chris Smith [R-NJ] (H.R. 3244) and Congressman Sam Gejdenson [D-CT], known as the Trafficking Victims Protection Act of 2000 (H.R. 3244). Senator Wellstone has also introduced legislation which closely mirrors the Smith-Gejdenson bill. Our primary difference is the methods for enforcement.[19]

The bipartisan nature of the Senate and the House bills was articulated by Senator Brownback in the *Congressional Record* of 14 June 2000. He mentioned the Smith-Gejdenson bill (H.R. 3244) that had passed the House, and stated that he and Senator Wellstone were

> seeking to get [the Senate version of that bill] passed, we hope by unanimous consent. . . . I will happily provide to any offices interested in this issue the hearing record Senator Wellstone and I have compiled on this bill, so Members can look into this issue. If they seek to make modifications to improve the bill, our office will be open to work with any office so we can reach unanimous consent on this important issue. It is something we need to and can address. The Administration wants this addressed as well and is working with us to make that happen.[20]

Senator Brownback further emphasized the bipartisan support for the legislation on 5 October 2000:

> I have put forward this bill on sex trafficking with Senator Wellstone. He and I don't get together on too many bills, so when we do, it is a bit noteworthy. We come from different perspectives, different viewpoints. I think we both have good hearts but our heads take us in different directions. But on this subject of stopping sex trafficking, we don't disagree. We have worked together all year to get this bill through which challenges this practice known as sex trafficking.[21]

The bill passed the Senate unanimously.

After reconciliation of the Senate version with the House bill, "An Act To combat trafficking in persons, especially into the sex trade, slavery, and involuntary servitude, to reauthorize certain Federal programs to prevent violence against women, and for other purposes," became the Victims of Trafficking and Violence Protection Act of 2000, which was signed by President Clinton on 28 October 2000.[22] The final legislation was passed only nineteen months after its introduction. It is a mixture of the bills proposed by Representatives Smith, Kaptur, and Gejdenson and those proposed by Senators Wellstone and Brownback.

Victims of Trafficking and Violence Protection Act of 2000

The TVPA specifically identifies trafficking in persons as a modern form of slavery.[23] This type of slavery was not recognized or, when recognized, was not prosecuted before the enactment of the TVPA. When setting forth the goals of the Act, Congress noted that "[n]o comprehensive law exists in the United States that penalizes the range of offenses involved in the trafficking scheme. Instead, even the most brutal instances of trafficking in the sex industry are often punished under laws that also apply to lesser offenses, so that traffickers typically escape deserved punishment."[24] The TVPA clearly identifies trafficking as a grave violation of human rights, which is a pressing international concern.[25]

Under the TVPA, the U.S. government is charged with working bilaterally and multilaterally to abolish the trafficking industry and to take steps to promote cooperation among countries linked by international trafficking routes to end trafficking and restore victims' rights.[26] Although there is an apparent conflict between the U.S. failure to sign the Rome Statute of the International Criminal Court and the mandate in the TVPA, the mandate may propel the United States into full cooperation with other countries on the issue of trafficking as a crime against humanity. In December 2000, after the passage of the TVPA, 81 of the 189 members of the United Nations, including the United States, signed a protocol encouraging the prevention of international trafficking as part of the United Nations Convention against Transnational Organized Crime (U.N. Protocol to Prevent, Suppress, and Punish Trafficking in Persons, Especially Women and Children, discussed above).[27]

The TVPA combats modern forms of slavery by penalizing the full range of offenses involved in trafficking and gives victims access to shelters, counseling, and medical care.[28] Under the TVPA, effective on the date of passage of the Act, alleged victims of trafficking who are willing to assist with the investigation and prosecution of severe forms of trafficking, and whose assistance the attorney general believes will help effect prosecution,[29] are given temporary legal immigration status and are to be housed in a safe location. The TVPA recognizes and criminalizes forced or involuntary servitude; forced labor; slavery; traffickers who recruit, harbor, transport, or provide others for forced or involuntary labor, servitude, or slavery; sex trafficking of children; and destroying, concealing, or confiscating another's passport or government document or restricting another's liberty or freedom of movement to obtain labor or services.

The Act makes document confiscation and destruction violations punishable by five years imprisonment and/or a fine.[30] It also amends the Federal Sentencing Guidelines to require the Sentencing Commission to take seriously and provide appropriate punishment ranges for offenses committed in violation of the TVPA.[31] Trafficking in persons is punishable by a maximum of twenty years imprisonment instead of the maximum ten-year imprisonment under prior law. The Act also provides that a fine may be imposed or that those convicted under the Act may be sentenced to both imprisonment and fine. In addition, a new section was added to the U.S. law by the TVPA providing that if death results from violations of the law or if the violations include kidnapping, aggravated sexual abuse, or an attempt to do any of those crimes, the defendant shall be fined, imprisoned for up to a life term, or both.[32] Also, in any case involving a child less than fourteen years of age, the offender may receive up to life imprisonment.[33]

The Act empowers the court to order restitution, a civil remedy, for offenses committed in violation of the TVPA.[34] The Order of Restitution may direct the defendant to pay the victim the full amount of his or her losses. The TVPA does not explicitly establish the framework for victims to seek civil compensation, including actual or punitive damages, from their offenders. The restitution section specifies that victims can seek restitution "under any other civil or criminal penalties authorized by law."[35] Some have suggested that trafficking victims should have a civil remedy under the Racketeering Influenced and Corrupt Organizations Act (RICO).[36] However, RICO requires "a pattern of racketeering," which could be difficult to prove if the victim was not trafficked by an organized trafficking ring. Another requirement of RICO is injury to the victim's business or property, which could also be problematic for victims to satisfy.[37] The Alien Tort Claims Act (ATCA) is another law under which trafficking victims could arguably seek civil compensation.[38] ATCA empowers the federal court to take jurisdiction over civil actions filed by aliens "based on a tort committed in violation of the law of nations or a treaty of the United States." However, ATCA has never been used in cases of trafficking victims.[39]

One of the most significant aspects of the TVPA is that it distinguishes between perpetrators of sex trafficking and the victims. Prosecution efforts have shifted from blaming the women forced into the sex trade or working without proper documents. The focus is now on criminal punishment of those found guilty of operating as traffickers in the United States. At the same time, a new immigration statute, a special "T" visa for trafficking, has been established to give victims a better chance of bringing charges against the traffickers.[40] Instead of being deported, up to 5,000 victims a year will be granted "interim immigration relief" for up to three years.[41] Thereafter, victims in the United States who have assisted the government in prosecuting the traffickers or who are minors can be protected from deportation past the three-year period of T-visas.[42] This visa helps not only the victims, but also the prosecution because it enables them to interview victims and obtain critical evidence of crimes that would otherwise not be available. As of 25 February 2003, the Bureau for Citizenship and Immigration Services (BCIS)[43] had granted 300 requests for continuing in the United States and is currently processing 150 T-visa applications. So far, twenty-three T-visas have been granted.[44] Since the passage of the TVPA, working under Section 107 of the Act, the Department of Justice (DOJ) has worked with the Office of Refugee Resettlement in the Department of Health and Human Services to certify more than 400 trafficking victims to allow them to receive federal and state benefits. The Criminal Section of the DOJ Civil Rights Division and other federal agencies have assisted approximately 370 victims of trafficking in obtaining immigration benefits.[45]

To fulfill the requirements of the TVPA, attorneys, agents, administrators, and other officials have had to be trained because the Act is complex and has many requirements. Further, prosecutorial and community outreach under the Act are labor intensive and time-consuming, often involving many victims, jurisdictions, and legal issues and requiring the full-time involvement of multiple attorneys and investigators. The National Advocacy Center was among the first to offer TVPA training. In December 2000, the National Advocacy Center held the first comprehensive training seminar on the implementation of the TVPA and trafficking cases for federal prosecutors, agents, and other officials. Assistant Attorney General Ralph Boyd, testifying before the U.S. House Committee on International Relations on 29 November 2001, stated: "the training consisted of presentations on structuring trafficking investigations and prosecutions from a victim-centered perspective, a panel on civil approaches to worker exploitation issues, a discussion of recent successful slavery prosecutions, and development of action plans by regional working groups of Assistant United States Attorneys and agents from the Federal Bureau of Investigation, BCIS and Department of Labor."[46]

Training and outreach to the community has continued. In October 2002, the Criminal Section of the DOJ Civil Rights Division trained prosecutors and agents at their training facility in South Carolina. This was the largest anti-trafficking training to date. Similar training was provided for federal victim-witness coordinators in October 2001. The Criminal Section of the Civil Rights Division also trains FBI agents on human trafficking issues at the FBI facility in Quantico. That section also works with local law enforcement to provide training on investigative strategies in trafficking cases.[47] Another example is the second annual Freedom Network Conference, "Two Year Review: Is the New Human Trafficking Law Working?" which included a specific training module, "Human Trafficking and Modern Day Slavery: Basic Tools for an Effective Response," offered in December 2003 in New York.[48]

The Department of Justice also funds a Trafficking in Persons and Worker Exploitation Task Force toll-free hotline (1-888-428-7581) and a community outreach program that works with local community groups, victims' and immigrants' rights organizations, shelters, and other interested groups to help local organizations identify and provide resources for trafficked persons.[49]

To provide wider education and dissemination about the TVPA, the DOJ has published two brochures on trafficking in persons. The first brochure was specifically created for BCIS and FBI law enforcement officials to distribute to the trafficking victims they encounter during investigations and prosecutions. This brochure was written at a second-grade reading level to inform victims of their rights, the availability of pro bono and low-cost legal services and translation services, and to provide information on contacting the Departments of Justice and State. The brochure has been translated into Russian, Spanish, Thai, Chinese, and Vietnamese, the most common languages spoken by trafficking victims. The Department of Justice, in collaboration with the Departments of State, Labor, and Health and Human Services, published a second brochure as a reference guide for nongovernmental organizations (NGOs) that offer assistance to trafficking victims.

The brochures were first distributed to appropriate federal agencies in March 2001 only five months after the passage of the TVPA.[50] The brochures emphasize the TVPA's enhanced punishment of traffickers with twenty years to life imprisonment for those convicted of trafficking offenses and the significant increase in severity over preexisting servitude statutes, which carried a maximum penalty of ten years imprisonment. Further, the brochures explain that the TVPA is designed to address the subtle means of coercion that traffickers often use to bind their victims in servitude, such as psychological coercion, trickery, and the seizure of documents—conduct that was difficult if not impossible to prosecute under previous servitude statutes.

In his 2001 testimony to the House Committee on International Relations, Boyd also announced that the attorney general had created two new attorney positions in the Civil Rights Division's Criminal Section, which specializes in investigating and prosecuting human trafficking cases and other civil rights crimes and has primary enforcement responsibility for the involuntary servitude and peonage statutes.[51] The increased prosecutorial resources were needed because of the increased caseload resulting from the enactment of the TVPA.

The increased resources allocated to trafficking cases pursuant to the TVPA have resulted in successful prosecutions. Since January 2001, the Criminal Section of the Civil Rights Division of the Justice Department has charged, convicted, or secured sentences against 109 human traffickers in thirty-three separate cases. Of those cases, twenty-one have specifically involved sex trafficking, and 78 of the 109 traffickers have been sex traffickers. As of 15 August 2003, there are 118 open trafficking investigations, nearly twice as many as were open in January 2001. Because the TVPA cannot be used to prosecute conduct that occurred prior to October 2000, its effective date, some of the cases have been brought under preexisting statutes such as the Mann Act.[52]

Of the cases brought to date, nineteen have been brought under the TVPA specifically. Twelve of these cases involve sexual exploitation against thirty-five traffickers. Of the nineteen cases, fourteen resulted in convictions against twenty-five defendants, twenty of whom were sex traffickers. Trial is pending in the remaining five cases.[53]

The Virchenko Case

Three of the cases brought under the TVPA involve sexual exploitation of women and children who were trafficked from former Soviet states to the United States. These three cases typify the issues that arise in sex trafficking cases, the deceit that is practiced, and the degradation that the victims undergo. The first case brought under the TVPA involving trafficking in women and children is *United States v. Virchenko, Agafonov, and Kennards.* In this case, four women and two sixteen-year-old girls were trafficked into the United States on 20 December 2000, shortly after passage of the TVPA, by Victor Nikolaevich Virchenko with the help of Pavel Agafonov and Tony and Rachel Kennard. The case was also brought under a section of the Mann Act prohibiting the transportation of minors for illegal sexual purposes. The defendants operated as a small group.[54] There is nothing in the record to indicate that they were tied to any large organized crime groups, although both Virchenko and Agafonov are from the same Black Sea area of Russia and the same hometown, Stanitsa Leningradskaya.[55]

On 20 December 2000, the women and children flew with Virchenko from Russia to Minnesota, and then to Anchorage, Alaska, where they were forced to

dance nude in strip clubs. They trusted Virchenko, "a well-known dance instruc-
tor in the Krasnodar region of Russia. He headed a folkloric dance troupe which
frequently toured Russia and other countries performing native and folk dances
in dance festivals and cultural exchanges."[56] Virchenko personally selected the
women and children and offered them an all-expense-paid trip to perform
dances in a nonexistent cultural festival in Anchorage called "Russian Winter in
Alaska."[57] He rehearsed them in native folklore dances. However, he did dis-
close to the women that in addition to performing folk dances, "they might also
dance in 'exhibitions' which could include partial nudity. The young women
expected these 'exhibitions' to be comparable to the type of dancing in a Las
Vegas show."[58] Virchenko obtained costumes for them, and even brazenly assured them that his daughter would be accompanying them.[59] At the last minute,
he told them that his daughter would be unable to join them. The victims were
forced to perform from 20 December 2000 until 4 January 2001 when they were
rescued by the U.S. government.[60]

Two other defendants in the case, Tony Kennard and his wife Rachel, who
were coconspirators in the scheme, are American citizens. They met the women
and girls at the airport and drove them to their residence in Chugiak, Alaska.
There, they gave the women and girls a single room to share with mattresses on
the floor, and a single bathroom. Tony Kennard later claimed that his was an
upscale suburban home where the women were housed in a "very large" single
bedroom with one "highly decorated bathroom," and a closet.[61]

After his arrest, Kennard characterized himself as a man with a "creative
personality" whose very creativity saddled him with a federal felony offense. He
characterized himself as a "man of varied talents," a man of the wilderness,
mountaineer and bow hunter, a lepidopterist, a collector of original art and professional quality digital cameras.[62] On their arrival at the Kennards' residence,
the women and girls had their documents confiscated and "were told that the
festival they had come to dance in was over, so they would be required to dance
in a club until February when another festival was scheduled."[63]

The final defendant was Pavel Agafonov, a naturalized U.S. citizen of Russian descent living in Marietta, Georgia, who operated a website that advertised
"Russian brides" and sex tours of St. Petersburg with "adult content."[64] Kennard, Virchenko, and Agafonov together made all visa arrangements for the
women. Kennard and Agafonov exchanged a number of e-mails in which they
discussed various ways to circumvent visa requirements of the Russian women
and girls. Kennard then "obtained a letter of invitation from the Chugiak River,
Alaska, Chamber of Commerce for a purported Russian dance troupe to perform
at a luncheon meeting of the Chamber, falsely stating that he was working on
behalf of a local legislator. On the basis of that letter, Kennard obtained a letter
of invitation from the city of Anchorage, which he later altered to state that the
members of the dance troupe were invited to perform at various functions in the
Anchorage/Homer areas during December 2000 and January 2001."[65] Kennard
then submitted the letter to the U.S. embassy in Moscow and to the Russian

Ministry of Culture in support of visa applications. Several days later, when the visas were issued, Kennard e-mailed Agafanov "WE ARE RICH!"[66]

> The dozens of e-mails between Kennard and Agafonov . . . over a period of nearly three months . . . demonstrate significant planning and painstaking attention to detail. For example, at one point, Tony Kennard critiqued the photographs that had been sent to him . . . complaining that the girls were not '10s.' . . . He suggested cosmetic make-overs at Nordstrom, and asked Agafonov if the girls would be willing to undergo bargain basement breast enhancements in Russia. . . . Kennard reasoned that the better looking and sexually attractive the women were, the more money he could realize from their labors.[67]

At one point Kennard grew apprehensive that the visas would not be issued. Consequently, he proposed an alternate means to bring the women to the United States:

> If we proceed with this process, we are surely going to get caught in a lie! We have already stretched this visa thing as far as we can. . . . So this is my suggestion, let's fly 2 girls to Mexico every week, they can pose as my wife and I can get them to Alaska. Once here, I can get one of my friends to marry them. They will live with me and Rachel as planned.[68]

Kennard's plan was broader than this one incident. He and Agafonov hoped to expand their business to the proposed Alaska natural gas pipeline route to provide nude dancers for the largely male workers on the pipeline. Kennard wrote in an e-mail: "For the next 5 years the Alaska population will double and will be 85% all men that are making a lot of money!!! If we don't take this opportunity now we are crazy. I would like to have 10 girls in Fairbanks and 15 girls in Anchorage then we are up to full go, do the math, if they make $400.00 a night, and even the ugly ones do that here."[69]

After the women and children arrived in Alaska, on 22 December 2000, they were taken to the Crazy Horse Saloon, a strip club in Anchorage, to dance nude and perform lap dances. When they wept, refused to dance, and asked to be sent back to Russia, Virchenko became verbally abusive, telling them they could not go back until they had earned enough money at the club to pay for their tickets and expenses. They were told that the tickets cost $1,500–$2,000, an amount impossible for them to earn in Russia where they were paid about $6–$8 per month.[70]

Virchenko confiscated the victims' passports, plane tickets, and visas on arrival in the United States. He further humiliated and demeaned them, treating them as inferior beings. They could not even have their meals until after he had finished eating. Further, "[t]hey were systematically isolated, they were not permitted to talk to customers at the club, particularly those who spoke Russian. [T]heir phone calls home were monitored, and they were escorted wherever they needed to go by [either Virchenko or the Kennards]." In addition, "Rachel Kennard provided the women with stripper costumes and took them shopping for provocative clothing." She also kept the books for the enterprise. Virchenko and Kennard taught the women how to perform striptease dances.[71]

Terrified and unable to speak English, the victims soon submitted to demands that they dance completely nude. They hoped that they would be able to leave on 19 January 2001, the return date of their confiscated plane tickets. One of two sixteen-year-old girls in the group experienced a breakdown a few days after first being forced to dance nude.[72]

Each night, the Kennards and Virchenko collected all the victims' earnings. "Rachel Kennard kept the accounting of the money in a notebook, but refused to tell the victims how much money they had earned or how much money they 'owed' for their plane tickets and living expenses."[73]

The nightmare ended for the trafficked women and children two weeks before the 19 January 2001 date on which they had hoped they would be freed. Astute BCIS investigators, who had been looking for evidence of trafficking and studying advertisements and other media, found them at the Crazy Horse Saloon after reading advertisements of Russian dancers working there as strippers.[74] The e-mail traffic between Kennard and Agafonov was retrieved from Kennard's computer, seized under a search warrant. Although Kennard had erased his hard drive, FBI computer experts were able to retrieve everything. This evidence was crucial to the investigation because it set forth in complete detail the scheme and its execution.[75]

Indictments against Virchenko, Agafonov, and the Kennards

Indictments were presented against Victor Virchenko, Pavel Agafonov, and Rachel and Tony Kennard on 18 January 2001. The three men were indicted for visa fraud and conspiracy to commit visa fraud. On 22 February, the Grand Jury returned a superseding indictment charging the three men and Rachel Kennard. Each of the three men was charged with one count of conspiracy, six counts of visa fraud, six counts of kidnapping, two counts of transporting minors for immoral purposes, and six counts of forced labor. Virchenko was charged with two additional counts of witness intimidation. Rachel Kennard was charged with conspiracy and six counts of forced labor.[76]

The indictment of Viktor Virchenko and his codefendants was the first application of the Victims of Trafficking and Violence Protection Act.[77] The case was investigated jointly by the BCIS, FBI, and the Anchorage Police Department, and was prosecuted by the Criminal Section of DOJ's Civil Rights Division[78] and the U.S. Attorney's Office for the District of Alaska. To prevent Virchenko from fleeing the country, his case was investigated and an indictment issued soon after the victims were freed from the control of Virchenko and his colleagues.[79]

Virchenko was arrested at the Anchorage International Airport as he attempted to leave with the two minors.[80] The Justice Department had evidence that for his role in the crime he was to be paid $6,000 ($1,000 for each woman he recruited), an amount equivalent to approximately ten years salary for him.[81] All of the victims are still in the United States on T-visas and are applying for permanent visas.[82] Virchenko entered into a plea agreement; he pled guilty to visa fraud and transportation for immoral purposes (violating the Mann Act).[83] In exchange, the government agreed to dismiss the remaining counts against him: conspiracy, kidnapping, forced labor, and witness intimidation. If Virchenko had been convicted of all or some of the remaining counts, the ultimate sentence would have been far more severe.

The Presentence Investigation Report, drafted to determine the appropriate sentence under the Federal Sentencing Guidelines, recommended that Virchenko receive from thirty-three to forty-one months imprisonment. The government recommended a lesser sentence, of from twenty-seven to thirty-three months with a three-year period of supervised release after the imprisonment and a special assessment of $100 for each of the twenty-one counts of the conviction. The government argued for the lesser punishment because Virchenko suffered an "immigration consequence"; on his release from prison, he would be deported for having entered the country by making false statements on his visa application.[84] The other defendants, Kennards and Agafonov, would not suffer this consequence. In addition, Virchenko had not received credit for time served in the halfway house (Cordova Center) while awaiting disposition of his case.[85] The government apparently concluded that his detention was equivalent to incarceration or time already served because, due to his limited English-language skills, he could not function outside the halfway house during his time there, and he was restricted to the center or his attorney's office.

On 28 August 2001, the U.S. District Court for Alaska sentenced Virchenko to thirty months imprisonment for immigration fraud and transporting minors from Russia to dance in an Anchorage strip club. Following his imprisonment, he was deported.[86] He received no fine because of his poverty. There is no evidence in the case records that profits of the trafficking scheme reached the level he and his partners expected.

In August 2001, Tony Allen Kennard pled guilty to visa fraud and transportation for immoral purposes. Although the plea agreement specifically stated that it was not based on the government's agreeing to drop the charges against Kennard's wife, those charges were dropped, and Kennard later asserted that they were dropped in exchange for his plea of guilty. The court rejected this assertion.[87] There was insufficient evidence to prosecute Rachel Kennard.[88]

As a result of Kennard's plea, the government agreed to dismiss the remaining counts and recommend a sentence at the low end of the applicable sentencing guideline range. The Presentence Investigation Report recommended that Kennard receive from forty-six to fifty-seven months of imprisonment for his crimes. The government determined that Kennard was the mastermind of this scheme. He had meticulously planned and plotted every detail from the false invitations, through visa trickery, to ultimately pocketing all of the monies the women and girls would make. Not satisfied with his sentence, Kennard argued that he did not know the two girls were under age eighteen. He asserted that, as a result, he did not know that transporting them across state and international lines for purposes of having them dance nude was a felony and that he should not receive an increased level of punishment for the more serious offense. The government argued that it had evidence and knowledge derived from stipulations in the record that Kennard did know that two of the girls were under age eighteen and that thereby he had knowingly violated the Mann Act.[89]

The government recommended that if Kennard accepted responsibility for his actions, he should be confined for forty-six months, have a period of supervised release of three years after confinement, and pay an assessment of $100 for each count of the conviction. The court entered its final judgment and commitment order on 21 September 2001.[90] Kennard received no fine. He is in federal custody serving his forty-six-month sentence, and is projected to be released on 12 September 2005.[91] Nonetheless, after pleading guilty and agreeing not to appeal his sentence, on 25 September 2001, Kennard filed an appeal seeking a reduction in sentence on the grounds that the government's dismissal of charges against his wife rendered his pleas involuntary. In response to his appeal, the government argued that Kennard was not entitled to a reduction in sentence because he had competent assistance of counsel to help him understand the plea, as fully evidenced in the record before the court. Kennard's plea agreement contained an express waiver of his right to appeal his sentence. The court affirmed his sentence and conviction on 29 August 2002.[92] For acts significantly more serious than Virchenko's, Kennard's sentence was only slightly higher, forty-six months to Virchenko's thirty months.

Pavel Agafonov also entered a plea of guilty to visa fraud and transportation for immoral purposes. In consideration of his guilty plea and his cooperation in the investigation, the government agreed to dismiss the remaining counts of the indictment at sentencing. Following the pattern set by the court in sentencing Virchenko and Kennard, Agafonov also received a sentence much less severe than he could have, eighteen months out of the forty-one months that the sentencing guidelines recommended. The Presentence Investigation Report prepared on Agafonov recommended that he be sentenced for from thirty-three to forty-one months, but the government sought only eighteen to twenty-four months imprisonment, a period of supervised release for two years, with no restrictions on Agafonov's use of computers, the Internet, or telephones, and a special assessment of $100 for each count of conviction. Because of the defendant's impoverished financial situation, the government requested that no fine be imposed, and none was.[93]

Effectiveness of Enforcement of the TVPA in the Virchenko Case

The Virchenko case was heralded nationally as the first brought under the TVPA, the tough new antitrafficking law. Alaska U.S. Attorney Robert Bundy stated, "We will vigorously enforce our anti-slavery laws against those who try to exploit others."[94] Officials further contended that the new law would allow immigration agents and prosecutors to identify more trafficking cases because it clearly defines crimes of forced labor, peonage, slavery, and involuntary servitude.[95] Previously, prosecutors had to string together charges, including charges related to immigration, in cases of trafficking for sex or forced labor. Those charges did not reflect the magnitude of the crimes that were committed. One Justice Department official said, "This isn't an immigration or morality issue. This is a human rights issue."[96]

However, the noble intentions that heralded the Virchenko case were not fulfilled. According to the *Washington Post,* federal prosecutors threw in the towel in some of the most serious aspects of the case, including charges dealing with kidnapping and forced labor that stem directly from the Victims of Trafficking and Violence Protection Act of 2000.[97]

"It [is] unclear why federal prosecutors in Anchorage agreed to dismiss the trafficking charges. Generally, plea deals that cut out major charges can be an indication of problems with the government's proof and witness testimony." However, this may not be the reason for the dismissal of major trafficking charges in this very difficult case with a significant language barrier. Judge James Singleton, Jr., suggested that the "government appeared to have mischaracterized some elements of the case." Prosecutors claimed that the case was about "child sexual abuse and exploitation." However, Judge Singleton said that "a review of the record [compelled] the conclusion that this [was] a mischaracterization of the case." He further maintained that the allegations involving minors under eighteen were only a small part of the case. "The case continues to sound primarily in fraud," he maintained. He agreed that "Alaska should not become a conduit for women from Eastern Europe to the United States for prostitution and sexual exploitation." He claimed that there should be enhanced surveillance by customs and immigration officials, but that this should not occur by turning a fraud case into a sex case.[98] It is not clear whether the dismissal of trafficking charges and the ultimate results in this case are because of an outmoded concept that fails to see slavery in its modern guises or whether the evidence was not sufficient to prove the alleged crimes beyond a reasonable doubt. Only a thorough study of many more cases and the passage of time will enable us to determine if even under the TVPA there is a pattern of nonrecognition of slavery.

United States v. Gasanov

The next case brought under the TVPA dealing with trafficking in Russian-speaking women is *United States v. Sardar and Nadira Gasanov.* This case broke new ground in prosecution under the TVPA because of its serious penalization of the traffickers. It marked the first use of the document confiscation and forfeiture provisions of the TVPA. The Gasanovs were indicted, convicted, and sentenced harshly in comparison to the sentences handed down in *Virchenko.* The penalties were more severe not only because of the seriousness of the trafficking charges, but also because of the charges filed under the document confiscation and forfeiture provisions of the Act.[99]

Sardar Gasanov, a research assistant in the Biological Science Department of the University of Texas at El Paso, together with his wife, Nadira, were indicted on 15 August 2001 on counts of conspiracy to commit document fraud, conspiracy to harbor illegal aliens, bringing aliens into the United States for the purpose of financial gain, and money laundering. The Gasanovs had recruited three women from their hometown of Tashkent, Uzbekistan, "to come to the United States, promising prosperous modeling jobs, extravagant lifestyles, and the ability to bring their family members to the United States." They used fraudulently obtained J-1 visas to bring the Uzbek women into the United States through El Paso.[100]

The visas obtained by the Gasanovs described the Uzbek women as scientists traveling to the United States to do research at the University of Texas at El Paso. When the women arrived in El Paso, "the Gasanovs confiscated their immigration documents, then required them to work seven days a week at strip clubs in El Paso for the benefit of the Gasanovs." The women were told that this was to pay back the alleged $300,000 fee for smuggling them into the United States and obtaining visas for them. The Gasanovs used confiscation of documents, threat of deportation, and threats against the victims' families to induce the Uzbek women to remain in their service, be productive dancers, and turn over all of their earnings to the Gasanovs.[101] The first of three trafficked Uzbek women arrived in the United States in January 1998. From February 1998 to August 1999 and from June 2000 to May 2001, she was forced to give the Gasanovs all of her earnings, approximately $120,000, from dancing topless. The second woman arrived in the United States in February 1999. From February 1999 to June 2001, with the exception of two months, she gave all the money she earned from dancing topless, approximately $350,000, to the Gasanovs. The third woman arrived in October 2000. From October 2000 to May 2001, she gave the Gasanovs all the money she earned from dancing topless, approximately $58,000.[102] Authorities estimate that the Gasanovs collected more than $500,000 from the women between 1998 and 2001 as a result of this criminal enterprise.[103]

The women trafficked and held in servitude by the Gasanovs were discovered as the result of a joint investigation by special agents of the Federal Bureau of Investigation working with the BCIS, the State Department, and the Texas Alcoholic Beverage Commission. The case was initiated after two of the victimized women sought assistance from the FBI. This joint investigation was also part of the initiative of Attorney General John Ashcroft to crack down on human trafficking and modern-day slavery.[104] When the Gasanovs were charged, the women were released from their control and given asylum for the three years provided under the TVPA.[105]

The Gasanovs were charged with violations of the TVPA on 15 August 2001. On 15 March 2002, a federal jury convicted them of conspiracy, alien smuggling conspiracy, and alien smuggling. On 17 May 2002, U.S. District Judge David Briones of El Paso, Texas, sentenced the defendants to sixty months in prison to be followed by three years supervised release. They were also ordered to pay $516,152 in restitution to their victims[106] and forfeit $650,000 in assets.[107]

On 24 May 2002, Nadira Gasanova appealed her case in the U.S. Court of Appeals for the Fifth Circuit. On 28 May 2002, Sardar Gasanov filed an appeal in the same court. On 22 May 2003, the court denied their appeals and affirmed the decision of the District Court.[108]

The Gasanov case proved that the new TVPA law had "teeth." The defendants were convicted in a timely manner, sentenced to significant time in prison, and had to make substantial restitution to the victims. It may be noteworthy that this case occurred in Texas, which historically tends to sentence criminals more harshly than many other states. An example of the enhanced punishment of crime is the fact that the rate of death penalty sentences is higher in Texas than in any other state.[109] It may be even more noteworthy that the case actually went to trial, unlike *Virchenko* where all the defendants pled guilty. Only after many more cases have been brought under the TVPA will it be possible to discern any patterns.

United States v. Trakhtenberg

The next case involving trafficking in Russian women and children is *United States v. Trakhtenberg*. This case is much larger in scope than the *Virchenko* and *Gasanov* cases, both because of the number of women trafficked and because it has alleged connections to Russian organized crime. At the time this chapter was written, this case was still being investigated. Because of the connections to organized crime and the reach of the trafficking scheme, this case stands out from the other two, and its successful prosecution may eventually help bring into focus the widespread tentacles of Russian organized crime and the problems facing the world as it commits to identifying and eradicating all guises of slavery and its degradations.

When this chapter was written, the following facts were known. On 28 August 2002, a federal grand jury in the U.S. District Court for Newark, New Jersey, returned an eleven-count indictment against Lev Trakhtenberg, his wife, Viktoriia L'lina, both United States naturalized citizens, and Sergei Malchikov, a Russian national in the United States on an expired visa. They were charged with conspiracy; forced labor; trafficking for forced labor; and conspiracy to commit extortion. As in *Gasanov*, the government sought to confiscate assets associated with or derived from the illegal activity. The conspiracy charge carries a maximum penalty of five years in prison and a $250,000 fine. Each of the other counts carries a maximum penalty of twenty years in prison and a $250,000 fine.

To obtain visas, the Trakhtenbergs and Malchikov submitted documentation to the BCIS that approximately thirty Russian women were coming to the United States to tour with two internationally recognized show groups, the Gurchenko Show Group and the Boyanova Show Group. To perform in these groups, the women had to have certain talents and abilities, and the defendants provided false documentation that the women possessed an array of musical talents from singing to being accomplished in several musical instruments, including the flute and the keyboard. In addition, the defendants stated that some of the women were to be "visiting specialists" at the Department of Performing Arts at the University of Illinois at Chicago. In actuality, the women's backgrounds ranged from nurse to chef. None were performing arts specialists or even performing artists.[110] On arrival in the United States, the women were brought to Delilah's Den in Perth Amboy and Dover Township, New Jersey, and Frank's Chicken House in Manville, New Jersey,[111] where they were required to dance nude six days a week, for eight to ten hours a day, with only one additional day off a month.[112]

According to the district court indictment, "the Russian women were lured to the United States with the promise that they would make large sums of money dancing at strip clubs. They were also misled as to the lascivious nature of the dancing they would be required to perform. . . . [T]he defendants also misled the women with regard to the amount of money they would be able to keep for themselves and for the benefit of their families." The women had to provide the defendants with detailed "emergency" contact information about family in Russia, which was later used to threaten them and their families to prevent them from leaving the defendants' control. If the women complained about the nature of the work or the insufficient money they were allowed to keep for themselves, they were reminded that the defendants had the addresses of their families back in Russia. If the women failed to pay the thousands of dollars demanded, the defendants told the women that the money was owed to Russian organized crime associates who would seek retribution against them and their families in Russia. The women were required to pay the defendants $1,200 per week, regardless of whether they earned sufficient money for dancing at the nude establishments, and even if they were ill or too tired to work. In those cases, the amount due was added to the following week's bill. The women's passports, visas, and return plane tickets were confiscated, which was another significant contributing factor in the case.[113]

Although still pending, the importance of this case is far-reaching. It addresses the global reach of the Russian organized crime group to which the Trakhtenbergs and Malchikov belong and adhere. The victims would never be able to escape, even if presented with the physical opportunity, because their families and contacts at home would be vulnerable to the reach of the group. Their trafficking captors held the women enslaved not only physically, but also because they recognized the reach of the organized crime group.

Several special agents of the FBI, special agents of the BCIS, and the New York Police Department/FBI Russian Organized Crime Task Force investigated the Trakhtenberg case. The trial was scheduled for 6 November 2002 in the U.S. District Court for Newark, New Jersey, but because the case is still under investigation due to the complexities of the issues, the multiple parties, and the reach of the trafficking group involved, the trial is now scheduled for 2004.[114] Law enforcement personnel, international human rights lawyers, and ROC groups will be watching to see if the TVPA finally starts to fulfill its promise of ending the rise of slavery and the possibilities of effectively combating it.

Conclusion

It is still too early to tell how the TVPA will affect trafficking in persons to the United States and whether it will inhibit traffickers from entering the United States. Effective enforcement of the Act should increase discovery of trafficking, prosecution, conviction, and punishment of traffickers and their co-conspirators and provide better protection for victims. The three cases examined do not yet provide clear precedents for strong enforcement. However, they establish clear intent to investigate, prosecute, and punish violations and provide restitution for victims. The heavy sanctions under the Act, including fines, restitution, and imprisonment up to life, support the clear legislative purpose and commitment to end trafficking.

With the existence of the TVPA, women are coming forward knowing that they have government protection and are not likely to be deported before their cases can be investigated and they can clear themselves and serve as key witnesses. These trafficked women and children now know that they are the "victim," not the "offender." Consequently, they do not fear deportation. The victims are granted temporary visas until the perpetrators of crimes against them are brought to justice. As evidenced in this chapter, trafficking cases take time to investigate and prosecute. If the TVPA is to be effective and end slavery, law enforcement must be given supplemental resources in terms of personnel. Resources must be allocated to hire additional U.S. attorneys to prosecute the cases and translators to interview the victims. In addition, the cooperation encouraged by the UN Protocol to Prevent, Suppress and Punish Trafficking in Persons, Especially Women and Children must be made mandatory, and the TVPA mandated trafficking statistics in the "Annual Country Reports on Human Rights Practices" must be used to publicize the far-reaching scope of trafficking.[115]

In the past, victims of trafficking, even if they were discovered by U.S. investigators, were either unable or fearful to come forward to law enforcement officials because they and their families had been threatened by the traffickers. In addition, trafficked women have in the past tended not to trust law enforcement personnel. Their experiences with law enforcement in their home countries were all too frequently fraught with the need to deal with corruption and terror. They bring those fears to the United States when dealing with investigators and officials. Nor has prior U.S. law, including the Mann Act, provided precedent that would reassure trafficked persons that the United States is committed to helping victims and to end trafficking.

Until the passage of the TVPA, sentences for drug convictions were far more severe than sentences for traffickers who caused women and children to suffer unspeakable horrors in the sex trade.[116] With the passage of the TVPA and the prosecutions under *Virchenko, Gasanov,* and the pending *Trakhtenberg* case, there is now evidence that the tide is turning against slavery. There is evidence that victims will be found and protected, that countries will work together to end the business of trafficking, and that traffickers will be punished. Although there are hopeful signs, it is still too soon to determine the ultimate effectiveness of the TVPA. Continuous dedication, allocation of resources, and hard work will be needed to fulfill the TVPA's goals and eradicate slavery once and for all.

Notes

I would like to thank Alicyn Siano and Hilary Talley for their research and editorial assistance. I would also like to thank Assistant United States Attorneys Holly Wiseman and Tom Firestone for their insights into the trafficking cases, and Margaret Weekes, associate dean, Washington Semester Program, American University, for her countless hours of editing the draft.

1. Walter Zalisko, "Russian Organized Crime, Trafficking in Women, and Government's Response," PMC International Inc., July 2003, http://www.monmouth.com/~wplz/Index1.htm (15 October 2003).

2. See Robert Friedman, *Red Mafiya: How the Russian Mob Has Invaded America* (Boston: Little, Brown & Company, 2000); James O. Finckenauer and Elin Waring, *Russian Mafia in America* (Boston: Northeastern University Press, 1998).

3. Zalisko, "Russian Organized Crime."

4. Zalisko, "Russian Organized Crime."

5. 18 U.S.C. 1589–1594.

6. Sections 108 and 109 of the Act, codified at 22 U.S.C. 2151 et seq.

7. Victims of Trafficking and Violence Protection Act of 2000, H.R. 3244, Pub. L. 106-386, 28 October 2000.

8. Section 110(d), TVPA 2000, H.R. 3244.

9. Law of 25 June 1910, Ch. 395, Sections 1, 2, 5, 8, 36 Stat. 825–827 (amended 1986); 18 U.S.C. 2421-2427 (all editions before 1998).

10. Pub. L. 99-628; 18 U.S.C. 2421–2427.

11. See the Protection Project, *Human Rights Report on Trafficking in Persons, Especially Women and Children* (Washington, D.C.: Johns Hopkins University, 2002), 589–90.

12. Protection Project, *Human Rights Report on Trafficking in Persons,* 589–90, citing section 102(a), TVPA of 2000, H.R. 3244.

13. "Universal Declaration of Human Rights," G.A. res. 217A (III), U.N. Doc A/810 (1948).

14. Rome Statute of the International Criminal Court, Final Act of the United Nations Diplomatic Conference of Plenipotentiaries on the Establishment of an International Criminal Court, Done at Rome on 17 July 1998, U.N. Doc. A/Conf.183/10, http://www.un.org/law/icc/statute/finalfra.htm (28 October 2003).

15. Article 7 of the Rome Statute of the International Criminal Court.

16. United Nations Protocol to Prevent, Suppress and Punish Trafficking in Persons, Especially Women and Children, supplementing the United Nations Convention against Transnational Organized Crime, Article 10 (3) G.A. res. 55/25, annex II, 55 U.N. GAOR Supp. (No. 49) at 60, U.N. Doc. A/45/49 (Vol. I) (2001). Articles V, VI, IX, and X. Also, see generally, Mohamed Y. Mattar, "Monitoring the Status of Severe Forms of Traffick-

ing in Foreign Countries: Sanctions Mandated under the U.S. Trafficking Victims Protection Act," *Brown Journal of World Affairs* 10, no. 1 (Summer/Fall 2003): 159, 169.

17. United Nations Protocol to Prevent, Suppress and Punish Trafficking in Persons, Especially Women and Children; Mattar, 169.

18. Mae M. Cheng, "US Border Control, New Law's First Test; Trafficking Statute to Be Used to Prosecute Alaska Case," *Newsday*, 15 March 2001, http://www.usbc.org/info/crime/0301newlaw.htm (28 October 2003).

19. Statements on Introduced Bills and Joint Resolutions, U.S. Senate, 13 April 2000, *Congressional Record*, http://thomas.loc.gov/cgi-bin/query/F?r106:1:./temp/~r106 badtrh:e380827: (26 October 2003).

20. http://thomas.loc.gov/cgi-bin/query/D?r106:1:./temp/~r106Qh2O77 (26 October 2003).

21. http://thomas.loc.gov/cgi-bin/query/D?r106:1:./temp/~r106ja2drg (26 October 2003).

22. The trafficking provisions of H.R. 3244, Pub. L. 106-386, are contained in sections 1 through 113 of the Act. The trafficking provisions are codified at 18 U.S.C. and are primarily contained at 18 U.S.C. 1589-1594.

23. Section 102(b)(1), TVPA of 2000, H.R. 3244.

24. Section 102(b)(14), TVPA, H.R. 3244.

25. Section 102(b)(23), TVPA, H.R. 3244.

26. Sections 102(b)(24) 108, 109, 110 TVPA, H.R. 3244.

27. Cheng, "US Border Patrol."

28. http://thomas.loc.gov/cgi-bin/query/F?r106:1:./temp/~r106u42dbC:e391953 (26 October 2003).

29. Section 107(b), TVPA, H.R. 3244.

30. 18 U.S.C. 1592.

31. 28 U.S.C. 994.

32. 18 U.S.C. 1581, 1583, 1584, 1589.

33. 18 U.S.C. 1591.

34. 18 U.S.C 1593.

35. 18 U.S.C. 1593. For further discussion of this section, see http://www.protectionproject.org (24 October 2003).

36. 18 U.S.C. 1961 et seq. The RICO civil remedy suggestion was first made by Lan Cao in "Note: Illegal Traffic in Women; A Civil RICO Proposal," *Yale Law Journal* 96, no. 6 (May 1987): 1297. See also The Protection Project, 593, note 123.

37. Protection Project, 594.

38. 28 U.S.C. 1350.

39. http://www.protectionproject.org/main1.htm (24 October 2003).

40. 8 U.S.C. 1101(a)(15)(T) and 1184(n).

41. 18 U.S.C. 1184(n) 1255.

42. 8 U.S.C. 1101(a)(15)(T)(i) and 8 U.S.C. 1255.

43. As of November 1999, the Immigration and Naturalization Service changed its name to the Bureau for Citizenship and Immigration Services.

44. Remarks of Attorney General John Ashcroft at the conference "Pathbreaking Strategies in the Global Fight against Sex Trafficking," 25 February 2003, http://www.state.gov/g/tip/rls/rm/17987.htm (22 July 2003).

45. DOJ Trafficking in Persons Fact Sheet, August 2003.

46. Testimony of Ralph F. Boyd, Jr., assistant attorney general for civil rights, Committee on International Relations, United States House of Representatives, "Implementation of the Trafficking Victims Protection Act," 29 November 2001.

47. DOJ Trafficking in Persons Fact Sheet, August 2003.

48. See http://www.nycagainstrape.org/home/nycaasa/stage.nycagainstrape.org/event 204html (30 October 2003).

49. DOJ Trafficking in Persons Fact Sheet, August 2003.

50. Boyd testimony.

51. Boyd testimony.

52. DOJ Trafficking in Persons Fact Sheet, August 2003.

53. DOJ Trafficking in Persons Fact Sheet, August 2003.

54. Trial Brief, *United States v. Virchenko, Agafonov, and Kennards*, No. A01-013 CR (JKS), United States District Court (D. Alaska) 9 March 2001.

55. Trial Brief, *United States v. Virchenko, Agafonov, and Kennards*.

56. Trial Brief, *United States v. Virchenko, Agafonov, and Kennards*; Superseding Indictment. *United States v. Virchenko, Agafanov, and Kennards*, United States District Court (D. Alaska), A01-013CR (JHS) (AHB).

57. Trial Brief, *United States v. Virchenko, Agafonov, and Kennards*.

58. Brief for the United States as Appellee, *United States v. Kennard*, United States Court of Appeals for the Ninth Circuit (No. 01-30346), 28 February 2002.

59. Superseding Indictment, *United States v. Virchenko, Agafanov, and Kennards*.

60. Trial Brief, *United States v. Virchenko, Agafonov, and Kennards*.

61. United States Response to Defendant Kennard's Sentencing Memorandum, *United States v. Kennards*, No. A01-013 CR (JKS), United States District Court (D. Alaska) 9 March 2001.

62. United States Response, *United States v. Kennards*. Kennard used digital cameras for commercial pornographic shoots, although he did not say so.

63. Trial Brief, *United States v. Virchenko, Agafonov, and Kennards*.

64. Superseding Indictment, *United States v. Virchenko, Agafonov, and Kennards*.

65. Trial Brief, *United States v. Virchenko, Agafonov, and Kennards*.

66. Trial Brief, *United States v. Virchenko, Agafonov, and Kennards*.

67. Government's Sentencing Memorandum. *United States v. Virchenko*, No. A01-013 CR (JKS), United States District Court (D. Alaska), 24 August 2001.

68. Government Sentencing Memorandum, *United States v. Virchenko, Agafonov, and Kennards*.

69. E-mail from Kennard to Agafonov dated 12 October 2000, quoted in Government's Sentencing Memorandum *United States. v. Kennard*.

70. Trial Brief, *United States v. Virchenko, Agafonov, and Kennards*.

71. Trial Brief, *United States v. Virchenko, Agafonov, and Kennards*.

72. Trial Brief, *United States v. Virchenko, Agafonov, and Kennards*.

73. Trial Brief, *United States v. Virchenko, Agafonov, and Kennards*.

74. Trial Brief, *United States v. Virchenko, Agafonov, and Kennards*.

75. E-mail to author from H. Wiseman, assistant United States attorney, 17 October 2003; Superseding Indictment, *United States v. Virchenko, Agafanov, and Kennards*, United States District Court (D. Alaska), A01-013CR (JHS) (AHB).

76. Brief for the United States as Appellee in the United States Court of Appeals for the 9th Circuit, *United States v. Tony Allen Kennard*. On Appeal from the United States District Court for the District of Alaska 28 February 2002.

77. Cheng, "US Border Patrol."

78. The Criminal Section of the Civil Rights Division is responsible for prosecuting TVPA cases.

79. "Alaska Man Sentenced to 30 Months for Immigration Fraud and Transporting Minors from Russia to Dance in Anchorage Strip Club," United States Department of Justice, 29 August 2001, http://usinfo.state.gov/topical/global/traffic/01083101.htm (1 July 2003).

80. "Alaska Man Sentenced."

81. Government's Sentencing Memorandum, *United States v. Virchenko.*

82. E-mail to author from Wiseman.

83. Brief for the United States as Appellee, *United States v. Kennard.*

84. As of the writing of this chapter, Virchenko had been deported and was back in his hometown of Stanitsa Leningradskaia, Russia, according to an e-mail to the author from Wiseman.

85. Government's Sentencing Memorandum, *United States v. Virchenko.*

86. E-mail to the author from Wiseman.

87. Unpublished Opinion, *United States v. Kennard,* No. 01-30346 (D.C. No. CR-01-00013-a-JMF) United States Court of Appeals for the 9th Circuit, 29 August 2002.

88. Brief for the United States as Appellee, *United States v. Kennard.*

89. Government's Sentencing Memorandum, *United States. v. Kennard.*

90. Government's Sentencing Memorandum, *United States. v. Kennard.*

91. Brief for the United States as Appellee, *United States v. Kennard.*

92. Unpublished Opinion, *United States v. Kennard,* No. 01-30346 (D.C. No. CR-01-00013-a-JMF) United States Court of Appeals for the 9th Circuit, 29 August 2002.

93. Government's Sentencing Memorandum, *United States v. Agafonov.*

94. USDOJ, Press Release, 22 February 2001.

95. USDOJ, Press Release, 22 February 2001.

96. Cheng, "US Border Patrol."

97. Anthony M. Destefano, "3 Plead Guilty to Visa Fraud," *Washington Post,* 23 June 2001, http://www.protectionproject.org/vt/ne625.htm (30 October 2003).

98. All quotes in this paragraph are from Destefano.

99. "Gasanovs Sentenced to Federal Prison for Alien Smuggling for Profit," United States Department of Justice, United States Attorney Western District of Texas Press Release, 17 May 2002.

100. "Gasanovs Sentenced to Federal Prison." J-1 visas are nonimmigrant visas for educated or cultural exchange programs designated by the Department of State, Bureau of Consular Affairs. The visas are designed to promote cultural interchanges in educations, arts and sciences. Participants include students, trainees obtaining on-the-job training, teachers, professors, research scholars, professional trainees in medicine or allied fields, and international visitors traveling or participating in organized people-to-people programs. Participants must demonstrate that they have sufficient funds to cover expenses. www.uscis.gov.

101. "Gasanovs Sentenced to Federal Prison."

102. Brief for the United States, *United States v. Gasanov,* United States District Court (W.D. Texas), 20 December 2002.

103. Brief for the United States as Appellee, *United States v. Gasanov,* United States District Court (W.D. Texas) (No. 02-50566), 22 May 2003.

104. "Russian Husband and Wife Arrested on Federal Indictment Charging Alien Smuggling for Profit and Money Laundering," Press Release of United States Attorney's office, Western District of Texas, 17 August 2001, www.usdoj.gov/usao/txw/gasanov.htm (15 October 2003).

105. Brief for the United States as Appellee, *United States v. Gasanov.*

106. The Gasanovs earned this money directly from the victims' dancing; other assets were held in their house, cars, and other bank accounts and they had to forefeit these assests. Under the Human Trafficking Act passed on 20 October 2002 the victims can claim only money directly made from the criminal activity, not all of the couple's assets.

107. "Gasanovs Sentenced to Federal Prison."

108. *United States v. Gasanov*, United States Court of Appeals for the 5th Circuit, No. 02-50566, 22 May 2003, http://www.ilo.com/lawyers/immigdaily/cases/2003,0527 Gasanova.pdf (30 October 2003).

109. See statistics from the Death Penalty Information Center, http://www .deathpenaltyinfo.org.

110. Background information provided to author by Assistant United States Attorney Tom Firestone.

111. Zalisko, "Russian Organized Crime."

112. Indictment, *United States v. Trakhtenbergs & Malchikov*, United States District Court (D. New Jersey), 27 August 2002; "Three Indicted for Bringing Russian Women into U.S. and Forced to Perform as Nude Dancers," Press Release of New Jersey's United States Attorney's office, 27 August 2002, http://www.njusao.org/files/tr0827r.htm (4 August 2003).

113. Indictment, *United States v. Trakhtenbergs & Malchikov*; "Three Indicted."

114. E-mail to author from assistant United States attorney Leslie Schwartz on 3 October 2003.

115. 22 U.S.C. 2151 (f).

116. See, for example, studies on disproportionate drug sentences, "Human Rights Watch Denounces Disproportionate Sentences," http://www.drcnet.org/rapid/1997/3-18 -1.html (30 October 2003); and United States Sentencing Commission, "Federal Sentencing Statistics by State, District and Circuit," http://www.ussc.gov/JUDPAK/JP2001.htm (30 October 2003).

ᥳᥳᥳ

Selected Bibliography

Alexander, Priscilla. "Prostitution: A Difficult Issue for Feminists." In *Sex Work: Writings by Women in the Sex Industry*. Edited by Frederique Delacoste and Priscilla Alexander. Pittsburgh, Pa.: Cleis Press, 1987.

Altink, Sietske. *Stolen Lives: Trading Women into Sex and Slavery*. London: Scarlet Press, 1995.

Andreas, Peter, and Timothy Snyder. *The Wall around the West: State Borders and Immigration Controls in North America and Europe*. Lanham, Md.: Rowman & Littlefield, 2000.

Bales, Kevin. *Disposable People*. Berkeley: University of California Press, 1999.

Barry, Kathleen. *Female Sexual Slavery*. New York: Prentice Hall, 1979.

Barry, Kathleen, Charlotte Bunch, and Shirley Castley, eds. *International Feminism: Networking against Female Sexual Slavery*. New York: IWTC, 1984.

Bertone, Andrea. "International Political Economy and the Politics of Sex." *Gender Issues* 18, no. 1 (2000): 4–22.

Bolz, Jennifer. "Chinese Organized Crime and Illegal Alien Trafficking: Humans as a Commodity." *Asian Affairs* 22, no. 3 (1995):147–58.

Caldwell, Gillian, Steven Galster, and Nadia Steinzor. "Crime and Servitude: An Exposé of the Traffic in Women for Prostitution from the Newly Independent States." Washington, D.C.: Global Survival Network, 1997.

Chin, Ko-Lin. *Smuggled Chinese: Clandestine Immigration to the United States*. Philadelphia: Temple University Press, 1999.

DeMore, Charles H. Testimony before the United States Senate Committee on the Judiciary Subcommittee on Crime, Corrections, and Victims Rights for the hearing "Alien Smuggling/Human Trafficking: Sending a Meaningful Message of Deterrence." 25 July 2003.

Doezema, Jo. "Forced to Choose beyond the Voluntary v. Forced Prostitution Dichotomy." In *Global Sex Workers: Rights, Resistance, and Redefinition.* Edited by Kamala Kempadoo and Jo Doezema. New York: Routledge, 1998.

Ehrenreich, Barbara, and Arlie R. Hochschild, eds. *Global Woman: Nannies, Maids, and Sex Workers in the New Economy.* New York: Metropolitan Books, 2003.

Finckenauer, James O. "Russian Transnational Organized Crime and Human Trafficking." In *Global Human Smuggling: Comparative Perspectives.* Edited by David Kyle and Rey Koslowski. Baltimore, Md.: Johns Hopkins University Press, 2001.

Firestone, Thomas. "The Russian Connection: Sex Trafficking into the U.S. and What the U.S. and Russia Are Doing about It," *International Organized Crime* 51, no. 5 (2003): 39–41.

Frank, Marcus. "Asian Criminal Enterprises and Prostitution." Edited version of paper delivered to the 24th International Asian Organized Crime Conference, Chicago, Illinois, 25–30 March 2002. http://usinfo.state.gov/regional/ea/chinaaliens/prostitution .htm.

Global Organized Crime Project. *Russian Organized Crime.* Washington, D.C.: Center for Strategic and International Studies, 1997.

Hughes, Donna. "The 'Natasha' Trade—The Transnational Shadow Market of Trafficking in Women." *Journal of International Affairs* 53, no. 2 (Spring 2000): 625–52.

———. "Trafficking for Sexual Exploitation: The Case of the Russian Federation." Geneva: International Organization for Migration, 2002.

Human Rights Watch/Asia. *Owed Justice: Thai Women Trafficked into Debt Bondage in Japan.* New York: Human Rights Watch, 2000.

International Organization for Migration. *Deceived Migrants from Tajikistan: A Study of Trafficking in Women and Children.* Dushanbe, Republic of Tajikistan, 2001.

———. *Information Campaign against Trafficking in Women from Ukraine.* Geneva, Switzeerland, 1998.

———. "Trafficking in Migrants, IOM Policy and Responses." Working Paper. 1999. www.iom.int/en/who/main_policies_trafficking.html.

———. *Trafficking in Women and Children from the Kyrgyz Republic.* Bishkee, Kyrgyz Republic, 2000.

James, Jennifer. "Motivations for Entrance into Prostitution." In *The Female Offender.* Edited by Laura Crites. Lexington, Mass.: Lexington Books, 1976.

Kaplan, David E., and Alec Dubro. *Yakuza Japan's Criminal Underworld.* Expanded edition. Berkeley: University of California Press, 2003.

Klein, Dorie. "The Etiology of Female Crime: A Review of the Literature." *Issues in Criminology* 8 (1973): 6ff.

Koh, Harold Hongju. Testimony before the House Committee on International Relations. "The Global Problem of Trafficking in Persons: Breaking the Vicious Cycle on 'Trafficking of Women and Children in the International Sex Trade.'" Washington, D.C., 14 September 1999. http://secretary.state.gov/www/picw/trafficking/tkoh.htm.

Koslowski, Rey. *Migrants and Citizens: Demographic Change in the European State System.* Ithaca, N.Y. : Cornell University Press, 2000.

Kyle, David, and Rey Koslowski, eds. *Global Human Smuggling: Comparative Perspectives.* Baltimore, Md.: Johns Hopkins University Press, 2001.

Landesman, Peter. "The Girls Next Door." *New York Times Magazine,* 25 January 2004, Section 6, 30.

Liang, Zai, and Wenzhen Ye. "From Fujian to New York: Understanding the New Chinese Immigration." In *Global Human Smuggling: Comparative Perspectives.* Edited by David Kyle and Rey Koslowski. Baltimore, Md.: Johns Hopkins University Press, 2001.

Lintner, Bertil. *Blood Brothers: The Criminal Underworld of Asia.* New York: Palgrave Macmillan, 2003.

Malarek, Victor. *The Natashas: The New Global Sex Trade.* Toronto: Viking Canada, 2003.

Malcolm, John. Testimony before the United States Senate Committee on the Judiciary Subcommittee on Crime, Corrections, and Victims Rights for the hearing "Alien Smuggling/Human Trafficking: Sending a Meaningful Message of Deterrence." 25 July 2003.

Masika, Rachel, ed. *Gender, Trafficking and Slavery.* Oxford: Oxfam, 2002.

Mattar, Mohamed Y. "Monitoring the Status of Severe Forms of Trafficking in Foreign Countries: Sanctions Mandated under the U.S. Trafficking Victims Protection Act." *Brown Journal of World Affairs* 10, no. 1 (2003).

Nozina, Miroslav. "Crossroads of Crime: The Czech Republic Case." In *Transnational Organized Crime: Myth, Power, and Profit.* Edited by Emilio C. Viano et al. Durham, N.C.: Carolina Academic Press, 2003, 147–32.

O'Neill, Maggie. *Prostitution and Feminism: Toward a Politics of Feeling.* Malden, Mass.: Blackwell, 2001.

O'Neill Richards, Amy. *International Trafficking in Women to the United States: A Contemporary Manifestation of Slavery and Organized Crime.* Washington, D.C.: Center for the Study of Intelligence, 2000.

Phongpaichit, Pasuk, et al. *Guns, Girls, Gambling, Ganja: Thailand's Illegal Economy and Public Policy.* Chiang Mai: Silkworm Books, 1998.

Ramesh, Asha, and H. P. Philomena. "The Devadasi Problem." In *International Feminism: Networking against Female Sexual Slavery.* Edited by Kathleen Barry et al. New York: IWTC, 1984, 82–87.

Reynolds, Helen. *The Economics of Prostitution.* Springfield, Ill.: Charles Thomas, 1986.

Richards, Lenore. "Trafficking in Misery: Human Migrant Smuggling and Organized Crime." *Gazette* (A Royal Canadian Mounted Police Publication) 63, no. 3 (2001). http://usinfo.state.gov/regional/ea/chinaaliens/rcmpexcerpt.pdf.

Shelley, Louise. "Changing the Position of Women: Trafficking, Crime and Corruption." In *The Legacy of State Socialism and the Future of Transformation.* Edited by David Lane. Lanham, Md.: Rowman & Littlefield, 2002, 207–22.

———. "Post-Communist Transitions and the Illegal Movement of People: Chinese Smuggling and Russian Trafficking in Women." *Annals of Scholarship* 14, no. 2 (2002).

———. Testimony at the Hearing before the Commission on Security and Cooperation in Europe on "The Sex Trade: Trafficking of Women and Children in Europe and the United States." 28 June 1999.

———. "The Trade in People in and from the Former Soviet Union," *Contemporary Crises* 40, nos. 2–3 (2003): 231–49.

———.. "Trafficking and Smuggling of Human Beings" delivered at the "Corruption within Security Forces: A Threat to National Security." Sponsored by George C. Marshall European Center for Security Studies. 14–18 May 2001, Garmisch-Partenkirchen, Germany.

———. "Trafficking in Women: The Business Model Approach." *Brown Journal of International Affairs* 10, no. 1 (2003): 119–32.

Skrobanek, Siriporn, Nataya Boonpakdee, and Chutima Jantateeroo, eds. *The Traffic in Women: Human Realities of the Sex Trade.* New York: Zed Books, 1997.

Smith, Paul J., ed. *Human Smuggling: Chinese Migrant Trafficking and the Challenge to America's Immigration Tradition.* Washington, D.C.: Center for Strategic and International Studies, 1997.

Spener, David. "Smuggling Migrants through South Texas: Challenges Posed by Operation Rio Grande." In *Global Human Smuggling: Comparative Perspectives.* Edited by David Kyle and Rey Koslowski. Baltimore, Md.: Johns Hopkins University Press, 2001.

Stoecker, Sally. "Child Homelessness and the Exploitation of Russian Minors: Realities, Resources, and Legal Remedies." *Demokratizatsiya: The Journal of Post-Soviet Democratization* 9, no. 2 (2001).

———. "The Rise in Human Trafficking and the Role of Organized Crime." *Demokratizatsiya: The Journal of Post-Soviet Democratization* 8, no. 1 (2000): 129–44.

Tiuriukanova, Elena V., and Liudmila D. Erokhina. *Torgovlia Liud'mi: Sotsiokriminologicheskii Analiz.* Moscow: Academia, 2002.

"Trafficking, Slavery and Peacekeeping: The Need for a Comprehensive Training Program." Conference Report, Turin, Italy, 9–10 May 2002. Organized by TraCCC and United National Interregional Crime and Justice Research Institute. http://www.unicri.it/TraCCC%20docs/TIP&PKO_EWG_Report_Final.PDF.

Truong, Thanh-Dam. "Organized Crime and Human Trafficking." In *Transnational Organized Crime: Myth, Power, and Profit.* Edited by Emilio C. Viano et al. Durham, N.C.: Carolina Academic Press, 2003, 53–72.

UN Protocol against the Smuggling of Migrants by Land, Sea and Air, supplementing the United Nations Convention against Transnational Organized Crime, Article 3 A. 2003.

U.S. Congress. "Trafficking Victims Protection Act of 2000."

U.S. Department of State, Office of Global Affairs, "Trafficking in Persons Annual Report." June 2002, 2003.

Von Lampe, Klaus. "Criminally Exploitable Ties: A Network Approach to Organized Crime." In *Transnational Organized Crime: Myth, Power, and Profit.* Edited by Emilio C. Viano et al. Durham, N.C.: Carolina Academic Press, 2003, 9–22.

Weitzer, Ronald. *Sex for Sale: Prostitution, Pornography, and the Sex Industry.* New York: Routledge, 2000.

Winer, Jonathan M. "Alien Smuggling: Elements of the Problem and the U.S. Response." *Trends in Organized Crime* 3, no. 3 (1998): 3–13.

ஒ⁄ஒ⁄ஒ

Index

❀❀❀

About the Contributors

Liudmila Erokhina holds a candidate's degree in philosophy from Moscow State University and serves as senior research fellow at the Vladivostok Center for the Study of Organized Crime. She is a member of the Russian Federation Duma's working group on the creation of an anti–human trafficking law. In 2002, she was the recipient of a four-month IREX Contemporary Issues Fellowship to conduct research into the recruitment of children into sexual exploitation and the sex tourism industry at the Transnational Crime and Corruption Center (TraCCC).

Mikhail Kleimenov holds a Ph.D. in legal sciences and is a professor and distinguished scholar of the Russian Federation. He works at the Omsk Academy of the Ministry of Internal Affairs of the Russian Federation. Kleimenov graduated from the Omsk Militia High School and received his college-level degrees at the All-Union Science and Research Institute of the USSR. His main academic interests include criminology, ethnology, sociology, religion studies, and statistics. Kleimenov is the author of 130 published research papers and is the vice president of the Russian Criminological Association.

Olga Pyshchulina is a candidate of sciences in sociology and a senior consultant for the Department of Social Relations and Civil Society at the National Institute for Strategic Research of the President of Ukraine in Kyiv, Ukraine. She is recognized as a leading Ukrainian expert in illegal migration and human trafficking. She is coauthor of Ukraine's first research study on human trafficking, sponsored by the International Organization for Migration in 1997. Pyshchulina is also the director of the nongovernmental organization "Humanitarian Initiative."

159

Anna Repetskaia holds her doctorate in judicial science and is a full professor and chair of criminal law and criminology in the Department of Judicial Investigations at Baikal State University of Economics and Law. Since 1995, she has served as director of the Irkutsk Center for the Study of Organized Crime and Corruption. Her main academic interests include organized crime and corruption and issues of victimology in fighting crime.

Stanislav Shamkov is a senior legal counsel for the Transportation Department of the West Siberian branch of Russia's Ministry of Internal Affairs. He works in the capacities of analyst, manager, tutor, team leader, researcher, and legal counsel. Shamkov received his university-level training in military operations, engineering, and law, and recently completed an FBI course on combating computer crime. He is the author of twelve research papers and twenty written works on incorporating research into practical work.

Louise Shelley is the founder and director of the Transnational Crime and Corruption Center (TraCCC) and a leading U.S. expert on organized crime and corruption in the former Soviet Union. Shelley is a professor in the Department of Justice, Law, and Society (School of Public Affairs) and the School of International Service at American University. Shelley received her undergraduate degree (cum laude) from Cornell University in penology and Russian literature. She holds an M.A. in criminology and a Ph.D. in sociology from the University of Pennsylvania.

Sally Stoecker is a consultant to the Transnational Crime and Corruption Center (TraCCC). From 1999 to 2002 she led two major projects on human trafficking sponsored by the U.S. Department of State. Before coming to American University in 1995, she worked for thirteen years as a research associate at the RAND Corporation in Washington, D.C. She holds a Ph.D. in international relations from the Paul H. Nitze School of Advanced International Studies, Johns Hopkins University.

Elena Tiuriukanova holds a degree from the Department of Demography of the Economics School of Moscow State University. In 1989, she received her candidate's degree by defending her thesis on family economic demographics. Since 1990, she has been employed at the Russian Academy of Sciences' Institute of Socio-Economic Population Issues, where she has been utilizing her extensive knowledge of economics, demography, and sociology to study complex and multidisciplinary issues of population migration. In 2003, she finished her doctoral degree work and is currently completing her doctoral dissertation.

Beatrix Siman Zakhari is academic director of both the "Justice" and the "Law Enforcement: Liberty versus Security" topics at the Washington Semester Program of American University. She earned her B.A. in sociology from Wilkes College and her doctoral degree in sociology with an emphasis on criminology from the University of Pennsylvania. The topic of her dissertation was crime during disasters. She has also studied decision-making processes among capital case jurors.